Prisons Of Delusion

OrangeBooks Publication

1st Floor, Rajhans Arcade, Mall Road, Kohka, Bhilai, Chhattisgarh 490020
Website: **www.orangebooks.in**

© Copyright, 2024, Author

All rights reserved. No part of this book may be reproduced, stored in a retrieval system, or transmitted, in any form by any means, electronic, mechanical, magnetic, optical, chemical, manual, photocopying, recording or otherwise, without the prior written consent of its writer.

First Edition, 2024

ISBN: 978-93-6554-021-5

PRISONS OF DELUSION
Our Past, Present, and Future

SUDDHIR REDDY REBALA

OrangeBooks Publication
www.orangebooks.in

"Prisons of Delusion: Our Past, Present & Future" © *2024, Suddhir Reddy Rebala. All rights reserved. No part of this publication may be reproduced, distributed, or transmitted in any form or by any means without prior written permission.*

Dedicated to my Dad

Acknowledgments

I extend my sincerest gratitude to my family, and friends who inspired me to write this book.

Preface

In the annals of human history, few tales underscore the perils of delusion as poignantly as that of the RMS Titanic. Heralded as the zenith of early 20th-century luxury and engineering prowess, the Titanic was marketed as "unsinkable," a testament to human ingenuity and hubris. This overconfidence, however, blinded its creators to the very risks they had sought to mitigate. The ship's insufficient number of lifeboats and dismissal of iceberg warnings proved to be fatal oversights. On its maiden voyage, the Titanic struck an iceberg and sank, claiming over 1,500 lives. This tragic event stands as a stark reminder of how delusions of invincibility can lead to catastrophic outcomes.

Yet, the story of the Titanic is more than a historical lesson; it is a metaphor for our contemporary predicament. As we navigate an era fraught with existential threats, our modern world finds itself perilously unprepared. Much like the Titanic, we are sailing forward with inadequate safeguards, often blinded by our own illusions of safety and certainty.

This book aims to unravel these illusions and explore the chains that bind us to a false sense of security. It delves into the myriad ways in which humanity has been ensnared by its self-imposed deceptions—delusions about history, state, religion, media and society—that have culminated in cultivating a slavish, subservient mindset that does not question. By examining historical and contemporary examples, we will uncover how these delusions have shaped our decisions, our societies, and ultimately, our fates.

In embarking on this journey, we must confront uncomfortable truths and question the very foundations of our beliefs and practices. To escape the existential threats that loom over us, we must first acknowledge the delusions that obscure our understanding and limit our potential for meaningful change. It is not enough to recognize these delusions; we must actively seek to dismantle them and replace them with grounded, evidence-based perspectives.

Economic progress, education, technology, culture and the urgent existential crises we face—such as climate change, superintelligence, depleting resources, geopolitical conflicts, and new pandemics—will unravel deep-rooted delusions and push us toward urgent, concerted action.

The time for complacency has passed. As we stand at the precipice of potential disaster, we must summon the courage to ask the right questions, seek the right answers, and confront the delusions that threaten our survival. This book is an urgent call to action—to break free from the shackles of our own making and forge a path toward a more informed, resilient future.

Introduction

Prisons of Delusion: Our Past, Present & Future is not just a critique of past and present deceptions but also a hopeful manifesto for a future where truth and integrity prevail. By dissecting these complex issues, I aim to empower readers to question, understand, and ultimately transform the world around them.

To provide a thorough analysis, I have divided the book into two distinct parts. Part A delves into the deceptions and historical perspectives, offering a critical examination in the first five chapters. In these chapters, we explore the foundational myths and manipulations that have perpetuated false beliefs and maintained oppressive systems.

Chapter 1, "Unraveling the Deception of Human History," sets the stage by dissecting the grand narratives that have obscured our understanding of the past.

Chapter 2, "Unmasking the Frauds of Religion and Embracing Humanism," challenges the dogmas and doctrines that have long dictated moral and social norms.

Chapter 3, "How the State Manipulates Humanity," reveals the subtle and overt ways in which state power exerts control over citizens.

Chapter 4, " The Media Mirage: Distorting Reality and Shaping Perception," examines how Media has been weaponized to construct false narratives.

Chapter 5, "The Grand Hoax: How Society Hoodwinks Humanity," uncovers the societal constructs that perpetuate illusions and control.

The second part of the book, encompassing Chapters 6 through 10, shifts focus to the catalysts for dismantling these false beliefs and unshackling the slavish mindset.

Chapter 6, "How Education Can Dismantle Historical Deceptions," explores the transformative power of education in challenging and changing entrenched narratives.

Chapter 7, "How Economic Progress Will Break the Illusions," discusses the potential of economic reforms to expose and rectify systemic manipulations.

Chapter 8, "Techno-Enlightenment: Shattering the Deceptions," examines how technological advancements can build greater transparency and understanding.

Chapter 9, "Art and Culture: Catalysts for Truth and Liberation," showcases how the intellectual development manifest in human expression challenging status quo and rebelling against oppression .

Finally, Chapter 10, "Navigating the New Age of Threats and Transformation," looks ahead to future challenges and opportunities for creating a more truthful and liberated society.

This book is an invitation to embark on a journey of discovery and liberation, to break free from the chains of delusion and embrace a future of clarity and truth.

Contents

Part: A

Chapter 1..3

Chapter 2..49

Chapter 3..95

Chapter 4..122

Chapter 5..137

Part: B

Chapter 6..181

Chapter 7..209

Chapter 8..262

Chapter 9..300

Chapter 10..336

Epilogue..382

Bibliography 385

Part: A

Chapter 1

Unravelling the Deception of Human History

History, as we know it, is often a tapestry woven from threads of conquest, power, and the victors' narratives. Yet, beneath the surface of commonly accepted truths lies a labyrinth of deception, manipulation, and untold stories that have been overshadowed or deliberately erased. This chapter attempts to peel back the layers of misinformation and uncover the hidden truths that have shaped our world. This chapter challenges the conventional chronicles, questioning the motives behind historical records and inviting readers to explore the complexities and contradictions of our past. Through meticulous research and a critical lens, we will delve into the forgotten voices, the suppressed facts, and the powerful forces that have sculpted our collective memory, revealing a more nuanced and authentic portrayal of human history.

The Evolution and Manipulation of Leadership

"History is written by the victors," declared Winston Churchill, encapsulating humanity's transformative journey from egalitarian bands to hierarchical civilizations. Our earliest ancestors roamed the earth in small, egalitarian groups, free from structured leadership. The transition to recognized leaders marked a pivotal turning point in human history, diverging from the natural order and setting the stage for complex social dynamics.

To grasp why and when humans accepted leadership, we must explore the intricate interplay of social, environmental, and psychological factors. The shift from the Pleistocene epoch to the more stable Holocene around 11,700 years ago brought significant climate changes and resource availability challenges. These environmental pressures necessitated new forms of social organization. As we transitioned to agriculture around 10,000 BCE, surplus food production became a reality, necessitating oversight and management. Historian Jared Diamond insightfully remarked, "The roots of inequality lay in the transition from hunter-gatherer bands to settled agricultural communities."

As human communities expanded, the need for complex social structures grew. Larger groups required coordinated activities such as hunting, gathering, and defence. Leaders naturally emerged to facilitate these activities and maintain order. Increased trade and interactions between groups further necessitated negotiators and representatives, solidifying the role of leaders. Social psychologist Daniel Kahneman aptly noted, "In a world where cooperation is key, leadership becomes essential."

Human Psychology

Humans share an evolutionary lineage with primates like chimpanzees, gorillas, and bonobos, who exhibit social hierarchies within their groups. In primate communities, dominant individuals hold higher status and control access to essential resources such as food, shelter, and mates. Alpha male chimpanzees, for instance, lead their groups and have priority in mating. Studies of primate behaviour, such as the work of Frans de Waal, reveal that effective leaders among chimpanzees often exhibit not just strength but also social intelligence, using grooming and alliances to maintain their status. The existence of dominance hierarchies in primates suggests an evolutionary advantage, extending to human tendencies to form hierarchies in various contexts.

Cognitive biases and heuristics play a crucial role in leadership dynamics. Authority bias, the tendency to attribute greater knowledge and competence to those in positions of power, makes it easier for leaders to gain and maintain authority. Social learning theory suggests that people model their behaviour after successful individuals. Malcolm Gladwell observed, "We learn by example and by direct experience because there are real limits to the adequacy of verbal instruction."

The example of Pericles amply demonstrates these biases. In the 5th century BCE, the Greek city-state of Athens was led by a statesman named Pericles. Pericles was not only known for his political acumen but also for his ability to leverage cognitive biases and heuristics to solidify his leadership during what is often referred to as the "Golden Age of Athens."

During the early years of the Peloponnesian War between Athens and Sparta, Pericles proposed a strategic defensive plan that involved bringing all Athenians inside the city walls and relying on their superior navy to strike at the

Spartans' allies. This strategy was unconventional and met with scepticism from many Athenians who were accustomed to traditional land battles.

Pericles' authority bias played a crucial role here. As the elected leader and a proven general, many Athenians deferred to his judgment, assuming his position granted him greater wisdom and competence. His past successes in expanding the Athenian empire and his role in the construction of the Parthenon had already created a halo effect around him, making his current decisions appear more credible.

Additionally, Pericles used social learning to his advantage. He was known for his eloquence and public speaking skills, often addressing the Assembly and the people of Athens to explain and justify his strategies. His speeches, filled with optimism and rationality, became a model for how Athenians thought about their city and its future. By presenting himself as calm and assured, he set an example that others sought to emulate.

Malcolm Gladwell's observation about learning by example is well-illustrated here. Pericles didn't just tell the Athenians what to do; he showed them how a leader should act in times of crisis. His behaviour provided a template for leadership that others followed, reinforcing his authority.

The psychological concept of the halo effect further cemented Pericles' authority. His achievements in cultural and military endeavours led to a general perception of him as an infallible leader. Even when his strategies were questioned, the overall impression of his competence and success in various areas made it difficult for dissenters to gain traction.

The core factor behind human subjugation throughout history lies in the deliberate manipulation of belief systems, which powerful leaders have used to entrench their authority and control over societies. By intertwining their rule with divine or ideological mandates, these rulers exploited the inherent human tendency to seek meaning, order, and security, effectively stifling dissent and promoting conformity.

At the heart of this subjugation is the exploitation of two key psychological weaknesses: the fear of chaos, the need for belonging and the human need for social cohesion and identity. By embedding their rule within religious and cultural frameworks, they offered a sense of unity and purpose among their subjects, who were made to believe that their individual fates were tied to the well-being of the ruler. This manipulation of identity not only discouraged rebellion but also made subjugation appear as a natural and even desirable condition, where questioning the established order was seen as a betrayal of one's community and, by extension, oneself.

The Divine Right

As societies grew, leadership roles became formalized. In Mesopotamia, around 3000 BCE, city-states emerged with priests acting as intermediaries between the people and gods. Their authority was institutionalized through religious rituals, legal codes, and administrative structures. These priestly leaders wielded both spiritual and secular power, shaping the destiny of their communities.

In ancient Egypt, the concept of divine right gained prominence. Pharaohs, believed to be earthly manifestations of gods, ruled with absolute authority.

In the 14th century BCE, the reign of Pharaoh Akhenaten marked a profound shift in ancient Egypt's religious and political landscape. Akhenaten, originally known as Amenhotep IV, ascended the throne and was determined to revolutionize the spiritual framework of his kingdom. He proclaimed that there was only one supreme deity, Aten, the sun disk, and declared himself the sole intermediary between Aten and the people.

Akhetaten (modern-day Amarna) was built in honour of Aten, and Akhenaten's vision was to create a physical manifestation of the divine order he represented. The rapid construction of grand temples and palaces was a testament to his absolute authority and divine status.

Amid the frenzy of construction, Akhenaten would often be seen participating in rituals and making offerings to Aten. During one such ritual, he stood at the Great Temple of Aten, bathed in the rays of the sun. In the eyes of the gathered priests and citizens, this sight was not merely symbolic; it was a direct representation of his divine connection. The pharaoh's actions and presence reinforced the belief that he was indeed the living embodiment of Aten on Earth.

Akhenaten's radical religious reforms and the establishment of Akhetaten were initially met with resistance, but his unwavering assertion of divine right gradually quelled dissent. The people of Egypt, conditioned to revere their pharaohs as gods, began to accept Akhenaten's new doctrine. The construction of Akhetaten and its magnificent structures served as a powerful reminder of his divine legitimacy and absolute rule.

This concept of divine right was mirrored centuries later in medieval Europe. Charlemagne, crowned Holy Roman Emperor by Pope Leo III in 800 CE, exemplified this notion. His coronation in Rome was a spectacle designed to convey that his rule was ordained by God. Charlemagne's subsequent efforts to revive learning and culture, known as the Carolingian Renaissance, left an enduring legacy on European history.

Resource Control

Control over resource distribution and wealth accumulation allowed leaders to reinforce their power through patronage and monument construction. In the ancient city-state of Ur, the power of its leaders was evident not only in their control over resources but also in the grand structures they erected. One such leader, King Ur-Nammu, is often remembered for his ambitious projects and strategic governance. Ur-Nammu understood that to maintain and reinforce his authority, he needed to showcase both his divine favour and his practical prowess.

One year, after a particularly bountiful harvest, Ur-Nammu decided to construct a monumental ziggurat dedicated to the moon god Nanna. This Ziggurat of Ur was not just a place of worship; it was a powerful statement of his centralized authority. The ziggurat's construction employed thousands of workers, creating jobs and distributing wealth throughout the city. This act of patronage ensured loyalty and stability, as the people saw tangible benefits from their king's rule.

Additionally, Ur-Nammu strategically distributed fertile land and controlled water access, which was critical in the arid Mesopotamian environment. By granting these vital resources to loyal subjects and allies, he secured their allegiance and strengthened his grip on power. His military campaigns further expanded Ur's territory, bringing new resources and trade routes under his control, which he skilfully managed to continue ensuring loyalty and economic prosperity.

The Ziggurat of Ur stood as a testament to Ur-Nammu's reign, symbolizing not only religious devotion but also the unification and strength of his city-state. Through a combination of resource management, military prowess, and monumental construction, Ur-Nammu's leadership was solidified, leaving a legacy that would be remembered for millennia.

Edifices of Control

In 221 BCE, Qin Shi Huang became the first Emperor of a unified China, a title he did not take lightly. Determined to solidify his rule and leave an indelible mark on history, Qin Shi Huang initiated a series of grand projects that would both defend his empire and showcase his might.

One such project was the construction of the Great Wall. Designed to protect his realm from northern invaders, the wall required vast resources and manpower. Qin Shi Huang imposed heavy taxes and seized lands to fund this monumental endeavour, mobilizing hundreds of thousands of labourers. These workers, including soldiers, peasants, and prisoners, toiled under harsh conditions, driven by the emperor's relentless vision.

Amidst the Great Wall's construction, another project unfolded in secret: the creation of the Terracotta Army. As a testament to his power and a means to ensure his dominance even in the afterlife, Qin Shi Huang commissioned an army of life-sized clay soldiers, each uniquely detailed and positioned to guard his tomb. This massive undertaking required skilled artisans, vast amounts of clay, and meticulous organization, further depleting the empire's resources.

Qin Shi Huang's reign was characterized by his belief in his divine mandate to rule. He often depicted himself as the intermediary between the gods and his people, a notion he reinforced through rituals and proclamations. This divine association legitimized his harsh methods and centralized control.

Simultaneously, halfway across the world in ancient Mesopotamia, the Sumerians had developed a groundbreaking innovation: writing. This invention allowed Sumerian leaders to codify laws, record transactions, and inscribe their achievements on clay tablets and monuments. These inscriptions not only facilitated governance but also served as propaganda, immortalizing their authority and divine favour.

In 44 BCE, the streets of Rome buzzed with tension and anticipation. Julius Caesar, having amassed significant power through his military conquests, was appointed dictator for life by the Senate. This unprecedented concentration of power marked a pivotal shift from the traditional Republican system of elected officials and checks and balances.

Amidst this political upheaval, a young Octavian, later known as Augustus, observed and learned. Following Caesar's assassination, Octavian swiftly navigated the treacherous waters of Roman politics. By 27 BCE, he had outmanoeuvred his rivals and was bestowed the title of Augustus, marking the official transition from Republic to Empire.

Augustus was acutely aware that maintaining control required more than just political manoeuvring and military might. He initiated the imperial cult, positioning himself as a semi-divine figure. Temples were built in his honour, and he was depicted in art and literature as a godlike figure, ensuring his subjects saw him as more than just a man.

One of the most significant acts during Augustus' reign was the establishment of the Pax Romana. This period of relative peace and stability, which lasted for over two centuries, was meticulously cultivated by Augustus. He reformed the Roman legal system, initiated vast construction projects, and promoted cultural activities that glorified Rome and, by extension, himself.

An incident that exemplifies Augustus' consolidation of power occurred during the dedication of the Ara Pacis, or Altar of Peace, in 9 BCE. This altar, commissioned by the Senate to honour Augustus' return from successful campaigns in Hispania and Gaul, symbolized the peace and prosperity he brought to Rome. The dedication ceremony was a grand affair, attended by senators, priests, and citizens. Augustus, draped in a toga with a laurel crown, performed the rituals, reinforcing his role as the bringer of peace and stability.

Through these religious and cultural means, Augustus cemented his authority. His reign not only marked the beginning of the Roman Empire but also set a precedent for the divine association of emperors, blending political power with religious reverence, and ensuring his legacy would be remembered for millennia.

These historical examples illustrate how rulers used the intertwining of political power and religious ideology to create a framework of control that extended beyond physical coercion to psychological manipulation.

Medieval Moment

In medieval Europe, the feudal system created a hierarchy of lords and vassals, with kings at the top. In the year 1215, tensions between King John of England and his rebellious barons reached a boiling point. King John, notorious for his heavy taxation and military failures, faced mounting opposition from the nobles who felt their traditional rights were being trampled upon. These barons, powerful vassals in the feudal hierarchy, demanded that the king acknowledge and respect their rights.

This clash of wills culminated at Runnymede, a meadow by the River Thames. On June 15, 1215, under considerable pressure, King John reluctantly agreed to affix his seal to a document that would become a cornerstone of modern governance: the Magna Carta. This "Great Charter" was a revolutionary step in medieval Europe, challenging the notion that the king's power was absolute.

One incident that vividly illustrates the significance of the Magna Carta occurred shortly after its sealing. The document stipulated that a council of 25 barons would be established to ensure the king adhered to its terms. This council could seize the king's castles and lands if he violated the charter, a radical departure from the idea of unquestionable royal authority.

Despite agreeing to the Magna Carta, King John had no intention of honouring it. He sought to annul the charter almost immediately, appealing to Pope Innocent III for support. The Pope, asserting the divine right of kings, declared the Magna Carta null and void, calling it a "shameful and demeaning agreement, forced upon the king by violence and fear."

However, the barons, now emboldened by the document, took up arms against King John, leading to the First Barons' War. Although the conflict was brutal and King John's reign ended with his death in 1216, the principles enshrined in the Magna Carta endured.

Over time, the Magna Carta's influence grew, reinforcing the idea that even the monarch was subject to the law. It laid the groundwork for future constitutional developments and the concept of due process, echoing through history as a pivotal moment in the struggle for the rule of law and the balance of power.

This incident at Runnymede exemplifies the medieval power struggle and the gradual shift towards a system where rulers could no longer claim absolute authority through divine right alone, setting the stage for the development of modern constitutional governance.

The Power and Consequences of Historical Manipulation

The story of human evolution and ancient migration is a fascinating tapestry woven from scientific discoveries, archaeological findings, and genetic research. Yet, like any narrative, it is subject to reinterpretation and manipulation. Historical revisionism in ancient history, particularly concerning human evolution and migration, serves various agendas, from national pride to political ideologies.

The desire for power and control is a fundamental aspect of human nature. Throughout history, leaders and ruling classes have leveraged their positions to shape historical narratives in ways that consolidate their authority.

Legitimizing Lies

Fear of losing power drives leaders to manipulate history to justify their rule. They create grandiose and often fictitious accounts of their achievements, ensuring their legacy endures through time. As Napoleon Bonaparte noted, "History is the version of past events that people have decided to agree upon."

In the early days of the Roman Republic, the founder Romulus used a clever historical manipulation to consolidate his power. According to legend, Romulus, the first king of Rome, fabricated a dramatic account of his founding of the city. After allegedly killing his twin brother Remus during a dispute over where the city should be located, Romulus portrayed himself as the sole and divinely ordained founder of Rome.

To cement his authority and ensure his place in history, Romulus claimed that the gods themselves had sanctioned his rule. He established various religious ceremonies and institutions, which were designed to glorify his achievements and reinforce his divine right to lead. The Roman historian Livy later recounted these events with reverence, creating the public perception of Romulus as a god-like figure who had established Rome's greatness. Romulus's manipulation of history ensured that the story of Rome's founding was one of divine providence and singular heroism.

When the actions of those in power conflict with societal ideals, they may alter historical narratives to reduce cognitive dissonance and present themselves more favourably. This justification of atrocities makes reprehensible actions more palatable to both rulers and the ruled.

Psychological factors alone do not explain the widespread manipulation of history. Social conditions also play a crucial role in enabling and perpetuating these distortions.

In many societies, those in power control access to information, allowing them to shape historical narratives with little opposition. High levels of illiteracy and lack of education among the general populace make it easier for leaders to impose their versions of history. Governments often institutionalize historical narratives through education systems, media, and cultural institutions, ensuring the official version of history is widely accepted.

The story of Pharaoh Hatshepsut (c. 1479–1458 BCE) provides an intriguing example of controlling historical narratives. Hatshepsut was one of the few female pharaohs and initially ruled as regent for her stepson, Thutmose III, before assuming full control as pharaoh. To solidify her authority and legitimize her rule in a male-dominated society, Hatshepsut undertook significant efforts to shape how history would view her reign.

Hatshepsut commissioned an extensive campaign of self-promotion through grand architectural projects, including the construction of her mortuary temple at Deir el-Bahari. These temples and monuments were adorned with inscriptions and reliefs that depicted her as the divine and rightful ruler of Egypt. She often portrayed herself in the traditional male attire of a pharaoh, complete with a false beard, to reinforce her legitimacy and challenge gender norms.

After Hatshepsut's death, Thutmose III, who eventually came to power, sought to erase her from history, possibly due to political motivations or a desire to restore the traditional male lineage of pharaohs. He ordered the defacement of her monuments and the removal of her name from official records. However, Hatshepsut's carefully crafted narrative and monumental legacy had already made a significant impact, and her achievements were remembered long after.

This historical manipulation illustrates how rulers have used control over monuments and inscriptions to enforce their version of history. Religious institutions have been complicit in building historical narratives to support the ruling class and maintain social order. Manipulated historical narratives often serve to reinforce existing social hierarchies and justify the privileged positions of the elite. Those who challenge official histories are often marginalized, silenced, or persecuted, further entrenching the dominant narratives.

Leveraging Fear

Fear played a pivotal role in maintaining the power of rulers. Subjects feared retribution, assassination, or arbitrary punishment. Cruelty often stemmed from rulers' paranoia—fearing betrayal, they pre-emptively eliminated potential threats. By cultivating fear, these kings ensured obedience, even if it meant committing atrocities.

Caligula (AD 12–41), the Roman Emperor, was infamous for his madness, sadism, and unchecked cruelty. He threw spectators into the arena to be torn apart by lions, indulged in arbitrary killings, and even planned to make his horse a Roman consul. His erratic behaviour instilled fear among his subjects, who dared not oppose him, knowing that defiance could lead to their demise. Similarly, Charles VI of France (1368–1422), known as "Charles the Mad," suffered from mental illness and took extreme measures to avoid shattering, believing he was made of glass. His erratic behaviour, including chasing around his palace naked, created fear among nobles and commoners alike, who tiptoed around him, fearing sudden outbursts or irrational decrees.

Vlad III, also known as Vlad the Impaler (1431–1476), ruler of Wallachia (modern-day Romania), earned his infamous nickname by impaling enemies on stakes, leaving forests of impaled bodies as a gruesome deterrent. The terror of Vlad's brutality struck fear into the hearts of his enemies, keeping rebellions at bay. Ivan IV of Russia (1530–1584), known as "Ivan the Terrible," ruled with an iron fist, executing thousands, including his own son, and establishing a secret police force. The fear of Ivan's unpredictable actions paralyzed the court, with nobles fearing being next on his list.

The manipulation of historical narratives is not a new phenomenon. Leaders have often rewritten history to glorify their achievements and erase their failures, manipulating collective memory to serve their agenda. Tacitus, the Roman historian, astutely observed: "The histories of Tiberius and Caligula, of Claudius and Nero, were falsified, during their lifetime, out of dread—then, after their deaths, were composed under the influence of still festering hatreds." Roman emperors manipulated accounts of their reigns to shape their legacies.

The Buried Truth

The fabrication of Piltdown Man supported a Eurocentric view of human evolution, reinforcing racial hierarchies. Discovered in 1912 by Charles Dawson, the Piltdown Man was presented as a crucial missing link between apes and humans, with features that seemed to confirm European superiority in the evolutionary timeline. For decades, this so-called discovery influenced scientific thought, leading many to believe that Europe was the cradle of modern humans. It was not until 1953 that the hoax was exposed, revealing that the Piltdown Man was a composite of a medieval human skull and an orangutan jaw. This deliberate manipulation of evidence was motivated by the desire to place Europe at the forefront of human evolution, thus bolstering Eurocentric and racially hierarchical views. The Piltdown Man hoax underscores the extent to which the desire for control and superiority can lead to the distortion of scientific understanding.

Shinichi Fujimura's fabricated discoveries similarly bolstered national pride and historical significance, skewing the understanding of Japan's prehistoric timeline. Fujimura, an amateur archaeologist, claimed to have uncovered ancient artifacts that significantly extended the known history of human habitation in Japan. These supposed findings elevated Japan's archaeological prestige and national pride, suggesting a more ancient and distinguished past. However, in 2000, it was revealed that Fujimura had planted the artifacts himself, staging the discoveries to fabricate a more illustrious prehistoric narrative for Japan. The exposure of Fujimura's deceit not only discredited him but also cast doubt on the integrity of Japan's archaeological record, demonstrating how nationalistic motives can distort historical understanding.

In 1869, workers digging a well in Cardiff, New York, discovered what appeared to be a 10-foot-tall petrified man. Dubbed the "Cardiff Giant," this figure was quickly declared a significant archaeological find, attracting thousands of curious visitors. Behind this elaborate hoax was George Hull, an atheist who created the giant to mock religious beliefs about giants mentioned in the Bible. Scepticism about the giant's authenticity arose swiftly, and experts soon determined that the giant was nothing more than a gypsum statue, artificially aged to appear ancient. The Cardiff Giant remains a classic example of how easily the public can be deceived by fabricated artifacts, highlighting the essential role of critical scrutiny in archaeology.

In 1866, miners in Calaveras County, California, claimed to have unearthed a human skull beneath a layer of lava, suggesting that humans existed in North America during the Pliocene epoch. This discovery, presented as evidence of prehistoric human presence, gained significant attention. However, geologists and anthropologists were sceptical of the claim from the start. Subsequent analysis revealed that the skull was of recent origin, likely planted by miners as a joke. The Calaveras Skull incident underscores the importance of contextual evidence and the dangers of misinterpretation in archaeological findings.

Throwing Sunshine

Over the years, various pseudoscientific theories have emerged regarding the construction and purpose of the Egyptian pyramids. Claims have ranged from the pyramids being built by aliens to them being energy generators, often ignoring or distorting well-established archaeological evidence. Figures like Erich von Däniken have popularized these theories through books and media, capturing public imagination but misleading many. Mainstream archaeologists and Egyptologists have consistently debunked these theories, demonstrating through research that the pyramids were built using sophisticated, but well-understood, engineering techniques by the ancient Egyptians. Despite this, pseudoscientific theories continue to divert public attention from genuine archaeological research and contribute to widespread misconceptions about ancient civilizations.

In 1971, the Tasaday, a purportedly isolated tribe living a Stone Age lifestyle, were "discovered" in the Philippines. The tribe was presented as a living example of prehistoric human society, largely due to the efforts of Manuel Elizalde, a Philippine government official who played a key role in publicizing the Tasaday. However, doubts about the authenticity of the Tasaday emerged in the 1980s. Investigations revealed that the Tasaday were not isolated and had been coached to behave primitively for visitors and researchers. This case highlighted how political and social agendas can distort anthropological research and the representation of indigenous peoples.

The consequences of historical distortions are profound and far-reaching. Manipulated histories have often reinforced social hierarchies and perpetuated inequality, ensuring the continued dominance of certain groups. For instance, the "Aryan invasion theory," which emerged in the 19th century, posited that a group of Indo-European invaders conquered the indigenous people of India, establishing a racial hierarchy that justified British colonial rule. This theory has since been largely discredited, but it served to legitimize colonial domination and marginalize the contributions of native populations.

Similarly, the erasure of marginalized groups' contributions drives a sense of inferiority and limits opportunities for social mobility. In the United States, the achievements of African Americans have historically been overlooked or undervalued in mainstream narratives, contributing to systemic racism and socioeconomic disparities.

Distorted narratives often promote the dominance of certain cultures and ideologies over others, leading to cultural homogenization and the loss of diversity. During the Cultural Revolution in China (1966-1976), Mao Zedong's regime sought to eliminate traditional cultural practices and promote a uniform socialist culture, resulting in the destruction of countless cultural artifacts and the suppression of minority cultures. These examples illustrate how the manipulation of historical narratives can have lasting impacts on societal structures, cultural diversity, and the recognition of contributions from various groups.

Ethnocentrism and nationalism further drive the creation of historical myths that glorify a nation's past and justify its present actions. The systematic minimization of women's contributions has reinforced patriarchal structures and limited women's roles in society. The erasure of indigenous histories has facilitated land seizures, cultural assimilation, and the marginalization of indigenous communities.

The Art of Historical Revisionism: Manipulating Facts to Shape Reality

The practice of historical revisionism—altering the perception of historical events to serve specific agendas—has profound implications for our understanding of the past and, consequently, our perception of the present and future.

But thanks to Historical revisionism, we can reinterpret historical events, figures, or periods. Sometimes, revisionism corrects inaccuracies or incorporates new evidence, but often, it distorts facts to influence public opinion or justify current policies. The power of revisionism lies in its ability to reshape collective memory, and this power has been wielded throughout history to various ends.

Twist the Rope

One of the most unacceptable forms of historical revisionism is Holocaust denial. The Holocaust, the systematic genocide of six million Jews and millions of others by Nazi Germany during World War II, is one of the most well-documented atrocities in history. Yet, despite overwhelming evidence, some groups and individuals deny its occurrence or minimize its scale. This form of revisionism, often motivated by anti-Semitism or political agendas, is not just a distortion of facts but a profound insult to the memory of the victims and survivors.

David Irving, a British historian, is one of the most notorious Holocaust deniers. His works questioned the existence of gas chambers and the scale of the genocide, leading to widespread condemnation and legal battles. Holocaust denial is illegal in several countries, including Germany and Austria, recognizing the dangerous implications of allowing such distortions to proliferate.

In the aftermath of the American Civil War (1861-1865), the Southern states faced devastation and the imposition of Reconstruction policies. In response, the Lost Cause narrative emerged, portraying the Confederate cause as noble and downplaying the role of slavery. This narrative emphasized states' rights and valorised Confederate leaders like Robert E. Lee, reframing the war as a struggle for Southern heritage rather than a fight to preserve slavery.

People like Edward A. Pollard and organizations such as the United Daughters of the Confederacy played significant roles in propagating this revisionist history. The Lost Cause narrative influenced the erection of Confederate monuments and the perpetuation of racial segregation policies, shaping public memory and historical discourse for generations.

Joseph Stalin's rule over the Soviet Union (1924-1953) was marked by extreme repression, purges, and widespread terror. Stalin manipulated historical records to erase enemies and glorify his achievements. Photographs were altered, documents edited, and a cult of personality was cultivated to maintain his grip on power. The Great Purge (1936-1938) saw millions executed or imprisoned, with their existence often erased from official records. This historical manipulation solidified Stalin's control but left a legacy of misinformation and trauma that persisted long after his death. The rewriting of history under Stalin was not just an act of erasure but a tool of totalitarian control, demonstrating the chilling power of revisionism.

Japan's actions during World War II, including atrocities in China and Korea, remain contentious to this day. Some Japanese textbooks downplay or omit events like the Nanking Massacre (1937) and the use of "comfort women" (forced prostitution), leading to accusations of historical revisionism. The Nanking Massacre involved the killing of an estimated 200,000 to 300,000 Chinese civilians and soldiers by Japanese troops. The minimization or denial of such events in educational materials has led to diplomatic tensions with China and Korea, as well as internal debates about historical accountability. This form of revisionism highlights the struggle between national pride and historical truth.

During World War I, the Ottoman Empire systematically exterminated an estimated 1.5 million Armenians in what is now widely recognized as the Armenian Genocide. However, the Turkish government has long denied that these events constitute genocide, labelling them as casualties of war or civil unrest. Various Turkish leaders have maintained this stance, with legislation criminalizing the acknowledgment of the genocide. This denial has hindered reconciliation efforts and strained Turkey's relations with Armenia and other countries recognizing the genocide. The refusal to acknowledge historical atrocities is a potent example of how revisionism can perpetuate conflict and impede healing.

Texas, the second-largest state in the U.S., wields significant influence over national textbook content. In recent years, the Texas State Board of Education has made changes to curriculum standards that critics argue distort historical facts. For example, references to the slave trade were altered to "Atlantic triangular trade," and the role of Moses in influencing the U.S. Constitution was emphasized. Various board members, including social conservatives, have pushed for these revisions, which affect the historical understanding of millions of students. These changes potentially shape their perception of American history, demonstrating how revisionism can influence future generations.

The Chinese Communist Party (CCP) has maintained strict control over historical narratives since its founding in 1949. The CCP has downplayed events like the Great Leap Forward (1958-1962), which led to a famine causing millions of deaths, and the Cultural Revolution (1966-1976), which saw widespread persecution and cultural destruction. Historical events are often depicted in a way that emphasizes the Party's successes while minimizing its failures. This control over historical narrative reinforces the Party's legitimacy and limits public discourse on past atrocities, illustrating how revisionism can be a tool of political power.

The Everlasting Impact of Mythologizing Leaders: From Ancient Gods to Modern Icons

Throughout history, leaders have been mythologized to embody ideals, instil national pride, and legitimize authority. This practice spans from ancient to modern times and across various civilizations, where the embellishment or fabrication of their virtues and achievements often serves political, social, or cultural agendas.

Mythology, the collection of myths belonging to particular religious or cultural traditions, has played a pivotal role in forming societies, controlling populations, and legitimizing power. From the dawn of human civilization, myths have been crafted to explain the unknown, instil moral values, and reinforce the authority of the ruling class. Mythology likely began with humanity's earliest attempts to understand the world. Natural phenomena, existential questions, and the need for social cohesion drove the creation of stories that explained the unexplainable. These stories evolved into elaborate myths that formed the foundation of ancient religions and cultures.

In prehistoric times, early humans lived in a world filled with mystery and danger. To make sense of natural events like thunderstorms, eclipses, and the changing seasons, they created myths. Cave paintings and artifacts suggest that early humans worshipped animal spirits and natural forces, embedding these beliefs in their daily lives and communal practices.

Mighty Myths

These primal myths established a shared worldview, building unity and cooperation within early human communities. Early civilizations such as Mesopotamia, Egypt, and Greece developed intricate pantheons of gods and goddesses. The Sumerian epic of Gilgamesh, the Egyptian Book of the Dead, and Hindu and Greek mythologies are rich with deities, heroes, and cosmological tales that explained life, death, and the afterlife. These myths reinforced social hierarchies, justified the authority of kings and priests, and established cultural norms.

Myths provided answers to questions that science could not yet explain. Creation myths like the Babylonian Enuma Elish or the Biblical Genesis explained the origins of the world and humanity. By offering explanations for natural and cosmic phenomena, myths reduced fear and provided a sense of order and purpose.

Myths often included moral lessons and codes of conduct. The Ten Commandments in the Judeo-Christian tradition, the teachings of Confucius in Chinese mythology, and the heroic virtues in the tales of Hercules and Odysseus are prime examples. These moral codes guided behaviour, promoted social harmony, and deterred actions that could disrupt communal life.

Myths were also instrumental in legitimizing the power of rulers and the elite. Once humanity has accepted and inculcated myths, it was easy for the rulers to leverage it for their benefit. The divine right of kings, as seen in the concept of pharaohs as gods in Egypt or the Mandate of Heaven in China, justified the rulers' authority as divinely ordained. By linking rulers to divine or supernatural forces, myths reinforced social hierarchies and discouraged rebellion.

The Catholic Church in medieval Europe wielded immense power by controlling access to religious texts and interpreting divine will. The Hindu caste system, reinforced by myths in texts like the Manusmriti, established a rigid social hierarchy. Religious myths often prescribed social roles and justified inequalities, keeping populations in line and preventing social upheaval.

Conquering civilizations imposed their mythology on subjugated peoples to consolidate power. The spread of Greek culture during Alexander the Great's conquests spread Hellenistic myths across the known world. Similarly, Roman conquests often incorporated and adapted local deities into the Roman pantheon.

By adopting and adapting local myths, conquerors could integrate diverse populations into their empires, reducing resistance and cementing loyalty. Modern nations have created their own myths to develop national identity and unity. The American myth of Manifest Destiny, the British myth of the Empire on which the sun never sets, and the Soviet myth of the proletarian hero are prominent examples. National myths inspire patriotism and a sense of collective destiny but can also justify imperialism, war, and social inequalities.

In the 20th and 21st centuries, political leaders have used myth-making and propaganda to consolidate power. The cult of personality around figures like Joseph Stalin, Adolf Hitler, and Kim Jong-un, who are often portrayed as infallible leaders with near-supernatural abilities, exemplifies this trend.

These modern myths are disseminated through state-controlled media, education systems, and public monuments, creating a narrative that supports the regime and stifles dissent.

The Epic of Gilgamesh portrays its hero as two-thirds god and one-third human, endowed with superhuman strength and wisdom, reinforcing the divine right of kingship. The myths say that he was immortal, built the great wall of Uruk single-handedly, killed the monster Humbaba single-handedly. Pharaohs like Ramses II, depicted as god-like figures in monumental inscriptions and temples, used myth to legitimize their rule. He is falsely depicted as the Pharaoh during the Exodus. He is also falsely praised to have won the battle of Kadesh.

Alexander the Great, depicted by ancient and later sources as a flawless military genius and cultural visionary, linked himself to Zeus as his son, pushing a legacy of Hellenistic culture and influencing leaders from Julius Caesar to Napoleon Bonaparte.

In classical and medieval times, figures like Julius Caesar, King Arthur, and Charlemagne were mythologized to bolster the legitimacy of their respective regimes. Caesar's own writings and later accounts portrayed him as a brilliant strategist and benevolent leader, his assassination leading to his deification.

The Arthurian legends such as the powerful Excalibur, the lady of the lake, the magician Merlin, and his Round table shaped British national identity and inspired chivalric ideals, while Charlemagne's mythologized image legitimized the Holy Roman Empire and influenced the medieval concept of kingship and Christendom.

The exaggeration and fabrication of leaders' achievements have profound effects on national identity, political legitimacy, and cultural values. From ancient demigods to modern political icons, mythologized leaders shape our understanding of history and influence contemporary society.

The Erased Histories: Rediscovering Marginalized Contributions Across Time

The early suppression of marginalized histories spans both ancient and medieval eras, revealing a persistent pattern of erasure that has shaped historical narratives. Women's contributions in ancient civilizations have frequently been downplayed or overlooked. Hypatia of Alexandria, who lived around 360–415 CE, stands as a poignant example. As a philosopher, mathematician, and astronomer, her intellectual prowess was widely recognized in ancient Egypt. Tragically, her works were largely forgotten after her murder by a Christian mob, illustrating how the triumph of one narrative often comes at the expense of another.

Similarly, women in the Roman Empire, such as Livia Drusilla, the wife of Emperor Augustus, wielded significant political influence. Despite their contributions, these women have often been sidelined in historical accounts, reinforcing patriarchal narratives that persist to this day.

Ancient Americas

The impact of European colonization on Mesoamerican cultures cannot be overstated, as it led to systematic destruction and suppression. The Spanish conquerors decimated the Maya civilization by destroying countless texts and codices, erasing vast amounts of historical and scientific knowledge. The achievements and rich history of the Aztec Empire were similarly overshadowed by the accounts of their defeat by Hernán Cortés in 1521. This deliberate erasure contributed to a broader narrative of European superiority, providing a distorted justification for colonial rule.

One of the most striking examples of the destruction of Mesoamerican knowledge by European colonizers is the fate of the codices created by the Maya civilization. The Maya were renowned for their advanced understanding of astronomy, mathematics, and complex writing systems. Their codices, made from bark paper or deerskin and adorned with intricate glyphs, contained vast amounts of scientific, historical, and religious knowledge.

When Spanish conquistadors, led by Pedro de Alvarado, arrived in the Yucatán Peninsula in the early 16th century, they were appalled by the Maya's sophisticated knowledge. The Spanish, driven by a mix of zealotry and a desire to assert their dominance, sought to eradicate what they saw as pagan knowledge. In 1562, Bishop Diego de Landa, a key figure in the Spanish colonization of the Maya region, conducted a dramatic and destructive campaign against Maya culture.

De Landa famously ordered the burning of numerous Maya codices, along with other cultural artifacts and texts. His aim was to eliminate what he considered heretical and idolatrous material, thereby imposing European religious and cultural norms. In one of his infamous proclamations, he expressed his desire to "exterminate the books of the ancient rites" and to forcefully convert the Maya to Christianity. As a result, of the many codices that existed, only a few fragments have survived to this day.

The systematic destruction of these texts had a profound impact. The Maya's rich history, scientific achievements, and cultural practices were severely diminished, leaving future generations with a fragmented understanding of their past. This deliberate erasure not only diminished the Maya's historical record but also reinforced the European narrative of superiority by portraying indigenous cultures as primitive and in need of European intervention.

Eclipse of Africa

The colonial period further entrenched the suppression of African contributions to global history. One notable example of the suppression of African history during the colonial period is the marginalization of the achievements of the Kingdom of Mali and its intellectual centre, Timbuktu. The Kingdom of Mali, which thrived from the

13th to the 16th centuries, was renowned for its immense wealth, advanced governance, and remarkable cultural and intellectual achievements.

The city of Timbuktu, in particular, was a thriving hub of scholarship and learning. Its University of Sankore, along with other madrasas, attracted scholars from across the Islamic world. The city boasted extensive libraries filled with manuscripts on a wide range of subjects, including astronomy, mathematics, medicine, and law. The wealth of knowledge and the sophistication of the Malian educational system were well-documented by contemporary Muslim scholars and travellers.

However, during the colonial period, European powers systematically downplayed or ignored these contributions. Colonial narratives often portrayed Africa as a land with little history or intellectual development, reinforcing the ideologies of European superiority and justifying colonial exploitation.

European colonial administrators and historians often emphasized the grandeur of Egypt while separating it from the rest of Africa. This artificial divide served to diminish the perception of Africa's historical contributions, portraying ancient Egypt as an anomaly rather than part of a continuum of African civilization.

By minimizing the achievements of African civilizations, colonial ideologies promoted the notion of African inferiority—a legacy that continues to influence global perceptions and discussions about African history and contributions.

American Erasure

Indigenous histories in the Americas faced a similar fate, as their contributions and experiences were marginalized amid European colonization. The Trail of Tears, which occurred between 1838 and 1839, involved the forced relocation of Native American tribes like the Cherokee, resulting in significant loss of life and cultural heritage. Furthermore, the rich agricultural, medicinal, and ecological knowledge of indigenous peoples was often dismissed or appropriated without acknowledgment. This suppression facilitated justifications for land seizures and cultural assimilation policies, further entrenching systemic injustices.

In the United States, the erasure of Black histories has been a consistent thread throughout American history. The Tulsa Race Massacre of 1921 serves as a stark reminder of this marginalization, as a prosperous Black community in Tulsa, Oklahoma, was destroyed in a racially motivated attack. This tragic event was largely omitted from mainstream history for decades.

The Civil Rights Movement also highlights this trend, with figures like Claudette Colvin—who famously refused to give up her bus seat before Rosa Parks—often overshadowed in historical accounts. The erasure of such significant contributions has reinforced systemic racism and hindered the recognition of African American achievements in society.

The hidden histories of gender and sexuality reveal further layers of suppression. The experiences and contributions of LGBTQ+ individuals have frequently been overlooked or minimized. The Stonewall Riots of 1969 were a pivotal moment in the LGBTQ+ rights movement, yet the roles of transgender women of color like Marsha P. Johnson and Sylvia Rivera are often overlooked. Alan Turing, a key figure in the development of computer science and cryptography, also faced persecution for being gay, overshadowing his monumental achievements. The suppression of LGBTQ+ histories has perpetuated discrimination and obscured the community's vital role in societal progress.

Women's contributions during wars have similarly been minimized in favour of male-dominated narratives. During World War II, women played crucial roles, such as the Night Witches, an all-female Soviet air force regiment, and Rosie the Riveter, who represented the women working in factories. Despite their significant contributions, these figures were frequently underrepresented in historical accounts.

In the American Civil War, Harriet Tubman, who served as a spy and scout for the Union Army, is another example of a remarkable woman whose achievements have been sidelined. This minimization of women's contributions in wartime has reinforced gender stereotypes and neglected the full scope of their impact.

Despite these historical erasures, there have been concerted efforts to reclaim and preserve marginalized histories. The Harlem Renaissance, spanning the 1920s and 1930s, emerged as a powerful cultural movement celebrating African American artistic, cultural, and intellectual achievements.

Thinkers like Langston Hughes, Zora Neale Hurston, and W.E.B. Du Bois played significant roles in challenging racist ideologies and highlighting the richness of African American culture. Their contributions have been instrumental in reshaping perceptions of Black identity and culture.

Indigenous rights movements have also emerged as a response to historical suppression. The American Indian Movement (AIM), founded in 1968, fought for the recognition of Native American rights and the preservation of their cultures.

Similarly, 'Idle No More', which began in 2012, is a Canadian movement advocating for indigenous sovereignty and environmental protection. These movements have brought greater visibility to indigenous issues and histories, challenging mainstream narratives that often ignore their experiences.

The Women's History Movement has sought to address the historical marginalization of women by recognizing and integrating their contributions into historical narratives. Women's History Month, established in 1987, serves as an annual reminder to highlight the achievements of women throughout history.

Scholars such as Gerda Lerner and Betty Friedan have worked tirelessly to uncover and celebrate women's roles, advocating for a more inclusive understanding of history that recognizes the vital contributions of women across time. These efforts not only acknowledge past injustices but also pave the way for a future that honours the diversity of human experiences.

Colonial Narratives: Justification of Colonization Through Distorted History

Colonialism, the practice of acquiring political control over another country, exploiting it economically, and imposing cultural dominance, was often justified through a series of distorted historical narratives. These narratives portrayed colonizers as benevolent bringers of civilization, while depicting indigenous populations as backward and in need of guidance.

The concept of "The White Man's Burden," popularized by Rudyard Kipling in his 1899 poem, suggested that it was the moral duty of white Europeans to civilize non-European peoples. This narrative provided a moral justification for imperialism, framing colonization as a noble enterprise despite its exploitative nature.

Similarly, in the 19th century, "Manifest Destiny" was the belief that the United States was destined to expand across North America, spreading democracy and capitalism. This ideology justified the displacement and genocide of Native American populations, portraying expansion as both inevitable and beneficial.

One of the most brutal examples of colonial atrocities occurred in the Belgian Congo from 1885 to 1908. King Leopold II of Belgium privately owned the Congo Free State, where millions of Congolese were subjected to forced labour, resulting in the deaths of an estimated 10 million people. Atrocities included amputations, floggings, and other forms of torture. Local traditions and governance structures were dismantled, and Christian missionaries often accompanied colonial administrators, undermining indigenous religious practices. Despite these horrors, Leopold's regime portrayed their actions as bringing civilization and Christianity to the region while systematically exploiting its people and resources.

The British Raj in India, lasting from 1858 to 1947, was marked by significant economic exploitation and cultural suppression. The Bengal Famine of 1943, exacerbated by British policies, led to the deaths of around 3 million people, while the Jallianwala Bagh Massacre in 1919 saw British troops killing hundreds of unarmed Indian civilians. The British systematically dismantled traditional industries, such as textile manufacturing, to benefit British economic interests. Education policies aimed at creating an English-speaking administrative class while neglecting indigenous knowledge systems. British propaganda highlighted the supposed benefits of British rule, such as railways and legal systems, while downplaying the economic exploitation and social disruption caused by their policies.

French colonization of Algeria, beginning in 1830 and lasting until 1962, was another instance of brutal colonial rule. The French military used harsh methods to suppress resistance, including massacres, forced relocations, and the destruction of villages. The Setif and Guelma massacres in 1945 resulted in thousands of Algerian deaths. French policies aimed to assimilate Algerians, suppressing local languages and customs in favour of French culture, and targeting Islamic schools and practices for suppression. French colonial authorities portrayed their presence as a civilizing mission, emphasizing infrastructure improvements while ignoring the violent suppression and economic exploitation of the Algerian people.

British colonization of Australia began in 1788, with devastating impacts on Aboriginal populations. Frontier violence, forced removals, and policies like the Stolen Generations, where Aboriginal children were taken from their families to be assimilated into white society, caused immense suffering. Aboriginal languages, traditions, and land rights were systematically undermined, and traditional knowledge systems were disregarded or destroyed. Colonial narratives often depicted Australia as an empty land ("terra nullius") ready for British settlement, ignoring the rich cultures and histories of Aboriginal peoples.

The late 19th-century partitioning of Africa by European powers led to widespread disruption and exploitation. Colonial administrations often employed brutal methods to maintain control, such as the Herero and Namaqua genocide in German South West Africa, Namibia today (1904-1908), where tens of thousands were killed. Colonial authorities imposed European languages, religions, and governance structures, often erasing or marginalizing indigenous cultures and traditions. Europeans justified their actions by claiming to bring civilization, Christianity, and progress to Africa while exploiting its resources and peoples for economic gain.

European colonization of the Americas began in the late 15th century, resulting in the near-extermination of indigenous populations. Conquistadors like Hernán Cortés and Francisco Pizarro used extreme violence to conquer the Aztec and Inca empires. Forced labour, disease, and deliberate killings decimated indigenous populations. Indigenous knowledge, languages, and cultural practices were systematically destroyed or suppressed.

The encomienda and later missions disrupted traditional societies and economies. European colonizers often depicted their conquests as divinely ordained missions to spread Christianity and civilization, ignoring the devastation wrought on native populations.

Colonial powers established education systems that promoted European languages, values, and histories. British colonial education in Africa and India, French mission schools in West Africa, and Spanish missionary schools in Latin America aimed to create a class of indigenous people who would support colonial rule while alienating them from their own cultures and histories.

Literature and media played significant roles in promoting colonial narratives. Works like Joseph Conrad's *Heart of Darkness* and Rudyard Kipling's *The Jungle Book* portrayed colonial subjects as exotic and inferior, justifying European dominance. These narratives reinforced stereotypes and justified the colonial project, building public perceptions in both the colonizing and colonized countries.

Post-colonial scholars and activists have been at the forefront of challenging the distorted narratives that have long dominated colonial history. Frantz Fanon's *The Wretched of the Earth,* Edward Said's *Orientalism,* and Chinua Achebe's *Things Fall Apart* are seminal works that highlight the destructive impacts of colonialism and reclaim indigenous voices.

These works have significantly impacted the academic and social discourse by prompting a re-evaluation of colonial histories, emphasizing the need to acknowledge and address the legacies of colonialism. They have laid the groundwork for a broader understanding of the complexities and brutalities of colonial rule, helping to dismantle the false narratives that have persisted.

In response to the historical injustices of colonialism, many formerly colonized countries are actively working to revive and preserve their indigenous cultures and traditions. Efforts to teach and preserve indigenous languages are gaining momentum in Australia, the Americas, and Africa.

These initiatives are accompanied by the celebration of traditional festivals and rituals, which serve to restore cultural pride. Additionally, the restitution of cultural artifacts, taken during colonial times, back to their countries of origin is a powerful step towards rectifying historical wrongs.

How the New Generation is Dispelling the Deceptions of Flawed History

The new generation is actively challenging the established narratives, critically examining history, myths, colonial legacies, and oppressive regimes. This shift reflects a broader global movement towards reclaiming marginalized voices and reassessing historical accounts that have long been accepted without question.

The new generation, equipped with advanced technology and a critical mindset, is actively challenging and dispelling the deceptions embedded in historical narratives. Through innovative research methods, critical analysis, and public discourse, young scholars, activists, and historians are uncovering truths long buried or distorted by flawed historical accounts. Tim Berners-Lee, the inventor of the World Wide Web, has significantly influenced the way historical data is accessed and shared, democratizing information and enabling researchers to cross-verify historical accounts, thus dispelling myths and biases entrenched in traditional narratives.

Prominent classicist and historian Mary Beard has been instrumental in revising historical narratives about the ancient world, emphasizing the importance of viewing history through multiple perspectives, especially those of marginalized groups. Beard's approach encourages a more nuanced understanding of history, prompting the new generation to question and re-examine established historical "truths." In the realm of public history, Hasan Kwame Jeffries, an associate professor at The Ohio State University, specializes in African American history and has been active in projects like "Teaching Hard History," which aims to bring accurate historical accounts to the public, particularly through social media and public history initiatives.

Shashi Tharoor, an Indian politician, diplomat, and author, has been vocal about the misrepresentations and omissions in colonial history. His book *Inglorious Empire: What the British Did to India* critically examines the impact of British colonial rule, challenging the often glorified narrative of the British Empire and sparking global discussions about the legacy of colonialism. Similarly, activist and historian Roxanne Dunbar-Ortiz has significantly contributed to the recognition and inclusion of Indigenous histories in mainstream narratives. Her book *An Indigenous Peoples' History of the United States* provides a comprehensive account of American history from the perspective of Indigenous peoples, helping to dispel many myths and inaccuracies about Native American history.

Priyamvada Gopal, a professor at the University of Cambridge, has been a leading voice in the movement to decolonize the curriculum. Her work advocates for the inclusion of diverse perspectives and the reassessment of historical content taught in academic institutions. Gopal's efforts are prompting educational institutions to rethink and restructure their curricula, ensuring that history education is more representative and accurate.

The methods and technologies employed by the new generation include digital humanities, social media campaigns, public history projects, and collaborative research. Digital tools such as text mining, GIS mapping, and digital archives allow for more comprehensive and accessible historical research. Social media platforms like Twitter, Instagram, and TikTok are used to share historical facts, challenge misconceptions, and promote critical discussions about history. Public history projects, including museums, documentaries, podcasts, and public lectures, engage wider audiences in historical research. Cross-disciplinary and international collaborations provide new insights and support a more holistic understanding of history.

The new generation's commitment to uncovering and disseminating the truth about our past is reshaping how history is understood and taught. This ensures that future generations have a more accurate and inclusive understanding of human history, moving away from the deceptions and biases that have long plagued historical narratives.

What Can We Expect in the Future?

In the future, we can expect a democratization of historical knowledge through digital archiving and open access, increased interdisciplinary approaches, and significant technological advancements like AI and VR. There will be a stronger focus on inclusivity and representation of marginalized groups, re-evaluation of historical monuments and symbols, and the influence of climate change on historical research. Global perspectives will become more prevalent, educational reforms will encourage critical engagement with history, and public history initiatives will grow, making history more accessible and relevant to broader communities. These changes will collectively ensure a more accurate and inclusive understanding of the past.

The convergence of archaeology, genetic studies, and technological advancements is transforming our understanding of history in unprecedented ways. Recent developments in these fields have provided groundbreaking insights into ancient civilizations and historical events, demonstrating the power of modern technology in unravelling the complexities of the past.

One notable example is the use of ground-penetrating radar (GPR) and LiDAR technology at the Ram Janmabhoomi site in Ayodhya, India. In the 2020s, archaeological surveys employing GPR and LiDAR revealed detailed information about the site's sub-surface structures. These technologies allowed researchers to identify the remnants of a large, ancient complex beneath the modern-day structures without extensive excavation. The non-invasive nature of these tools enabled the discovery of a series of walls and foundations, providing critical evidence that supported historical claims about the site's significance. This technological approach preserved the integrity of the site while offering new insights into its historical context.

Similarly, advancements in genetic studies and technology have shed light on the enigmatic Indus Valley Civilization. For many years, the Indus Valley Civilization was shrouded in mystery due to its undeciphered script and limited archaeological exploration. However, recent breakthroughs in ancient DNA analysis have transformed our understanding. In 2018, researchers analysed genetic material from remains found in Indus Valley sites, revealing a complex genetic heritage that included contributions from both ancient Near Eastern populations and indigenous South Asians. This revelation overturned previous assumptions about the isolation of the Indus Valley Civilization and highlighted its connections with other ancient cultures.

Moreover, the application of AI and machine learning has revolutionized the analysis of archaeological and genetic data. AI tools have helped researchers analyse inscriptions, genetic markers, and spatial data, leading to new insights into migration patterns, cultural interactions, and the development of ancient societies.

These technological advancements exemplify how integrating archaeology, genetics, and modern technologies can lead to more comprehensive and nuanced historical narratives. By combining these disciplines, researchers are uncovering the complexities of human history, shedding light on both well-known and obscure aspects of our past, and offering a more detailed understanding of ancient civilizations and their environmental and cultural contexts.

Chapter 2

Unmasking the Frauds of Religion and Embracing Humanism

The unnatural aspects of religion are evident in its suppression of natural human instincts and desires, enforcing celibacy, dietary restrictions, and other ascetic practices that contradict biological and psychological needs. Additionally, religion's reliance on supernatural explanations for natural phenomena prevents the understanding and acceptance of scientific truths, resulting in ignorance and superstition. This disconnection from reality and the promotion of divisive ideologies have historically led to significant societal harm and conflict.

The Origins of Religious Thought

Religion, with its profound impact on human civilization, has shaped societies, cultures, and individual lives throughout history. Its origins are deeply entwined with humanity's early attempts to understand and control the natural world, driven by fear, ignorance, and a desire for order. The emergence of religious thought can be traced back to ancient times when humans faced existential questions and sought answers beyond the tangible world. This quest for understanding led to the birth of various belief systems, many of which laid the groundwork for both genuine spiritual exploration and deceptive practices.

The earliest forms of religion emerged from humanity's interaction with the environment and the deep mysteries of existence. In prehistoric societies, animistic beliefs were among the first religious systems to develop. These beliefs attributed spiritual agency to animals, plants, and natural phenomena, creating a framework that allowed early humans to interact with their surroundings in a meaningful way. Animism offered a way to explain the unpredictable and often terrifying aspects of nature, such as storms, disease, and death. By ascribing these forces to the will of spirits, early humans could frame their experiences within a more comprehensible construct.

In the dense forests of ancient Siberia, the Evenki people revered the Amur tiger as a spiritual guardian. The tiger was not merely an animal but a powerful spirit with the ability to influence the fate of the tribe. This reverence was reflected in their rituals and daily practices. For instance, they would avoid hunting tigers not only out of respect but also in the belief that doing so would invite misfortune upon their community. The Amur tiger's majestic presence was seen as a symbol of the untamed forces of nature that held sway over their lives, embodying the animistic belief that animals could hold spiritual significance.

Moving south to the Amazon Rainforest, the Yanomami tribe also illustrates early animistic practices. For the Yanomami, the forest itself was alive with spirits. They believed that each plant, animal, and even the rivers were imbued with a spiritual essence that could influence their wellbeing. A fascinating story tells of a shaman who, during a particularly harsh drought, performed a ritual to appease the river spirit, believing it would bring rain. The shaman danced through the night, invoking the spirit with chants and offerings. As dawn broke, the skies cleared, and rain began to fall, reinforcing the belief that their spiritual practices could directly affect natural events.

The Australian Aboriginal cultures offer another example. The Dreamtime, or "The Dreaming," is a cornerstone of their belief system. It is a time when ancestral spirits shaped the world, creating its landforms, animals, and laws. One Aboriginal story speaks of the Rainbow Serpent, a powerful deity that travels through the land, carving rivers and valleys as it moves. This serpent's journey is not just a myth but a way to interpret the natural landscape, serving as a bridge between the spiritual and physical worlds.

One of the earliest known animistic cultures was the San people of southern Africa. Dating back over 20,000 years, the San's rock art and oral traditions reveal a rich tapestry of beliefs centered around nature and the spirit world. The San shamans performed trance dances and rituals, often using hallucinogenic substances like the African plant Tobacco to enter altered states of consciousness. These practices allowed shamans to purportedly communicate with spirits and influence the natural world. While the San's rituals were deeply embedded in their cultural practices, they also provided opportunities for shamans to manipulate and control their communities by claiming special access to spiritual realms.

Similarly, ancient animistic traditions were prevalent among the indigenous peoples of the Americas, such as the Native American tribes. The Lakota Sioux, for instance, practiced a form of animism that revered the natural world and its elements, viewing them as imbued with spiritual significance. Their rituals, including the Sun Dance, were intended to connect them with the spirit world and ensure harmony with nature. However, the hierarchical nature of these spiritual practices often placed certain individuals, such as shamans or spiritual leaders, in positions of power where they could influence the beliefs and actions of others.

Shamanic Traditions and Strange Religions

Shamans conducted rituals, provided healing, and offered guidance based on their claimed connection to the spiritual realm. However, the power wielded by shamans often led to exploitation and manipulation, illustrating the darker side of these ancient practices.

A striking example of shamanic exploitation involves the use of hallucinogenic substances in rituals. Shamans often employed drugs like Ayahuasca, a powerful hallucinogen derived from Amazonian plants, to induce altered states of consciousness. In traditional contexts, these substances were used to facilitate spiritual experiences and healing. However, the use of such substances also provided a convenient means for shamans to claim communication with the spirit world, thereby reinforcing their authority and control over their communities. In recent years, this practice has been commercialized, with some shamans in the Amazon charging exorbitant fees for Ayahuasca ceremonies aimed at tourists. This exploitation undermines the genuine spiritual intent of the ritual, turning it into a profitable venture and potentially jeopardizing the well-being of participants seeking authentic spiritual experiences.

The Aztec religion offers another example of how religious practices can become tools of manipulation and control. Central to Aztec worship was the ritual of human sacrifice, believed to be essential for appeasing their gods and ensuring the continuation of the natural order. The Aztecs performed these sacrifices on a massive scale, with thousands of captives from wars being ritually killed to offer their blood to the gods. The sacrifice was thought to ensure the sun's rise and the fertility of crops, integrating a profound sense of cosmic significance into the ritual. The priesthood wielded this belief to consolidate their power, manipulating fear and superstition to justify their actions and maintain their dominance over the populace. The gruesome nature of these rituals, which often involved elaborate ceremonies and public displays of violence, highlights the extent to which religious authority can exploit deeply ingrained beliefs to exert control and instill fear.

In other regions, strange and often cruel religious practices have similarly exploited followers for the benefit of religious leaders. For instance, the Thuggee cult in India, active from the 14th to the 19th centuries, involved a network of devotees who carried out ritualistic murders of travelers. The Thugees believed that their acts of murder, carried out in the name of the goddess Kali, were a form of divine service that ensured their spiritual purity. This practice was shrouded in secrecy and mysticism, allowing the cult leaders to manipulate their followers into committing heinous acts under the guise of religious duty. The British colonial authorities eventually dismantled the Thuggee network, but the extent of their exploitation demonstrates how religious ideologies can be perverted to justify extreme violence.

Similarly, in some African and Caribbean cultures, Voodoo and Santería practices have included elements of human sacrifice and ritualistic violence. Although these religions are often misunderstood and misrepresented, some practitioners have used these beliefs to exploit their followers. Rituals involving animal sacrifices and, in rare and extreme cases, human sacrifices were believed to appease spirits or gods. The secrecy and mysticism surrounding these practices have often facilitated the exploitation of vulnerable individuals seeking spiritual guidance.

While these religious practices initially served to provide spiritual insight and community cohesion, they have also been exploited by those in power to manipulate, control, and exploit their followers.

The Rise of Organized Religion

The transition from shamanic traditions to organized religion marked a profound shift in human religious thought, bringing with it formalized doctrines, rituals, and hierarchies. As human societies evolved from small, tribal communities to complex civilizations, religious institutions grew in sophistication and influence. This transformation saw the emergence of major world religions, each establishing its own set of beliefs and practices that further entrenched the power of religious leaders.

Hinduism

In the heart of the ancient Indus Valley Civilization archaeologists unearthed a remarkable artifact known as the "Dancing Girl" statue from Mohenjo-Daro. This bronze figurine, depicting a young woman in a confident pose, adorned with bangles and a playful smile, is believed to represent not just a figure of beauty but possibly a deity or a priestess involved in religious rituals. Her posture and attire suggest that dance and music were integral to the spiritual practices of the time, reflecting a sophisticated understanding of the divine through artistic expression.

A striking find from this period is the so-called "Great Bath" of Mohenjo-Daro. This large, public bathing facility, with its intricate system of drainage and waterproofing, hints at the ritual importance of water. Early inhabitants likely used this space for purification rites, which became a central feature in later Hindu rituals. The emphasis on cleanliness and ritual bathing in Hinduism can be traced back to these ancient practices, showing how the sacredness of water persisted through the millennia.

Hinduism is viewed by a few as a synthesis of Indus Valley Civilization and migrating tribe from Persia. These tribes called Aryans (from Iran), were fire-worshippers- just like the other sect, the Zoroastrians. They spoke Sanskrit.

Hindus developed a complex pantheon of gods and goddesses, intricate rituals, and elaborate temples. However, the Brahmins, the priestly class, wielded their religious authority to exploit their followers for personal gain. They often manipulated religious texts to reinforce their dominance, imposing strict societal norms that reinforced social hierarchies and demanded offerings from the faithful. This manipulation not only cemented their control but also perpetuated social inequality and exploitation.

The Rigveda, one of the oldest sacred texts in Hinduism, is a treasure trove of ancient rituals and hymns that date back to the early Vedic period, succeeding the Indus Valley Civilization. This collection of hymns and mantras reflects the evolution of religious thought and practice over time. Interestingly, the Rigveda includes references to a mysterious ritual called the "Ashvamedha" or horse sacrifice, which involved the ritualistic sacrifice of a horse to assert royal power and divine favor. This ritual underscores how early Hindu practices intertwined with political power, forming the socio-religious landscape of the time.

The role of the Brahmins in instituting early Hinduism cannot be understated. These priestly figures were not only custodians of religious knowledge but also wielded significant influence over the spiritual and social lives of their communities.

In the realm of social stratification, the Brahmins played a critical role in perpetuating the caste system, a hierarchical social structure that divided people into different classes. The Manusmriti, a foundational text attributed to the sage Manu, outlined the duties and responsibilities of each caste, reinforcing the Brahmins' position as the highest class. This text's influence persisted for centuries, shaping social norms and practices in Hindu societies and illustrating how religious authority was used to maintain social order and control.

One particularly intriguing aspect of Brahminical influence involves the preservation and interpretation of ancient texts. For instance, the Brahmins were responsible for memorizing and orally transmitting vast amounts of Vedic literature. Their rigorous training and disciplined methods ensured that sacred texts were preserved accurately over generations. However, this control over sacred knowledge also allowed them to manipulate religious teachings to reinforce their own power and influence, a practice that would have profound implications for Hindu society.

One of the most painful examples of exploitation within Hinduism is the ritual of Sati. This practice involved widows being forced to immolate themselves on their husbands' funeral pyres. While Sati was not mandated by the core Hindu scriptures, certain Brahminical authorities justified and perpetuated it to maintain social control. Women were coerced into this horrific act, stripped of their agency, and subjected to unimaginable suffering. Although the British colonial government banned Sati in 1829, the practice had already inflicted immense suffering and illustrated the brutal consequences of religious exploitation.

Judaism

In Judaism, the evolution of organized religion also brought about significant changes. Ancient Jewish religious practices were initially focused on tribal worship and rituals. However, with the establishment of the Kingdom of Israel and later the formation of the Rabbinic tradition after the destruction of the Second Temple in 70 CE, Judaism became more codified. The Talmud, a central text of Rabbinic Judaism, played a crucial role in this transformation. While the Talmud contributed to the preservation and development of Jewish law and ethics, it also led to the entrenchment of hierarchical structures and dogmas that sometimes stifled intellectual debate and marginalized dissenting voices.

In ancient Israel, the worship practices of the early Israelites were deeply entwined with their tribal identity. One captivating story from this period involves the Ark of the Covenant, a sacred chest said to contain the tablets of the Ten Commandments. According to biblical accounts, the Ark was carried into battle by the Israelites as a divine standard. During the battle of Jericho, the Ark was paraded around the city's walls, and when the Israelites blew their trumpets, the walls famously fell down. This story underscores the central role of ritual and sacred objects in early Jewish worship.

The destruction of the Second Temple in 70 CE was a watershed moment in Jewish history, leading to profound changes in religious practice. The Temple had been the center of Jewish worship and sacrifice, so its loss was a significant blow. In the wake of this destruction, Jewish scholars and leaders convened at Yavne, a town on the Mediterranean coast, to establish new religious norms and practices. This period marked the transition from a Temple-based religion to one focused on rabbinic teachings and synagogue worship, laying the groundwork for Rabbinic Judaism.

The Talmud, a monumental work of Jewish law and tradition, emerged from this transformative period. It consists of two parts: the Mishnah, a compilation of oral laws, and the Gemara, a commentary on the Mishnah. An interesting anecdote about the Talmud's development involves the famed Rabbi Akiva, who, despite being a latecomer to rabbinic studies and initially lacking formal education, became one of its most influential scholars. His enthusiasm and dedication to studying the Torah were so profound that he was known to have memorized vast amounts of scripture, demonstrating the power of intellectual perseverance in shaping religious tradition.

The Talmud's role in codifying Jewish law was not without controversy. For example, the debates recorded in the Talmud often reflect intense discussions and disagreements among rabbis. One story tells of a famous debate between Rabbi Hillel and Rabbi Shammai, two leading scholars with opposing views on numerous issues. Their disagreements were so fervent that their followers would often find themselves caught in disputes, reflecting how rabbinic authority and interpretation could both clarify and complicate religious practice.

A lesser-known fact about the Talmud is its role in the development of Jewish humor. The Talmud contains numerous anecdotes and stories that reflect a sophisticated sense of humor and irony. For instance, there is a story about a rabbi who, when asked why he was so optimistic despite the many troubles of life, responded that he was like a "broken jug"—always filled with hope despite being cracked. This light-hearted approach highlights how humor and wisdom were intertwined in rabbinic thought.

The evolution of Jewish law and ethics through the Talmud also led to the establishment of various practices that have become central to Jewish life. For example, the Talmudic discussions on dietary laws gave rise to the kosher dietary practices observed today. The intricate details of these laws, including the separation of meat and dairy and the specific requirements for slaughtering animals, reflect a deep concern for spiritual and physical purity that has shaped Jewish identity over centuries.

Despite its role in codifying Jewish law, the Talmud also faced criticism for its complexity and perceived rigidity. Some scholars argue that the Talmudic focus on detailed legalism sometimes stifled broader intellectual inquiry and marginalized dissenting voices. Nevertheless, the Talmud remains a vital text for understanding the development of Jewish thought and practice, embodying a tradition of rigorous debate and scholarship.

Christianity

Christianity, which emerged as a sect within Judaism in the 1st century CE, quickly grew into a major world religion, driven by the teachings and missionary work of its early followers. One of the most fascinating figures in early Christianity was the Apostle Paul, originally named Saul. Once a fierce persecutor of Christians, Paul experienced a dramatic conversion on the road to Damascus, where he reported seeing a vision of Jesus. This event transformed him into one of Christianity's most ardent evangelists, and his letters, or epistles, to early Christian communities became foundational texts of the New Testament.

The early Church Fathers, such as St. Augustine and St. Jerome, were pivotal in forming Christian doctrine and consolidating the religious texts. St. Augustine's *Confessions* is not only a profound spiritual autobiography but also a cornerstone of Christian philosophy and theology. In it, Augustine details his journey from a life of sin to his conversion to Christianity, providing deep insights into the human condition and the nature of divine grace. St. Jerome, on the other hand, is renowned for his translation of the Bible into Latin, known as the *Vulgate*, which became the Catholic Church's official Bible for many centuries.

The suppression of Gnostic texts and early Christian heresies reveals the Church's efforts to establish a unified doctrine. The Gnostics, for example, believed in secret knowledge (gnosis) that could lead to spiritual salvation. Their texts, such as the *Gospel of Thomas*, offered alternative perspectives on Jesus's teachings and emphasized personal spiritual experience over institutional authority. However, these texts were deemed heretical and were largely suppressed, only to be rediscovered in the 20th century with the Nag Hammadi library find in Egypt, which provided new insights into early Christian diversity.

The dominance of the Catholic Church during the medieval period is a vivid example of religious control. The practice of selling indulgences reached its peak in the 16th century, where these documents were marketed as a means to reduce punishment for sins in the afterlife. The funds raised were often used for grand projects, such as the construction of St. Peter's Basilica in Rome. This practice was infamously criticized by Martin Luther, a German monk and theologian, who nailed his Ninety-Five Theses to the door of the Wittenberg Castle Church in 1517. Luther's theses condemned the corruption and greed of the Church, particularly the sale of indulgences, and called for a return to true Christian values.

Martin Luther's protest sparked the Protestant Reformation, a seismic shift in Christian history that led to the formation of numerous Protestant denominations and significantly challenged the Catholic Church's authority. One captivating story from this period involves the Diet of Worms in 1521, where Luther was summoned to recant his teachings. Standing before the Holy Roman Emperor Charles V and other high-ranking officials, Luther famously declared, "Here I stand, I can do no other," refusing to retract his statements and cementing his role as a leading figure in the Reformation.

Despite the Reformation, the Catholic Church continued to wield considerable influence. The Council of Trent (1545-1563) was convened as a part of the Counter-Reformation efforts to address the issues raised by

Protestant reformers and to reform the Church from within. This council reaffirmed core Catholic doctrines and implemented measures to combat corruption, such as stricter regulations on the sale of indulgences.

A particularly intriguing aspect of the Catholic Church's history involves its manipulation of religious dogma to maintain control. For instance, the concept of papal infallibility, formalized in the First Vatican Council of 1869-1870, asserted that the Pope was incapable of error when proclaiming doctrines of faith and morals. This doctrine reinforced the central authority of the Pope and the Church, further consolidating their influence over the faithful.

Islam

In Islam, the rise of organized religion also led to complex and sometimes troubling developments. The early Islamic Caliphates, such as the Umayyad and Abbasid dynasties, were instrumental in the spread of Islamic civilization and culture. One of the most fascinating figures from this period is Caliph Harun al-Rashid, who ruled during the height of the Abbasid dynasty's Golden Age. His court in Baghdad was renowned for its opulence and intellectual vibrancy. The legendary tales of *One Thousand and One Nights* often depict Harun al-Rashid wandering the streets of Baghdad in disguise to experience the lives of his subjects firsthand. This period saw remarkable advancements in science, medicine, mathematics, and philosophy, with scholars like Al-Khwarizmi, the father of algebra, and Avicenna, a polymath whose works influenced both Islamic and European thought.

Despite the flourishing of Islamic culture under these caliphates, the establishment of formal religious and political institutions also led to hierarchical structures that often stifled dissent. For example, the theological and philosophical debates between the Mutazilites and the Ash'arites in the 9th and 10th centuries highlighted the tensions within Islamic thought. The Mutazilites advocated for the use of reason and rationalism in interpreting Islamic texts, while the Ash'arites emphasized divine revelation and traditionalism. The eventual triumph of the Ash'arites led to the marginalization of rationalist thought in many Islamic regions.

The rise of Salafism and Wahhabism in the modern era, particularly in Saudi Arabia, has further exemplified the dangers of radical interpretations of Islamic doctrine. Salafism, which seeks to return to what its adherents consider the purest form of Islam practiced by the earliest generations (the Salaf), often promotes a strict and literalist approach to Islamic teachings. Wahhabism, a branch of Salafism founded by Muhammad ibn Abd al-Wahhab in the 18th century, has been particularly influential in Saudi Arabia. One striking anecdote involves the alliance between Muhammad ibn Abd al-Wahhab and the Saudi tribal leader Muhammad ibn Saud. This pact, made in 1744, laid the foundation for the modern Saudi state and the spread of Wahhabi doctrines.

These movements have had significant impacts on both global and local scales. For example, the destruction of historical sites and cultural heritage in Mecca and Medina, carried out under the guise of religious purity by Wahhabi followers, has drawn widespread condemnation. This includes the demolition of the graves of the Prophet Muhammad's family and companions, which were seen as potential sites of idolatry.

A lesser-known but fascinating fact is the role of coffee in Islamic culture. Coffeehouses, known as qahveh khaneh, became popular in the Middle East during the Ottoman Empire. These establishments were not only places for drinking coffee but also centers of social interaction, political discussion, and intellectual exchange. However, they also faced opposition from religious authorities who viewed them as venues for idle gossip and potential dissent. Despite this, coffeehouses became integral to the social fabric of Islamic societies and played a significant role in the cultural and intellectual life of the time.

In the realm of religious tolerance, it's worth noting the example of Al-Andalus, the Muslim-ruled region of medieval Spain. Under the rule of the Umayyad Caliphate of Córdoba, Al-Andalus became a melting pot of cultures and religions, where Muslims, Christians, and Jews coexisted and contributed to a vibrant and diverse society. This period saw remarkable achievements in architecture, such as the Great Mosque of Córdoba, and advancements in science, philosophy, and the arts. However, this era also faced periods of tension and conflict, reflecting the complexities of religious and cultural coexistence.

Buddhism

Similarly, in Buddhism, the transition to organized religious institutions led to the development of hierarchical structures and dogmas that sometimes stifled intellectual and spiritual freedom. In Buddhism, the transition to organized religious institutions indeed led to the development of hierarchical structures and dogmas. The establishment of the Sangha, the monastic community, was a pivotal moment in early Buddhism. One fascinating aspect of this development is the Vinaya, a set of rules for monks and nuns that govern their conduct. The Vinaya contains not only ethical guidelines but also detailed procedures for resolving disputes and maintaining harmony within the monastic community. An interesting trivia is that the Buddha himself is said to have instituted these rules in response to specific incidents among his followers, illustrating his pragmatic approach to monastic life.

The Tibetan Buddhist tradition, under the leadership of the Dalai Lama, has made significant contributions to spiritual and intellectual development. The institution of the Dalai Lama dates back to the 14th century, with the first Dalai Lama, Gedun Drupa, being recognized as the reincarnation of Avalokiteshvara, the Bodhisattva of Compassion. The current Dalai Lama, Tenzin Gyatso, the 14th Dalai Lama, is one of the most recognized spiritual leaders in the world and has played a crucial role in promoting Tibetan Buddhism and advocating for peace and human rights. An interesting fact about the 14th Dalai Lama is that he was awarded the Nobel Peace Prize in 1989 for his nonviolent struggle for the liberation of Tibet.

However, the hierarchical structures in Tibetan Buddhism have sometimes stifled intellectual and spiritual freedom. One compelling story involves the controversy over the recognition of the Panchen Lama, the second-highest figure in Tibetan Buddhism. In 1995, after the 10th Panchen Lama's death, the Dalai Lama recognized a young boy named Gedhun Choekyi Nyima as the 11th Panchen Lama. However, the Chinese government intervened and installed their own candidate, Gyaltsen Norbu, leading to a complex and ongoing dispute. The whereabouts of Gedhun Choekyi Nyima remain unknown, and he is often referred to as the "world's youngest political prisoner."

Despite these hierarchical challenges, Tibetan Buddhism has also fueled incredible intellectual and spiritual achievements. The Tibetan monastic university system, with institutions like Sera, Drepung, and Ganden, has produced some of the most profound philosophical and scholastic works in Buddhist history. The Gelug school, founded by Je Tsongkhapa in the 14th century, emphasized rigorous study and debate, contributing to a rich tradition of scholasticism. Je Tsongkhapa himself was a prolific writer and reformer, known for his works on Madhyamaka philosophy and for establishing the Great Prayer Festival (Monlam Chenmo) in Lhasa, which became an important religious and social event in Tibet.

Another fascinating aspect of Tibetan Buddhism is the practice of Tulkus, or reincarnated lamas. This system of recognizing the reincarnations of high lamas has created a unique blend of continuity and renewal within the tradition. One of the most famous Tulkus is the Karmapa, the head of the Karma Kagyu lineage. The selection of the 17th Karmapa was marked by controversy, with two competing candidates being recognized by different factions within the Karma Kagyu school. This dispute highlights the complexities and challenges of maintaining religious authority and tradition in Tibetan Buddhism.

An interesting anecdote about Tibetan Buddhism's influence beyond the Himalayas involves the travels of the great Indian Buddhist master, Padmasambhava, also known as Guru Rinpoche. Invited to Tibet in the 8th century by King Trisong Detsen, Padmasambhava is credited with subduing the local spirits and establishing Buddhism in Tibet. His legendary exploits, filled with miraculous events and spiritual conquests, are vividly depicted in Tibetan art and literature. Padmasambhava's influence extends to Bhutan, where he is revered as the "Second Buddha" and credited with establishing Buddhism as the state religion.

Despite the hierarchical structures, Tibetan Buddhism has also been a source of profound spiritual inspiration and innovation. The practice of Dzogchen, or "Great Perfection," within the Nyingma school, offers a direct and experiential approach to enlightenment, emphasizing the innate purity and perfection of the mind. This practice has inspired many contemporary teachers and practitioners, contributing to the diversity and richness of Tibetan Buddhist thought.

Organized religion therefore, in its many forms, has historically subjugated humanity by imposing rigid doctrines, promoting narrow-mindedness, and engaging in systematic indoctrination. These institutions have often diluted fundamental ethical principles, with many religious leaders succumbing to corruption. By perpetuating ignorance, promoting hollow rituals, and inciting hatred and violence against other faiths, organized religion has too often served as a tool for control rather than a source of moral guidance.

Religious Dogma and Suppression of Inquiry

The imposition of dogma and the suppression of scientific inquiry have been deeply entrenched in organized religions across different cultures and eras. These practices have often stifled intellectual progress and maintained control over followers through fear and repression.

A prominent example of this phenomenon is the medieval Catholic Church's treatment of Galileo Galilei. In the early 17th century, Galileo's support for the heliocentric model, which posited that the Earth revolves around the Sun, directly contradicted the Church's geocentric doctrine that placed the Earth at the center of the universe. This clash with the Church's official teaching led to Galileo's trial by the Roman Catholic Inquisition. Accused of heresy, Galileo was forced to recant his views and spent the remaining years of his life under house arrest. This suppression of Galileo's groundbreaking scientific work exemplifies how religious dogma can hinder intellectual progress and reinforce ecclesiastical authority by discouraging dissent and critical thinking.

The Inquisition itself, established in the 12th century by the Catholic Church, represents another severe measure used to enforce religious orthodoxy. This institution was notorious for its use of torture and execution to root out heresy. The Spanish Inquisition, in particular, is infamous for its brutality, targeting Jews, Muslims, and suspected witches. The systematic persecution and execution of those who deviated from established Church teachings resulted in countless deaths and imprisonments, illustrating the extreme lengths to which religious authorities would go to maintain control and suppress alternative viewpoints.

The dogmatic suppression of scientific inquiry is not unique to Christianity. In Islam, the early medieval period saw the flourishing of intellectual pursuits during the Islamic Golden Age, with scholars making significant advances in science, mathematics, and philosophy. However, over time, rigid interpretations of Islamic doctrine began to stifle scientific and philosophical inquiry. The rise of conservative movements and the implementation of Sharia law in various countries have sometimes led to the suppression of scientific progress. For instance, the enforcement of strict religious laws in countries like Saudi Arabia has led to the curtailment of educational and scientific freedoms.

Similarly, in Hinduism, certain sects and dogmas have also impeded intellectual freedom. The caste system, deeply rooted in Hindu religious texts and traditions, has perpetuated social inequality and discrimination, discouraging social mobility and critical inquiry into its unjust practices. The dogmatic adherence to the caste system has been challenged by reformers like B.R. Ambedkar, who sought to dismantle these oppressive structures. Yet, resistance to such reforms has often come from those who maintain traditional interpretations of religious texts that support the caste hierarchy.

In Buddhism, particularly in its more traditional forms, there have been instances where religious authorities have suppressed dissent and discouraged critical examination of established doctrines. For example, the Tibetan Buddhist tradition under the Dalai Lama's leadership has faced criticism for maintaining hierarchical structures and controlling religious teachings, potentially stifling reformist ideas and intellectual diversity within the tradition.

These examples across different religions illustrate a broader pattern where religious institutions and dogmas have historically suppressed scientific inquiry and intellectual freedom.

Monetization of Faith

The exploitation of followers for financial gain remains a deeply ingrained issue in organized religion, with many religious institutions historically amassing significant wealth through various means. This monetization of faith has often enriched religious leaders and perpetuated social inequality and corruption.

The sale of indulgences became a significant source of revenue, with vast sums of money flowing into the Church's coffers.

In contemporary times, the exploitation of followers for financial gain continues through various religious organizations and figures. Televangelists and prosperity gospel preachers have carried forward this tradition, often using sophisticated media strategies to solicit funds from their followers. Figures such as Jim Bakker and Benny

Hinn are notable examples. Bakker, who once led the PTL (Praise The Lord) Club, was convicted of fraud and conspiracy in the 1980s. Despite his conviction, he continued to solicit donations through his new ministry, often appealing to the financial hopes of his followers with promises of divine blessings and miraculous healings. Benny Hinn, known for his extravagant healing crusades, has similarly amassed a considerable fortune by convincing his audience that financial donations would result in personal and spiritual rewards. Hinn's lavish lifestyle, funded by the contributions of his often impoverished followers, starkly contrasts with the promises of prosperity and blessings he preaches.

In India, the exploitation of followers by self-styled gurus has also been pervasive. Swami Nithyananda, for instance, has faced numerous accusations of sexual abuse and fraud. Despite legal troubles, he continues to deceive his followers by claiming supernatural powers and spiritual authority, amassing wealth and influence through donations and offerings in his new pseudo-nation called 'Kailasa.' Asaram Bapu, another notorious figure, was convicted of raping a minor in 2018. His ashrams, which attracted millions of followers, provided him with significant resources and the means to evade justice for years. Both Nithyananda and Asaram Bapu exemplify how religious figures exploit the faith of their followers for personal gain.

These examples underscore a troubling pattern within organized religion, where financial exploitation is often disguised as spiritual necessity. The vast sums of money collected through tithes, donations, and offerings are frequently used to support lavish lifestyles and institutional power rather than the welfare of the followers. This exploitation is not only a betrayal of the trust placed in these leaders but also a perpetuation of social and economic inequalities under the guise of spiritual guidance.

The Predators of Faith. Cults, often centered around charismatic leaders, have been notorious for sexual exploitation. Jim Jones, the founder of the Peoples Temple, used his charismatic influence to manipulate and control his followers, ultimately leading to the tragic Jonestown massacre. Jones initially attracted followers with promises of social equality and communal living. However, he increasingly demanded financial contributions from his congregation, coercing them into signing over their paychecks, social security benefits, and even life insurance policies. By exploiting their devotion and creating a climate of fear and dependency, Jones amassed substantial wealth, which he used to fund his lavish lifestyle and the establishment of Jonestown in Guyana. His control culminated in the 1978 Jonestown massacre, where over 900 people died, illustrating the extreme dangers of unchecked religious authority.

David Koresh, leader of the Branch Davidians, claimed divine status to justify sexual relationships with numerous women and underage girls in his community. The 1993 Waco siege, resulting in 76 deaths, exposed the extent of his manipulative and abusive practices. He exercised strict control over his followers, demanding absolute loyalty and obedience. Koresh exploited his followers' beliefs by convincing them that he was the final prophet and that their material possessions should be surrendered to support their religious community. He amassed wealth by compelling followers to contribute their savings and assets, which he used to stockpile weapons and build a compound in Waco, Texas. Koresh's authoritarian rule and the financial exploitation of his followers culminated in a tragic standoff with federal authorities in 1993, resulting in the deaths of Koresh and many of his followers.

Shoko Asahara, the founder of Aum Shinrikyo, used a blend of Eastern and Western religious ideologies to attract followers, whom he systematically exploited for financial gain. Asahara promised spiritual enlightenment and supernatural powers, which enticed followers to donate large sums of money and personal property. Through intimidation, manipulation, and promises of spiritual advancement, Asahara amassed significant wealth, which he used to fund his elaborate lifestyle and the development of chemical weapons. His organization sold his semen to this followers for vast sums of money. His leadership ultimately led to the infamous Tokyo subway sarin attack in 1995, revealing the extent of his control and the devastating consequences of his financial and psychological exploitation of his followers.

Osho Rajneesh, an Indian spiritual leader, founded a movement that attracted a global following with its promise of enlightenment and liberation through meditation and free love. He preached that humans can attain complete freedom and realization of god in a state of sexual orgasm. His disciples engaged in free sexual activities. Rajneesh's commune in Oregon, USA, known as Rajneesh Puram, became a hub for his teachings and amassed considerable wealth through donations from wealthy followers, the sale of books, and other commercial ventures. Despite his teachings on simplicity and detachment, Rajneesh led a luxurious lifestyle, owning a fleet of Rolls-Royces and other opulent possessions. His movement was marred by allegations of financial mismanagement, fraud, and even bioterrorism, highlighting the stark contrast between his public persona and the behind-the-scenes exploitation of his followers' wealth and trust.

Holy Wars and Religious Violence

Religion has often justified violence and conflict, leading to devastating holy wars and persecution. Throughout history, religious beliefs have been used to legitimize acts of aggression, conquest, and genocide. The Crusades, a series of religious wars between the 11th and 13th centuries, illustrate this dangerous aspect of religion.

The Crusades were initiated by the Catholic Church to reclaim the Holy Land from Muslim control. Tens of thousands of people participated in these wars, driven by promises of spiritual rewards and absolution of sins. However, the Crusades resulted in widespread destruction, loss of life, and deep-seated animosities between different religious groups. These conflicts underscore how religion can be manipulated to justify violence and achieve political goals.

The Thirty Years' War (1618-1648), one of the most destructive conflicts in European history, also demonstrates the deadly impact of religious conflict.

Initially sparked by tensions between Protestant and Catholic states within the Holy Roman Empire, the war devastated much of Europe, resulting in the deaths of an estimated 8 million people. The war's brutalities, including widespread famine, disease, and atrocities committed by both sides, highlight the catastrophic consequences of religiously fueled violence.

False Prophecies and Manipulation

Promoting false prophecies and manipulating religious texts are tactics frequently employed by religious leaders to maintain control and influence. Throughout history, individuals claiming to possess divine knowledge or prophetic abilities have misled followers for personal gain.

One notorious example is Nostradamus, a 16th-century French astrologer and seer. Nostradamus's cryptic quatrains have been interpreted as prophecies, leading many to believe in his supernatural abilities. However, his vague and ambiguous predictions can be retroactively fitted to various events, demonstrating the manipulative nature of his claims. Despite this, Nostradamus gained a significant following, illustrating how easily people can be deceived by false prophecies.

Modern-day cults also demonstrate the dangers of false prophecies and manipulation. The Heaven's Gate cult, led by Marshall Applewhite, convinced its members that they would be taken to a higher existence aboard an alien spacecraft following the Hale-Bopp comet. In 1997, 39 members committed mass suicide, believing they were transitioning to this new life. Applewhite's charismatic leadership and manipulation of his followers' beliefs underscore the perilous power of false religious claims.

Fake Gurus and Tantrics

In various cultures, the phenomenon of fake gurus and fraudulent religious leaders illustrates a profound abuse of faith for personal gain. These individuals, often charismatic and persuasive, exploit the trust of their followers by presenting themselves as embodiments of divine power or wisdom. Through deception and manipulation, they promise miraculous healings, spiritual enlightenment, and supernatural insights, while engaging in unethical and often illegal activities. The case of such leaders reveals the vulnerabilities within spiritual communities and underscores the pressing need for vigilance against fraudulent practices.

The impact of such fraudulent leaders extends beyond individual cases, reflecting a broader pattern of exploitation across different religious and spiritual traditions. For example, in the realm of tantric practices, some self-styled gurus and practitioners have been known to exploit the mystique of tantra for personal gain. Tantric practices, which originated in Hinduism and Buddhism, are often shrouded in secrecy and complexity. This opacity makes them ripe for exploitation by fake gurus who claim to offer powerful rituals or spiritual benefits. These practices sometimes involve elaborate rituals that can include symbolic acts of violence or sacrifice, though authentic tantric traditions do not condone actual harm. Unfortunately, some fraudulent practitioners have used the guise of tantra to deceive and manipulate vulnerable individuals, promoting dangerous and unethical practices under the pretense of spiritual advancement.

The Aghori Sadhus and Naga Sadhus are Hindu ascetics known for their extreme and often shocking practices, which they claim are part of their spiritual path to achieving enlightenment and liberation. Aghoris are notorious for their rituals involving human skulls, cremation ashes, and cannibalism, which they argue are ways to transcend worldly attachments and defy taboos. Similarly, Naga Sadhus engage in severe austerities, including nudity, and public displays of self-mortification, intended to demonstrate their renunciation of worldly life. However, these practices often attract attention and curiosity, which some individuals exploit for financial gain and notoriety. Reports have surfaced of fraudulent activities where so-called sadhus deceive followers and tourists, demanding money for blessings or rituals, and leveraging their shocking practices to create a mystique that can be monetized. Such actions undermine the genuine spiritual traditions they claim to represent, revealing a darker side of exploitation and fraud masked by the guise of religious devotion.

Voodoo practices, particularly in certain regions, have also been exploited by charlatans posing as practitioners with magical abilities. In some cases, individuals claiming to be voodoo priests or priestesses use fear and superstition to control and defraud their followers. They might promise protection from malevolent forces, success in love, or financial prosperity in exchange for large sums of money or other material goods. In the worst cases, these fraudulent practitioners have been known to perpetuate myths about human sacrifice or other harmful rituals, preying on the gullibility of those seeking spiritual guidance.

Vama Tantra, a controversial branch of Tantric practice, is often associated with ritualistic use of substances and activities typically considered taboo in traditional Hinduism, such as liquor, sex, meat, fish, and grain. Practitioners claim these elements are used to transcend societal norms and achieve spiritual liberation. However, this mystique and allure of forbidden practices create a fertile ground for exploitation. Unscrupulous individuals pose as Tantric gurus, manipulating the credulous by promising miraculous results and spiritual enlightenment through expensive and elaborate rituals involving these taboo substances. Followers are often coerced into providing large sums of money, personal favours, or even sexual services under the guise of sacred rites.

The cases of these fake gurus and their fraudulent practices serve as a stark reminder of the dangers inherent in religious and spiritual deception. The charisma and persuasive abilities of these individuals can easily mask their true intentions, making it crucial for followers to approach spiritual claims with skepticism and critical thinking. As these examples illustrate, the exploitation of faith and spiritual beliefs for personal gain is a pervasive issue that requires ongoing vigilance and education to prevent and address.

Sexual Exploitation by Religious Leaders and Institutions

Religion, revered for its moral guidance and spiritual solace, has often concealed a sinister reality where leaders exploit their positions to commit sexual abuse. This pattern of exploitation transcends geographical boundaries and historical periods, revealing a disturbing consistency in how power can corrupt even the most sacred institutions.

This systematic cover-up allowed abusers to continue their misconduct, perpetuating a cycle of suffering and betrayal. The Church's failure to address these crimes transparently and justly has eroded its moral authority and highlighted the dangers of unchecked religious power.

Similarly, in Hinduism, the practice of Devadasi, where young girls were dedicated to temples and subjected to sexual exploitation, persisted for centuries. Despite being officially banned, this practice continued due to the complicity and concealment by religious authorities. The exploitation of these girls, often under the guise of religious service, exemplifies the deep-seated corruption and abuse within religious institutions.

The Catholic Church's sexual abuse scandals are among the most well-documented and pervasive. For decades, priests like Father John Geoghan in the Boston Archdiocese molested countless children, with church authorities, including Cardinal Bernard Law, systematically covering up the abuse. The Boston Globe's "Spotlight" investigation in 2002 revealed that Geoghan alone had abused over 130 boys, and similar stories emerged from dioceses worldwide. The Church's response was often to reassign rather than defrock abusive priests, prioritizing the institution's reputation over victims' safety. This systemic failure led to a crisis of faith for many Catholics and billions in settlements to victims.

Similarly, Keith Raniere of NXIVM created a secret society where women were branded and coerced into sexual servitude, masking abuse as spiritual empowerment.

Sexual scandals within evangelical and Protestant communities highlight another dimension of religious exploitation. Televangelist Jimmy Swaggart's downfall began in 1988 when his involvement with prostitutes was exposed. His tearful confessions and subsequent relapse into scandal underscored the hypocrisy within some evangelical circles. Ted Haggard, once a prominent evangelical leader, was found engaging in drug-fueled sexual encounters with a male escort, despite his public anti-homosexuality stance.

Bill Hybels, founder of Willow Creek Community Church, faced multiple allegations of sexual misconduct. His 2018 resignation shocked the evangelical community, revealing how power and prestige can shield predatory behavior. These cases underscore the need for transparency and accountability in religious leadership.

Eastern religions and new spiritual movements have also seen significant abuse cases. Swami Bhimanand ran a prostitution ring under the guise of spiritual leadership, exploiting followers' faith for financial gain.

The sexual exploitation by religious leaders profoundly impacts victims, undermines moral authority, and exposes deep hypocrisy. These leaders, entrusted with spiritual guidance, betray their followers' trust in the most intimate and devastating ways. The scandals reveal a pattern of using religious authority to silence victims and evade accountability, perpetuating cycles of abuse.

Charles Manson, the notorious leader of the Manson Family cult, manipulated his followers through a combination of psychological control and charismatic persuasion. Manson's followers, primarily young women, were convinced to sever ties with their families and turn over their assets to him. Manson exploited their devotion, using it to support his own needs and his twisted vision of an apocalyptic race war, which he called "Helter Skelter." Although Manson's primary objective was not financial gain, his control over his followers ensured that their resources were at his disposal, providing him with a communal living arrangement and the means to sustain his influence.

To address this pervasive issue, systemic changes are necessary within religious institutions. Greater transparency, accountability, and victim support are essential. Religious leaders must be held to higher ethical standards, and independent oversight bodies should be established to investigate and address allegations of abuse.

While religion aims to uplift humanity, it has often been a cover for exploitation and abuse. Religious institutions and their leaders have often employed various methods to secure monetary and sexual advantages. Millions flock to these so-called spiritual leaders, becoming unwittingly enslaved to these institutions. Most people only begin to question their authority after scandals are exposed. Yet, in a perplexing twist, many continue to follow these charlatans, even in the face of overwhelming evidence of their deceit.

Radical Elements and Dangers of Religion

Radical elements within religions pose significant threats to global peace and stability. Extremist ideologies, often rooted in fundamentalist interpretations of religious texts, have fueled terrorism, discrimination, and violence. These groups exploit religious narratives to justify their acts of terror and recruit followers, demonstrating the dangerous potential of radical beliefs.

Groups like Al-Qaeda and ISIS have become synonymous with radical Islamic terrorism. Al-Qaeda, founded by Osama bin Laden in the late 1980s, orchestrated the September 11, 2001, attacks, killing nearly 3,000 people in the United States. This act of terror marked a significant escalation in global jihadist violence, with Al-Qaeda promoting a militant interpretation of Islam that calls for violent jihad against perceived enemies of Islam, including Western nations and moderate Muslims.

ISIS, or the Islamic State of Iraq and Syria, emerged from the remnants of Al-Qaeda in Iraq. Under the leadership of Abu Bakr al-Baghdadi, ISIS declared a caliphate in 2014, capturing vast territories in Iraq and Syria. The group's brutal tactics included mass executions, sexual slavery, and the destruction of cultural heritage sites. ISIS used sophisticated propaganda to recruit fighters globally, emphasizing a radical and puritanical interpretation of Islam that justified extreme violence and aimed to establish a global Islamic state.

Both Al-Qaeda and ISIS exploited religious texts and narratives to brainwash followers, portraying their violent acts as divinely sanctioned. They targeted vulnerable individuals, often through online platforms, promising glory, martyrdom, and a sense of belonging.

In Christianity, the Westboro Baptist Church (WBC) exemplifies radical extremism. Founded by Fred Phelps in 1955, the WBC is notorious for its hateful rhetoric and protests at funerals. The church preaches an extreme interpretation of the Bible that condemns LGBTQ+ individuals, Jews, Muslims, and soldiers, among others. Their infamous slogan, "God hates fags," underscores their virulent anti-LGBTQ+ stance.

The WBC's actions include picketing military funerals with inflammatory signs, claiming that the deaths of soldiers are divine punishment for the United States' tolerance of homosexuality. This radical ideology not only deepens division and hatred but also misrepresents the core tenets of Christianity, which emphasize love, compassion, and forgiveness. The WBC's extremism demonstrates the destructive potential of radical beliefs within any religious tradition.

Some peaceful religions such as Hinduism also took to radical extremism in response to the violence perpetrated by the Muslim League led by Jinnah. But anti-social elements under the guise of protectors of the religion make targeted attacks on innocent Muslims in India. Such violence suits the politicians as they harness this hatred for their communal agenda.

Extremist leaders often use sophisticated techniques to brainwash and recruit followers. This includes exploiting socio-economic grievances, providing a sense of purpose and identity, and using religious texts to justify violence. For instance, ISIS recruiters promised recruits a utopian Islamic state and used graphic propaganda to desensitize them to violence.

Addressing the threat of religious extremism requires multifaceted strategies, including promoting education, facilitating interfaith dialogue, and enhancing social integration. De-radicalization programs aim to reintegrate former extremists into society by challenging their beliefs and providing support networks.

Prominent religious leaders and scholars also play a crucial role in countering extremism by emphasizing moderate and inclusive interpretations of religious texts. For instance, Islamic scholars worldwide have condemned ISIS and Al-Qaeda, arguing that their actions are antithetical to Islamic teachings.

The Dangers of Absence of Religion

Throwing out Religion is like throwing the baby with the bathwater. The absence of religion, particularly when accompanied by nihilism or atheism, presents profound challenges to both individuals and societies. While religion has historically subjugated humans and instilled fear and slavish mindset, it also provided moral guidance, community, and a sense of purpose.

The absence of religion raises complex questions about psychological stability, social order, and legal systems. The potential dangers of a world devoid of religious frameworks must be examined to understand how the absence of such structures might impact human behavior and societal functioning.

At its core, nihilism—the belief that life is without objective meaning, purpose, or intrinsic value—can lead to psychological disarray. When individuals confront the idea that life lacks inherent meaning, it can precipitate a profound existential crisis. This crisis may manifest as a sense of futility or despair, driving some individuals towards apathy or self-destructive behaviors. For instance, Friedrich Nietzsche, a prominent philosopher known for his exploration of nihilism, warned that the decline of religious and metaphysical beliefs could lead to a void in values, potentially causing a sense of disorientation and a loss of moral compass. The absence of religious or spiritual anchors can lead to heightened anxiety and depression, as individuals struggle to find purpose and meaning in a seemingly indifferent universe.

In the realm of law and order, the absence of religious moral frameworks poses significant challenges. Many legal systems have historically been influenced by religious principles that underpin concepts of justice, equity, and morality. For example, the Ten Commandments have had a profound impact on Western legal traditions, creating notions of theft, murder, and perjury. Without a religious foundation, societies must rely on secular ethical systems to uphold legal norms. While secular ethics can be robust, the transition from religious to secular moral systems can lead to debates over the nature of justice and the basis for laws. Societies might struggle to develop universally accepted standards of morality and justice, potentially leading to legal uncertainty and fragmentation.

Social order is similarly affected by the absence of religion. Religious institutions often provide social cohesion through community activities, rituals, and shared beliefs. They can create a sense of belonging and collective identity, which can be crucial for social stability. For instance, churches, mosques, temples, and synagogues frequently serve as centers for social support, charitable activities, and community engagement. The absence of such institutions may result in the erosion of social bonds and a decline in community-oriented values. This gap might be filled by other forms of social organization, such as secular clubs or online communities, but these alternatives may not always provide the same depth of connection or support.

Moreover, the rise of nihilistic or atheistic perspectives can sometimes lead to moral relativism, where the lack of absolute ethical standards results in diverse and conflicting moral viewpoints. This relativism can create tension and instability, as individuals and groups may find it difficult to agree on fundamental ethical principles. In extreme cases, it can lead to the normalization of behaviors that were previously deemed unacceptable, potentially undermining social norms and contributing to moral ambiguity.

How is the present Generation viewing Religion?

The present generation is increasingly scrutinizing organized religion, questioning its doctrines, and embracing humanism as an alternative ethical framework. This shift is driven by a desire for rationality, equality, and an evidence-based understanding of the world. The impact of this movement is evident in various parts of the world through changing demographics, rising secularism, and the growing influence of humanist organizations.

In the United States, a 2021 Gallup poll found that the percentage of Americans identifying as members of a church, synagogue, or mosque has dropped below 50% for the first time in history, down from 70% in 1999. This decline is particularly pronounced among younger generations, with only 36% of Millennials identifying as religious. Similarly, in Europe, secularism is on the rise. A 2018 survey by the Pew Research Center found that 72% of people in Sweden, 55% in the United Kingdom, and 60% in France identify as non-religious. This trend is mirrored across other Western European countries.

The global humanist movement is gaining prominence through organizations such as Humanists International and the American Humanist Association. Humanists International's 2020 Global Report indicated that there are now humanist organizations in over 100 countries, with substantial growth in regions like Latin America, Africa, and Asia. Humanist values are being integrated into education systems and public policies. For example, in the

Netherlands, humanist counseling is available as part of public healthcare. In Norway, humanist ceremonies for weddings, funerals, and naming are legally recognized and increasingly popular, accounting for 17% of all weddings in 2019.

The shift towards humanism is associated with advances in social progress and equality. Countries with high levels of secularism, such as the Nordic nations, often rank highly on indices of gender equality, LGBTQ+ rights, and overall happiness. For instance, Norway, Sweden, and Denmark are consistently among the top performers in the World Happiness Report. Embracing humanism promotes scientific literacy and rational thinking. Countries with strong humanist movements, like Finland and Estonia, perform exceptionally well in international educational assessments, particularly in science and mathematics, according to the OECD's PISA reports. Legal reforms influenced by humanist principles are evident in changes to marriage laws, abortion rights, and euthanasia policies. For example, Ireland's legalization of same-sex marriage in 2015 and the repeal of the Eighth Amendment (which prohibited abortion) in 2018 were significantly influenced by secular and humanist campaigns.

Exposing religious fraud and abuse has led to significant societal and institutional changes. High-profile cases like the Catholic Church's sexual abuse scandals have prompted widespread calls for accountability and transparency. A 2019 Pew Research Center survey found that 81% of U.S. Catholics were aware of these scandals, and many have distanced themselves from the Church as a result. Individuals like Richard Dawkins, author of *The*

God Delusion, and Ayaan Hirsi Ali, a critic of Islamic fundamentalism, have been pivotal in challenging religious dogma and advocating for secularism. Their works have sparked global debates and inspired many to question religious authorities and embrace humanist values.

The present generation's shift away from organized religion towards humanism reflects a broader desire for rationality, equality, and evidence-based understanding. This movement is leading to significant social, educational, and legal transformations worldwide, promoting a more inclusive and progressive society. As humanist principles continue to gain traction, we can expect further advancements in human rights, scientific literacy, and ethical governance.

Future Implications of Transformation of Religion Humanism as the True Religion

In stark contrast to the deceptions and dangers often associated with organized religion, humanism offers a rational and compassionate alternative. This philosophy emphasizes the intrinsic value and agency of human beings, advocating for reason, ethics, and justice. Rejecting supernatural beliefs, humanism focuses on improving the human condition through science, education, and social progress.

Prominent humanists like Carl Sagan and Bertrand Russell have championed this philosophy. Sagan, a renowned astronomer and science communicator, famously said, "We are a way for the cosmos to know itself." This perspective encourages a direct connection with the universe and a sense of wonder that does not rely on religious dogma. Sagan's works, such as *Cosmos,* have inspired millions to appreciate the vastness of the universe and our place within it, pushing a profound sense of awe and responsibility for our planet.

Bertrand Russell, a philosopher and Nobel laureate, argued for the importance of critical thinking and skepticism. In his essay "Why I Am Not a Christian," Russell critiqued the logical inconsistencies and moral failings of organized religion, advocating for a secular and rational approach to ethics and knowledge. His contributions to humanism highlight the importance of reason and evidence in understanding the world, encouraging a mindset that values inquiry and evidence over blind faith.

Direct Conversation with God

For those who seek a spiritual dimension, a direct conversation with God or a higher power can be a fulfilling and authentic form of religion. This approach, transcending organized institutions, allows individuals to develop a personal and meaningful connection with the divine.

Mystics and spiritual seekers throughout history have pursued this path, emphasizing inner experience over external rituals. Figures like Rumi, a 13th-century Persian poet and Sufi mystic, have inspired countless individuals with their profound insights and devotion. Rumi's poetry, which celebrates divine love and unity, encourages a direct and personal relationship with God. His verses, such as "The wound is the place where the Light enters you," have become timeless expressions of spiritual longing and fulfillment.

Similarly, the Quakers, a Christian denomination founded in the 17th century, emphasize the importance of an inner light and direct experience of God. Quakers reject formal rituals and clergy, focusing instead on personal spiritual experiences and communal decision-making. This approach promotes a more egalitarian and authentic religious practice, free from the corruption and dogma often found in organized religion.

In Hinduism, numerous genuine mystics and saints have attained profound spiritual realization through ascetic practices and penance. Revered figures such as Sai Baba, Swami Vivekananda, Ramana Maharshi, and Baba Sant Nagpal Ji (also known as Chattarpur Baba) are celebrated for their intense dedication to meditation, simplicity, and spiritual enlightenment. They lived austere lives, often in isolation, focused solely on their spiritual quest without seeking fame, wealth, or recognition. Similarly, in Islam, pious leaders like Khwaja Moinuddin Chishti and other revered Sufi saints, known as Peer Babas, devoted their lives to spiritual growth and serving humanity, spreading messages of love, unity, and peace. In Christianity, figures like Saint Francis of Assisi and Mother Teresa exemplified humility, compassion, and selfless service to others. The Buddha in Buddhism renounced worldly pleasures to seek enlightenment. These true mystics and saints, across various faiths, upheld the highest spiritual and ethical standards, guiding their followers through personal example rather than seeking to amass followers or material gains.

The Societal Impact of Humanism

As humanism continues to gain traction, we can expect a profound transformation in societal values and governance. The emphasis on rationality, scientific literacy, and equality will likely lead to more progressive policies that prioritize human rights and social justice. Education systems will increasingly incorporate critical thinking and evidence-based learning, promoting a generation that values inquiry over dogma.

This shift will enhance global cooperation as countries adopt more inclusive and equitable approaches to address shared challenges such as climate change, public health, and economic inequality. Furthermore, the decline of religious influence in public life will prompt a reevaluation of laws and cultural norms historically shaped by religious doctrines. Legal reforms concerning marriage equality, reproductive rights, and end-of-life choices will become more prevalent, reflecting the values of a secular, humanist society.

The rise of digital technology and social media will continue to democratize access to information, allowing for greater scrutiny of historical and religious narratives. This increased transparency and accountability will lead to a more informed and empowered populace, capable of driving ethical and sustainable progress on a global scale.

The Future of Religion

Ultimately, the future of religion lies in its transformation. As society evolves, religion must adapt to new understandings and priorities. This transformation involves shedding harmful practices, embracing inclusivity and equality, and nurturing a genuine connection with the divine or the universe. Most importantly, new religious thinking should focus on promoting decency and respect for all humans and nature. By doing so, we can create a world where religion contributes positively to human flourishing rather than perpetuating deception and division.

In essence, the transition to humanism and the direct personal experience of spirituality present pathways to a future where human dignity, rational thought, and ethical conduct form the foundation of societal progress. Humanity can overcome the pitfalls of organized religion and move towards a more just and compassionate world, by learning from the past and embracing a more enlightened approach.

Chapter 3

How the State Manipulates Humanity

The intricate dance between power and control has shaped human societies from the dawn of civilization to the complexities of the modern era. In examining the evolution of governance, one uncovers a recurring theme: the state's persistent manipulation of its citizens, often under the guise of order and progress. From the earliest empires to contemporary democracies, governments have employed various strategies—both overt and covert—to consolidate power, manage resources, and control populations. This exploration delves into how states, through diverse mechanisms such as legal systems, propaganda, and resource appropriation, have maintained their grip on societies. We will navigate the dark side of government power, highlight the resistance movements that challenge oppression, and consider the revolutionary potential of a non-party-based parliamentary democracy. By understanding these dynamics, we can better appreciate the ongoing struggle for transparency, accountability, and justice in governance.

The Seed of the State: Origins Rooted in Power and Fear

The concept of the State is ancient, emerging from the convergence of necessity, fear, and the pursuit of power. Across various civilizations, states were formed to address the growing complexity of human societies, offering security, organizing resources, and managing populations. However, from the outset, the State was a double-edged sword—a force for both protection and suppression, shaping the course of human history with profound implications.

The State's authority is founded on the collective decision to relinquish individual rights in exchange for safety and order. Yet, this pact often leads to the opposite outcome—subjugation, control, and the erosion of freedoms.

The Philosophical Foundations of Government Power

Philosophically, the nature of government power has been debated for centuries. Thomas Hobbes, in his work *Leviathan,* argued that a strong central authority was necessary to avoid the chaos of a "state of nature." In contrast, John Locke's theories in *Two Treatises of Government* advocated for the protection of individual rights and the idea that governments should be based on the consent of the governed.

These philosophical foundations have influenced how governments operate and justify their authority. For instance, the concept of the social contract, as articulated by Locke, is a concept that continues to influence democratic theories today. It asserts that the legitimacy of a government stems from its ability to protect the rights and interests of its citizens. However, the practical application of this idea often falls short when power becomes concentrated or corrupted.

In contemporary discussions, philosophers like Michel Foucault have expanded on how power operates beyond traditional government structures, analyzing how power dynamics pervade all aspects of society, including institutions, discourse, and everyday interactions. Foucault's ideas reveal how government power is not only enacted through laws and regulations but also through subtler forms of control, such as social norms and surveillance.

The Formation of the State: A Global Perspective
Mesopotamia: The Dawn of Centralized Power

Mesopotamia, often referred to as the cradle of civilization, offers one of the earliest examples of state formation. Around 3000 BCE, the city-states of Sumer emerged, marking a significant shift toward centralized power. These city-states were governed by a ruling class, usually led by a king who claimed divine right to rule. This centralization was driven by the need for organized irrigation, defense against external threats, and the management of trade and resources.

However, the concentration of power also led to exploitation. The ruling class maintained control through religious authority and military strength, effectively subjugating the population. Monumental architecture, like the ziggurats, served not only as religious centers but also as symbols of the ruling class's dominance. The

State, even in its earliest form, was a mechanism for both order and oppression.

Ancient India: The Emergence of the Rajya

In ancient India, the formation of the State, or Rajya, can be traced back to the Vedic period, around 1500 BCE. The concept of kingship and governance evolved as Aryan tribes settled in the Indo-Gangetic plains, transitioning from a nomadic lifestyle to settled agriculture. The need for protection against rival tribes, management of agricultural surplus, and the administration of justice led to the establishment of early states.

The Mahajana Paadas (great kingdoms) that emerged by 600 BCE were among the first significant political entities in India. These states were governed by kings who often claimed divine sanction for their rule, similar to the Pharaohs of Egypt or the Mandate of Heaven in China. However, the centralization of power also resulted in rigid social hierarchies, codified in texts like the Manusmriti, which institutionalized social divisions and subjugation.

The Arthashastra, attributed to the ancient Indian philosopher Chanakya, offers a detailed treatise on statecraft and the exercise of power. It emphasizes the importance of a strong centralized state to maintain order, but it also highlights the potential for corruption and tyranny. The Arthashastra's realpolitik approach reflects the inherent tension between governance and control, a theme that resonates throughout the history of state formation.

Egypt: Divine Kingship and Absolute Power

In ancient Egypt, the State was deeply intertwined with the concept of divine kingship. The Pharaoh was not just a political leader but a god on earth, wielding absolute power over the people. The unification of Upper and Lower Egypt around 3100 BCE under Pharaoh Narmer marked the beginning of a state that would endure for millennia.

The construction of the pyramids, colossal tombs built to honor the Pharaohs, stands as a testament to the State's ability to mobilize vast resources and labor. These projects were more than religious expressions; they were also displays of the State's power over its subjects. Egypt maintained control through a combination of religious ideology, military might, and an extensive bureaucracy that penetrated every aspect of life.

China: The Mandate of Heaven and Dynastic Rule

In ancient China, the concept of the State was closely linked to the "Mandate of Heaven," a doctrine that justified the rule of emperors as divinely sanctioned. The Zhou dynasty (1046-256 BCE) introduced this idea to legitimize the overthrow of the Shang dynasty, establishing a precedent for the divine right to rule that would persist throughout Chinese history.

The State's formation in China was also driven by the need for defense and resource management. The construction of the Great Wall, a monumental project spanning thousands of miles, exemplifies the State's role in both protecting and controlling its population. While the wall was intended to defend against nomadic invaders, it also served to delineate the boundaries of the State's power and to keep its subjects in check.

The Indus Valley Civilization: The Harappan Enigma

The Indus Valley Civilization, which flourished around 2500 BCE in what is now Pakistan and northwest India, presents a unique case in the study of early state formation. Unlike other ancient civilizations, the Harappan cities of Mohenjo-Daro and Harappa show little evidence of centralized power or monumental architecture that typifies state control. Instead, these cities were highly organized with advanced urban planning, including sophisticated drainage systems and standardized weights and measures.

The absence of overt signs of rulership or a visible ruling class in the archaeological record has led to much debate among historians. Some scholars suggest that the Indus Valley Civilization may have operated under a more collective form of governance, possibly resembling a city-state confederation. However, the eventual decline of this civilization around 1900 BCE, possibly due to environmental changes or invasions, raises questions about the sustainability of such a system without a strong centralized state.

Europe: Feudalism and the Rise of Monarchies

In medieval Europe, the State evolved within the framework of feudalism, a decentralized system where power was based on land ownership. Kings and lords held authority over vast territories, while the common people were bound to the land, working as serfs with limited rights. Feudalism emerged as a response to the collapse of centralized Roman authority, leading to a fragmented but interconnected network of power.

However, as monarchies began to consolidate power, the State took on a more centralized form. The rise of nation-states in the early modern period, such as France, Spain, and England, was marked by the centralization of authority in the hands of the monarchy. This shift was often justified by the need for defense, the administration of justice, and the maintenance of order, but it also led to the suppression of dissent and the erosion of local autonomy.

The State as a Tool of Control

Across different civilizations, the State has been a mechanism for centralizing power, often at the cost of individual freedoms. From religious ideologies to military force and bureaucratic administration, states have employed various methods to maintain control over their populations.

In the modern era, the power of the State has only expanded. Surveillance technologies, militarized police forces, and the extension of government powers under the guise of security have all contributed to a situation where individuals are increasingly subordinate to the State. What was once a social contract designed for collective security has become a tool for maintaining control and perpetuating delusion.

The accumulation of power has never been a straightforward or peaceful process. Throughout history, the struggle for dominance has consistently led to both oppression and moments of progress. Various regimes have used power to enforce their will, often at the expense of the masses, while those oppressed have resisted, sometimes driving significant social and political changes. However, these struggles rarely dismantled the underlying systems of control; instead, they often reinforced them in new forms.

How Agriculture Enabled State Control

The development of agriculture was a turning point in human history, fundamentally altering the structure of societies and giving rise to the first complex states. The ability to produce surplus food allowed certain individuals and groups to accumulate wealth, leading to the emergence of social hierarchies and the need for systems of management and control.

In Ancient Egypt, for example, the predictable flooding of the Nile River created fertile lands capable of producing abundant crops. This surplus allowed the state to centralize control, managing irrigation and food distribution, which in turn supported the construction of monumental projects like the pyramids. However, this centralization of power also meant that those who controlled the surplus—namely the pharaoh and the priestly class—could exert significant influence over the population.

Similar dynamics can be observed in Mesopotamia, where the control of irrigation systems along the Tigris and Euphrates rivers enabled the rise of city-states and the development of early forms of government. The need to manage agricultural surplus led to the creation of complex bureaucracies, codified laws, and the enforcement of social hierarchies.

The relationship between agricultural productivity and state formation is not just a historical phenomenon. Even in the modern era, the World Bank has noted that countries with high agricultural productivity tend to have more developed and complex administrative systems. Conversely, regions with less productive agriculture often have simpler, less centralized forms of governance.

For example, in Southeast Asia, the introduction of wet-rice agriculture allowed for the rise of powerful kingdoms like Angkor in Cambodia, where the management of water resources became a central aspect of state control. On the other hand, in regions where agriculture was less intensive, such as in parts of Sub-Saharan Africa, political systems remained more decentralized and less hierarchical.

Mobilization of Labor and Resource Appropriation

States have historically mobilized labor to support their objectives, often through both overt and covert means. In ancient Egypt, the construction of monumental architecture like the pyramids was facilitated by a system of labor conscription. The labor was often extracted through a combination of tribute and forced work, reflecting a system where state needs took precedence over individual rights.

In the 20th century, resource appropriation and labor mobilization were starkly visible in totalitarian regimes. For example, Stalin's Soviet Union utilized forced labor camps known as Gulags to extract labor for state projects, from infrastructure development to military production. According to some estimates, up to 18 million people passed through the Gulag system between 1930 and 1953, underscoring the extreme measures states have taken to control and utilize labor.

Control over the Citizens: From Early States to the Modern

The state, as we know it today, is the product of centuries of evolution. However, the roots of modern governance can be traced back to the early states, which laid the groundwork for centralized authority, control, and the subjugation of individuals under the guise of order and stability. These early states not only established the foundations of statecraft but also set precedents for the concentration of power that continue to shape our world.

The nature of governance has shifted dramatically over the centuries. In ancient Greece, particularly in Athens, early forms of democracy allowed citizens to participate directly in decision-making. This form of governance was revolutionary but limited to a small segment of the population, excluding women, slaves, and non-citizens.

In medieval Europe, feudalism dominated, characterized by a hierarchy of lords and vassals. The Magna Carta of 1215 was a pivotal document that sought to limit the king's power and establish certain legal protections for subjects. This early attempt at creating a balance of power set the stage for future democratic principles.

The Enlightenment era brought about significant changes in governance with the rise of constitutionalism and the notion of separating powers. Figures like Montesquieu advocated for dividing governmental powers into branches to prevent any one branch from becoming too dominant. These ideas influenced the creation of modern democratic systems, as seen in the U.S. Constitution and the French Declaration of the Rights of Man and of the Citizen.

The Treaty of Westphalia: The Birth of the Nation-State

The Peace of Westphalia in 1648 is often cited as the beginning of the modern nation-state system. This treaty, which ended the Thirty Years' War in Europe, established the principles of state sovereignty and territorial integrity, which remain the cornerstones of international law today. However, the Westphalian system also entrenched the idea of centralized state control, with rulers granted absolute authority within their borders.

This concept of sovereignty has been both a blessing and a curse. On one hand, it has allowed for the development of stable nation-states, but on the other, it has also justified the suppression of internal dissent and the aggressive expansion of state power. For example, the principle of sovereignty has often been invoked to justify authoritarian regimes that use state power to crush opposition, as seen in numerous dictatorships throughout the 20th century.

The Modern Surveillance State: A Continuation of Early Control Mechanisms

In today's world, the legacy of early states is perhaps most evident in the rise of the surveillance state. Modern governments, armed with advanced technology, have taken the centralized control mechanisms of early states to new heights. Surveillance systems, data collection, and digital monitoring allow states to exercise unprecedented control over their citizens, often under the pretext of national security.

For instance, China's social credit system, which monitors and rates citizens based on their behavior, is a direct descendant of early state practices of monitoring and controlling populations. This system, which combines traditional methods of state control with modern technology, reflects the enduring legacy of centralized authority. Similarly, in the United States, the post-9/11 expansion of surveillance capabilities under the Patriot Act has given the government broad powers to monitor citizens, echoing the control mechanisms of early states like Rome and Mesopotamia.

Legal Systems as Instruments of Power and Control

There are several major legal systems in the world, each governing different nations and populations. The civil law system, derived from Roman law, is the most widespread, covering approximately 60% of the world's population across nations such as France, Germany, Japan, and much of Latin America. The common law system, rooted in English law, is prevalent in countries like the United

States, the United Kingdom, Canada, and Australia, influencing around 30% of the global population.

Islamic law, or Sharia, is the primary legal framework in many Muslim-majority countries, including Saudi Arabia, Iran, and Pakistan, affecting about 15% of the world's population. Additionally, customary law systems, which are based on traditional practices and community norms, are predominant in some African and Pacific nations. Lastly, mixed legal systems, which combine elements of the above, are found in countries like South Africa, Israel, and the Philippines, impacting a smaller but significant portion of the global population.

Legal systems throughout history have not merely functioned as mechanisms for dispensing justice but have often served as powerful tools for consolidating state authority and maintaining control over populations. From ancient civilizations to modern states, the law has frequently been shaped to reinforce existing power structures and suppress dissent.

Ancient Rome: Law as a Pillar of Empire

In Ancient Rome, the development of a sophisticated legal system was instrumental in consolidating the power of the state. Roman law, particularly through the Lex Hortensia and Corpus Juris Civilis (Body of Civil Law), was designed to ensure the dominance of the ruling class while providing a semblance of order and fairness. While these laws regulated property rights, contracts, and social behavior, they also reinforced the status quo by codifying the privileges of the Patrician class and the authority of the state over its subjects.

For example, the Lex Hortensia of 287 B.C. was introduced as a response to the demands of the Plebeians, who sought greater political representation. While it granted the decisions of the Plebeian Council the force of law, effectively integrating the Plebeian class into the Roman legal framework, it also entrenched the power of the Senate and the elite. This law showcased how legal reforms could be used to pacify demands for change while simultaneously strengthening the state's control.

Feudal Europe: Legal Codes as Tools of Subjugation

In medieval Europe, the feudal system was underpinned by legal codes that enshrined the obligations of serfs to their lords, effectively binding the majority of the population to a life of servitude. These legal frameworks were not just local customs but were often reinforced by the Church and the monarchy, which used them to justify the social hierarchy as divinely ordained.

One notable example is the Domesday Book, commissioned by William the Conqueror in 1086, which was not merely a survey of land and resources but also a legal document that solidified the king's authority over his newly acquired territories. By documenting the rights and duties of landholders, the Domesday Book served as a legal tool that reinforced the feudal system, ensuring that the peasants remained legally bound to their lords while the monarchy exerted control over the nobility.

The British Empire: Law as a Colonial Weapon

The British Empire's expansion across Asia, Africa, and the Americas also relied heavily on legal systems to maintain control over its colonies. The introduction of British common law in these regions was not merely an effort to impose a uniform system of justice but also a strategic move to solidify colonial authority and exploit local populations.

For example, in India, the British implemented the Permanent Settlement Act of 1793, which created a new class of landlords who were loyal to the British Crown. This law transformed traditional landholding systems and tied the rural population to exploitative landlords, leading to widespread poverty and unrest. The British legal system in India also enforced harsh penalties for rebellion and dissent, as seen during the suppression of the 1857 Indian Rebellion, where martial law was declared, and thousands were executed without trial.

Modern China: Legal Reforms as Instruments of State Power

In contemporary times, the manipulation of legal systems to maintain state control is perhaps most evident in China. The Chinese Communist Party (CCP) has systematically used legal reforms to consolidate its authority and suppress dissent. The National Security Law of 2015, for instance, grants the state broad powers to crack down on activities deemed as threats to national security, which often includes political dissent and human rights advocacy.

The CCP's control over the judiciary is another tool for maintaining power. Courts in China are not independent but are instead directly influenced by the Party, which uses the legal system to legitimize its actions. For instance, the conviction rate in Chinese courts is notoriously high, at over 99%, according to official statistics, indicating that the judiciary is more of an instrument of state policy than a guardian of justice. This system ensures that those who challenge the state face severe legal repercussions, often without a fair trial.

One particularly striking example is the treatment of Uyghur Muslims in Xinjiang, where the legal system has been used to justify mass detentions in what the Chinese government terms "reeducation camps." According to reports from human rights organizations, over a million Uyghurs have been detained, with legal justifications provided by anti-terrorism laws that allow for indefinite detention without trial. This illustrates how legal systems can be weaponized to oppress minorities and maintain state control under the guise of national security.

The United States: Legal Manipulation in the War on Drugs

The use of legal systems to exert control is not limited to authoritarian regimes. In the United States, the War on Drugs, initiated in the 1970s, has been widely criticized for disproportionately targeting minority communities and expanding the power of the state over individuals' lives. The implementation of mandatory minimum sentencing laws, particularly for drug-related offenses, has led to the mass incarceration of African Americans and Hispanics, contributing to the U.S. having the highest incarceration rate in the world.

Statistics reveal the extent of this legal exploitation: African Americans are incarcerated at more than five times the rate of white Americans, despite similar rates of drug use. The War on Drugs has been used as a tool to enforce social control, marginalize minority communities, and expand the reach of the legal and prison systems in ways that perpetuate systemic inequality.

Deception and Control: Propaganda, Misinformation, and Governmental Manipulation

Throughout history, governments have honed the art of deception, using various tools to manipulate public perception, control the narrative, and maintain their grip on power. From ancient empires to modern democracies, the strategies of misinformation and propaganda have evolved, but their core purpose remains the same: to subdue the populace, suppress dissent, and ensure the dominance of the state.

The Historical Roots of Propaganda: From Rome to Nazi Germany

Propaganda is not a modern invention. Its roots can be traced back to ancient civilizations where rulers understood the power of controlling information to shape public opinion. The Roman Empire, for instance, was adept at using public inscriptions, statues, and coinage to propagate the image of the emperor as a divine and invincible leader. These messages were carefully crafted to reinforce the legitimacy of the emperor's rule and to dissuade any thoughts of rebellion among the populace.

Fast forward to the 20th century, and the Nazi regime in Germany took propaganda to unprecedented levels. Joseph Goebbels, the Reich Minister of Propaganda, orchestrated a comprehensive and relentless campaign to control every aspect of information in Germany. The regime utilized films, radio broadcasts, newspapers, and public rallies to spread a narrative that dehumanized Jews, glorified Aryan supremacy, and justified the regime's aggressive policies. This manipulation of public perception played a crucial role in garnering widespread support for the Holocaust and the broader war efforts of the Third Reich. Goebbels' mastery of propaganda demonstrated how state-sponsored misinformation could be used to justify even the most horrific actions.

The Digital Evolution of Propaganda: Misinformation in the 21st Century

In the digital age, propaganda has taken on new and more insidious forms, enabled by the rapid advancement of technology and the rise of social media. Today, state-sponsored misinformation can be disseminated more quickly, widely, and effectively than ever before, reaching millions of people in an instant and shaping opinions on a global scale.

A stark example of this is the Russian government's interference in the 2016 U.S. presidential election. This interference involved a sophisticated campaign of misinformation, largely carried out through social media platforms like Facebook, Twitter, and YouTube. Russian operatives created fake accounts, spread divisive content, and circulated false information, all aimed at sowing discord, deepening political polarization, and undermining trust in the democratic process. The success of this campaign highlighted the vulnerability of even the most robust democracies to digital manipulation and underscored the growing power of state-sponsored propaganda in the 21st century.

In addition to election interference, state-sponsored misinformation has been used to suppress dissent and control populations in authoritarian regimes. In China, for instance, the government's strict control over the internet, coupled with a well-coordinated campaign of online censorship and propaganda, ensures that dissenting voices are silenced and the Communist Party's narrative remains unchallenged. The Chinese government's use of the "Great Firewall" to block foreign websites, combined with its promotion of pro-government content through state-controlled media, exemplifies how modern technology can be harnessed to maintain state control over the flow of information.

The Consequences of Misinformation: Eroding Freedom and Trust

The use of propaganda and misinformation by governments has far-reaching consequences for society. One of the most significant impacts is the erosion of freedom—freedom of thought, speech, and action. When governments control the narrative and manipulate information, they effectively limit the ability of citizens to make informed decisions, engage in critical thinking, and express dissent.

Moreover, the widespread use of misinformation undermines trust in institutions, both governmental and non-governmental. When citizens are repeatedly exposed to conflicting information, fake news, and propaganda, they become increasingly skeptical of all sources of information, leading to a general mistrust of media, government, and even scientific facts. This erosion of trust can destabilize societies, as seen in the growing polarization and political instability in many parts of the world today.

The Global Reach of State Deception: Examples from Around the World

State-sponsored deception is not confined to any one region or political system; it is a global phenomenon. In North Korea, the government's propaganda machine works tirelessly to maintain the cult of personality around the ruling Kim family, presenting them as infallible leaders and guardians of the nation. The regime's control over information is so complete that most North Koreans have little to no access to outside news, keeping them in a constant state of ignorance and subjugation.

In Venezuela, the government of Nicolás Maduro has used state-controlled media to spread propaganda that blames the country's economic collapse on foreign conspiracies rather than on its own mismanagement and corruption. This narrative is designed to deflect blame from the government and to rally nationalist sentiments, even as the country sinks deeper into crisis.

Breaking the Chains: How the Present Generation is Challenging State Control and Reclaiming Freedom

The modern world, with its complex web of governments and institutions, continues to exert significant control over individuals, often curbing freedom of thought and action.

However, the present generation is increasingly aware of these challenges and is actively working to break free from the delusions and deceptions that have historically been imposed by the state. This chapter explores the various ways in which people today are addressing these issues, using innovative methods and technologies to resist control and reclaim their autonomy.

The Digital Revolution: A Double-Edged Sword

The advent of the internet and digital technology has transformed the way people access information, communicate, and organize. While governments have exploited these technologies to increase surveillance and control, the present generation has also harnessed them to resist state power and promote freedom of thought.

One notable example is the role of social media in facilitating grassroots movements. In 2011, the Arab Spring swept across the Middle East and North Africa, as people used platforms like Twitter and Facebook to organize protests, share information, and rally against oppressive regimes. These digital tools allowed citizens to bypass state-controlled media and coordinate large-scale demonstrations that challenged entrenched power structures. Although the outcomes of these uprisings were varied, the use of social media as a tool for resistance demonstrated the potential for technology to empower individuals against state control.

However, the digital revolution is a double-edged sword. Governments have also adapted, using the same technologies to monitor and suppress dissent. China's "Great Firewall" and the use of surveillance technology in

Xinjiang to monitor the Uyghur population are stark reminders of how the state can use digital tools to enforce control. Despite these challenges, the present generation continues to develop new methods to counteract these efforts, such as using encrypted messaging apps like Signal and Telegram to communicate securely and organizing decentralized platforms to avoid state surveillance.

Decentralization and Blockchain: Challenging Centralized Power

As awareness of government overreach grows, many individuals and groups are turning to decentralized technologies as a means of resisting state control. Blockchain, the technology behind cryptocurrencies like Bitcoin, has emerged as a powerful tool for challenging centralized power structures.

In 2020, more than 1.4 billion people around the world participated in online activism, using digital platforms to organize protests, sign petitions, and campaign for change, often in direct defiance of government restrictions.

Blockchain's decentralized nature means that no single entity, including the state, has control over the entire system. This makes it difficult for governments to manipulate or censor transactions, offering individuals a way to conduct business and store wealth outside the purview of state-controlled financial systems. For instance, in countries with unstable economies and oppressive regimes, such as Venezuela and Zimbabwe, cryptocurrencies have provided a lifeline for citizens who face hyperinflation and currency devaluation, allowing them to preserve their wealth and conduct transactions without government interference.

Moreover, blockchain technology is being used to create decentralized autonomous organizations (DAOs), which operate without centralized control. These organizations allow for decision-making processes that are transparent and free from the influence of governments or corporations, giving power back to the people. The rise of DAOs represents a significant shift towards decentralized governance, where individuals have a greater say in how their communities and resources are managed.

The Rise of Citizen Journalism: Reclaiming the Narrative

In the face of state-controlled or biased mainstream media, citizen journalism has emerged as a powerful force for truth and transparency. Equipped with smartphones and social media accounts, ordinary people around the world are documenting events as they happen, often providing a more accurate and unfiltered view than traditional media outlets.

One powerful example of citizen journalism is the documentation of police violence during the Black Lives Matter protests in the United States. In 2020, after the murder of George Floyd, videos captured by bystanders showing police brutality sparked a global outcry and widespread protests. These videos, shared on social media, bypassed traditional media gatekeepers and brought the reality of systemic racism and police violence to a global audience. The impact of these images was profound, leading to a national reckoning on race and policing and demonstrating the power of citizen journalism to challenge state narratives.

In authoritarian countries like Myanmar, citizen journalists have played a crucial role in exposing government atrocities. During the military coup in 2021, the junta attempted to suppress information by shutting down the internet and arresting journalists. However, ordinary citizens continued to document and share evidence of the military's brutality through encrypted channels and social media, bringing international attention to the situation and countering the state's efforts to control the narrative.

Global Movements for Transparency and Accountability

The present generation is also pushing back against government secrecy and corruption through global movements that demand transparency and accountability. Organizations like WikiLeaks and the International Consortium of Investigative Journalists (ICIJ) have exposed state secrets, revealing corruption, human rights abuses, and the misuse of power at the highest levels of government.

For example, the Panama Papers leak in 2016, facilitated by the ICIJ, exposed how politicians, business leaders, and celebrities around the world used offshore tax havens to hide their wealth and evade taxes. The leak implicated over 140 politicians from more than 50 countries, leading to resignations, criminal investigations, and calls for greater financial transparency. This unprecedented exposure of global corruption highlighted the power of collective action in holding governments and elites accountable.

Moreover, the rise of whistleblower protections and the support for those who expose wrongdoing is gaining momentum. Whistleblowers like Edward Snowden and Chelsea Manning have brought to light extensive government surveillance programs and military abuses, challenging the narrative of state infallibility and encouraging a broader conversation about the balance between security and civil liberties.

Education and Awareness: Breaking the Chains of Deception

Education and critical thinking are essential tools for the present generation in breaking free from the delusions imposed by the state. Across the globe, educators, activists, and independent organizations are working to promote media literacy, critical thinking, and awareness of state propaganda.

In Finland, for example, the government has implemented a comprehensive media literacy program aimed at teaching students how to critically evaluate information and recognize misinformation. This initiative, which began in response to Russian disinformation campaigns, has been credited with making Finland one of the most resilient countries in Europe to fake news. By empowering citizens with the skills to discern truth from falsehood, such programs are helping to create a more informed and less easily manipulated populace.

However, the fight for freedom is far from over. As governments continue to adapt and find new ways to assert control, it is essential for people to remain vigilant, informed, and engaged. By continuing to push back against deception and manipulation, the present generation can pave the way for a future where freedom of thought, speech, and action are truly protected, and the delusions that have held humanity captive for so long are finally shattered.

Non-Party-Based Parliamentary Democracy: The Future of Governance

Looking to the future, a non-party-based parliamentary democracy represents a promising alternative to traditional party-based systems. This model seeks to address many of the issues inherent in party politics, such as corruption, partisanship, and the influence of special interests.

In a non-party-based system, candidates are selected based on merit rather than party affiliation. This approach reduces the influence of political donations and party loyalty, allowing elected officials to focus on serving their constituents rather than advancing party agendas. By eliminating political parties, the system aims to create a more transparent and accountable form of governance.

The non-party-based model involves a transparent entrance exam for candidates, ensuring that only qualified individuals stand for election. Debates among candidates and public voting based on merit rather than party affiliation further enhance accountability and voter engagement. Additionally, a merit-based selection process for ministerial positions and regular progress reports from elected officials promote transparency and effective governance.

As future generations confront the limitations of current political systems, the non-party-based parliamentary democracy offers a potential pathway to a more just and equitable form of governance. By addressing the root causes of corruption and promoting direct accountability, this model embodies the principles of democracy in a more effective and transparent manner.

Chapter 4

The Media Mirage: Distorting Reality and Shaping Perception

From the earliest days of print to the rapid dissemination of information in the digital age, media has been a powerful force in shaping human perception. It has influenced wars, revolutions, social movements, and even the mundane aspects of daily life. But beneath the veneer of enlightenment lies a darker reality—media as a tool of manipulation, a mirage that distorts reality and entraps the masses in a web of deception. This chapter delves into how the media has enslaved humanity, creating delusions that persist across generations, and how future societies might confront and overcome these challenges.

The Historical Roots of Media Manipulation

The manipulation of media to control public perception is not a new phenomenon. As early as the 16th century, rulers and religious authorities understood the power of printed materials to sway public opinion. The invention of the printing press revolutionized communication, but it also provided the means for controlling the narrative. During the Protestant Reformation, for instance, both the Catholic Church and Protestant leaders used pamphlets, posters, and books to advance their agendas, often distorting facts to serve their purposes.

In the 20th century, media manipulation became more sophisticated with the advent of radio and television. World War I marked one of the earliest large-scale uses of media as a propaganda tool. Governments on both sides of the conflict understood that controlling the flow of information was as crucial as winning battles on the ground. The British government's establishment of the Ministry of Information in 1917 was a testament to this understanding. The Ministry orchestrated a vast propaganda campaign, utilizing newspapers, posters, and cinema to maintain public support for the war effort. Similar tactics were employed by the United States with the Committee on Public Information, which used pamphlets, films, and speeches to sell the war to a skeptical American public.

But it was World War II that truly showcased the power of media in shaping public perception. Joseph Goebbels, the Nazi Minister of Propaganda, orchestrated one of the most notorious media campaigns in history, using film, radio, and print to indoctrinate the German population with the ideology of the Third Reich. Goebbels understood the psychological power of repetition and emotional appeal, famously stating, "If you tell a lie big enough and keep repeating it, people will eventually come to believe it." This statement, chilling in its simplicity, captures the essence of media manipulation—a process that taps into the psychological vulnerabilities of individuals to create and sustain delusions.

The Media Mirage in the Modern Era

In the modern era, the media's role in shaping perception has become even more pervasive, thanks to the advent of the internet and social media. The 24-hour news cycle, the rise of infotainment, and the explosion of online platforms have created an environment where information is ubiquitous, yet often unreliable. The sheer volume of content available at any given moment has led to a paradox where, despite being more connected than ever, we are also more susceptible to misinformation and manipulation.

One of the most hard-bitting examples of media manipulation in recent times is the case of the 2016 U.S. presidential election. The role of fake news and targeted social media campaigns in influencing voter behavior has been widely documented. A study conducted by researchers at Stanford University and New York University found that fake news stories were shared millions of times on Facebook, often reaching more users than legitimate news sources. These stories were not just misinformation—they were deliberately crafted to appeal to existing biases and prejudices, creating an echo chamber effect where falsehoods were amplified and reinforced.

The impact of media manipulation extends beyond elections. The rise of social media platforms like Facebook, Twitter, and Instagram has given rise to new forms of propaganda, where algorithms play a crucial role in determining what content users see. These algorithms are designed to maximize engagement, often by promoting sensational or emotionally charged content.

This has led to the proliferation of conspiracy theories, pseudoscience, and extremist ideologies, which thrive in the echo chambers created by social media.

A particularly alarming example of this is the spread of anti-vaccine misinformation. Despite overwhelming scientific evidence supporting the safety and efficacy of vaccines, a small but vocal minority has used social media to spread false claims about vaccine dangers. A 2019 study published in the journal Vaccine found that the majority of anti-vaccine content on social media came from just a handful of accounts, yet these accounts were able to reach millions of users, creating a significant public health challenge. The World Health Organization identified vaccine hesitancy as one of the top ten global health threats in 2019, illustrating the real-world consequences of media-driven delusion.

Media Manipulation

The phenomenon of media manipulation is not confined to any one country or region; it is a global issue with far-reaching implications. In Russia, state-controlled media has been used to maintain the authority of the government and suppress dissent. The Russian government's control over major television networks and newspapers ensures that the official narrative dominates public discourse. This has been particularly evident in the coverage of conflicts in Ukraine and Syria, where Russian media has portrayed events in a manner that aligns with the government's geopolitical interests.

In China, media manipulation is even more overt, with the state exercising strict control over all forms of communication. The Chinese government employs a vast censorship apparatus known as the Great Firewall to restrict access to information and suppress dissent. In addition to censorship, the government actively promotes its narrative through state-run media outlets like CCTV and the People's Daily. These outlets present a sanitized version of events, omitting or distorting information that could challenge the government's authority. The Chinese government also employs a massive online propaganda operation, often referred to as the "50 Cent Army," which is tasked with flooding social media platforms with pro-government content and disinformation.

In India, media manipulation has taken on a different form, with the rise of corporate-owned media conglomerates that often prioritize profit over journalistic integrity. The concentration of media ownership in the hands of a few powerful individuals and corporations has led to a situation where news coverage is often biased or sensationalized to attract viewership and advertising revenue. This has been particularly evident in the coverage of political events, where media outlets have been accused of favoring certain political parties or candidates.

One striking example of media manipulation in India is the 2020 Delhi riots. During the violence, several media outlets were criticized for their biased coverage, which often framed the events in a manner that aligned with the government's narrative. This biased reporting contributed to the polarization of public opinion and the spread of misinformation, further exacerbating the violence.

In general, the mass media of the country, including television channels, often exhibit clear alignments with political parties, particularly the ruling BJP and the opposition. This alignment influences the tone, content, and editorial stance of various outlets, with some media favoring the government's narrative and policies, while others are more critical and supportive of opposition viewpoints. This polarization results in a divided media landscape where viewers gravitate towards channels that reflect their political preferences, contributing to a fragmented and ideologically driven public discourse.

In Brazil, the rise of far-right populism has been fueled in part by media manipulation. During the 2018 presidential election, disinformation campaigns on social media played a significant role in shaping voter perception. Fake news stories, often spread through WhatsApp, targeted political opponents and promoted the candidacy of Jair Bolsonaro, who went on to win the election. The Brazilian example highlights how media manipulation can be used to undermine democratic processes and install authoritarian regimes.

The Psychological Foundations of Media Deception

To understand why media manipulation is so effective, it is essential to examine the psychological mechanisms that make individuals susceptible to deception. Humans are not purely rational beings; our perceptions are shaped by cognitive biases, emotions, and social influences. These psychological factors create vulnerabilities that can be exploited by media to distort reality.

One of the most powerful psychological mechanisms at play is confirmation bias—the tendency to seek out and interpret information in a way that confirms one's existing beliefs. Media manipulators exploit this bias by creating content that resonates with the audience's preconceived notions. This is particularly evident in the proliferation of echo chambers on social media, where users are exposed only to information that aligns with their views, reinforcing their beliefs and making them resistant to contrary evidence.

Another psychological factor that contributes to media manipulation is the availability heuristic—a cognitive shortcut that leads people to overestimate the importance of information that is readily available. Media outlets often exploit this heuristic by bombarding the audience with sensational or emotionally charged content, making these stories seem more significant than they are. For example, the extensive coverage of terrorist attacks, despite their statistical rarity, has led to widespread fear and the perception that such events are more common than they actually are.

The emotional appeal is another powerful tool used by media manipulators. Humans are emotional beings, and our emotions often override our rationality. Media outlets capitalize on this by creating content that elicits strong emotional responses, such as fear, anger, or sympathy. This emotional manipulation is evident in the coverage of tragic events, where the focus is often on personal stories and graphic imagery rather than a balanced analysis of the situation.

Moreover, social proof—a psychological phenomenon where people assume the actions of others in an attempt to reflect correct behavior—also plays a crucial role in media manipulation. When individuals see that a particular narrative or piece of information is widely accepted or shared by others, they are more likely to accept it as true, regardless of its accuracy. Social media platforms, with their likes, shares, and retweets, amplify this effect, creating a feedback loop where popular content is perceived as credible simply because it is popular.

Statistics and Data: The Scale of the Problem

The extent of media manipulation can be quantified through various statistics and data, revealing the scale of the problem and its impact on society. According to a 2018 report by the MIT Media Lab, false news stories are 70% more likely to be retweeted on Twitter than true stories. The study, which analyzed data from 2006 to 2017, found that falsehoods spread significantly faster and farther than accurate information, highlighting the vulnerability of social media platforms to manipulation.

In the realm of traditional media, a 2019 survey by the Pew Research Center found that 71% of Americans believe that their news media tends to favor one side of an issue, indicating widespread distrust in the impartiality of news coverage. This distrust is further compounded by the increasing concentration of media ownership.

The Impact of Concentrated Media Ownership

The concentration of media ownership is a significant factor contributing to the distortion of reality and the shaping of public perception. When a small number of conglomerates control the majority of media outlets, the diversity of viewpoints is significantly diminished. This lack of diversity can lead to a homogenized narrative that reflects the interests of those in power, rather than presenting a balanced or truthful account of events.

For instance, in the United States, just six corporations control about 90% of the media landscape, including television networks, radio stations, newspapers, and online platforms. This concentration has led to concerns about the ability of these corporations to influence public opinion and policy decisions. The interests of these conglomerates often align with those of the political and economic elite, which can result in biased reporting that favors the status quo and marginalizes dissenting voices.

Globally, the impact of concentrated media ownership is equally troubling. In many countries, media conglomerates have close ties to the government, leading to a situation where the media acts as a mouthpiece for the state rather than a watchdog. This dynamic is particularly evident in authoritarian regimes, where the media is used to reinforce the legitimacy of the ruling party and suppress opposition. However, even in democratic societies, the concentration of media ownership can lead to a situation where the public is presented with a narrow range of perspectives, limiting the scope of public discourse and the ability of citizens to make informed decisions.

The Role of Technology in Amplifying Media Manipulation

The advent of digital technology has revolutionized the way media is produced, distributed, and consumed. While this has democratized access to information, it has also created new opportunities for manipulation. Social media platforms, in particular, have become powerful tools for spreading misinformation and shaping public perception.

One of the key challenges posed by digital technology is the algorithmic nature of content distribution. Platforms like Facebook, Twitter, and YouTube use algorithms to determine what content is shown to users, based on their previous interactions and preferences. While this can create a personalized experience, it also reinforces existing biases and creates echo chambers where users are only exposed to information that aligns with their beliefs. This can lead to the entrenchment of false narratives and the polarization of public opinion.

Moreover, the anonymity and speed of digital communication have made it easier for bad actors to spread misinformation. Troll farms, bot networks, and fake accounts can be used to amplify false stories and create the illusion of widespread support for a particular viewpoint. This can be particularly effective in shaping public opinion during critical moments, such as elections or social movements.

How the Present Generation is Handling the Issue

The present generation faces the complex and evolving challenge of media manipulation with a mix of awareness, innovation, and education. Younger people, who are the most active on social media, have become increasingly conscious of the prevalence of misinformation. This awareness has spurred a global movement toward fact-checking and accountability. Independent organizations, such as FactCheck.org in the United States, Full Fact in the UK, and Alt News in India, have emerged as key players in verifying the accuracy of news stories. These organizations work tirelessly to debunk false claims and provide the public with reliable information.

Social media platforms themselves have also responded, albeit with mixed results. For instance, Facebook and Twitter have introduced measures to flag misleading content and reduce the spread of fake news. During the COVID-19 pandemic, these platforms played a crucial role in combating misinformation by directing users to authoritative sources like the World Health Organization. However, these efforts have not been without controversy. In some cases, the platforms have been accused of censorship or of not doing enough to curb the spread of harmful content. The struggle to balance free speech with the need to prevent the spread of false information remains a contentious issue.

Another critical development is the growing emphasis on media literacy. Recognizing the need for individuals to navigate the complex information landscape, many countries have begun integrating media literacy into their educational curricula. In Canada, the Media Smarts initiative provides educators with resources to help students develop the skills needed to become informed and responsible digital citizens.

Despite these positive steps, the challenge remains immense. The sheer volume of information, combined with the sophisticated tactics used by those spreading misinformation, continues to overwhelm efforts to maintain the integrity of public discourse. Social media platforms, which were once celebrated as tools for democratizing information, have increasingly become arenas for the spread of ideological extremism and conspiracy theories. For example, in Myanmar, Facebook was used to incite violence against the Rohingya Muslim minority, illustrating how social media can be weaponized in ethnic and religious conflicts.

In the United States, the polarization of public opinion has been exacerbated by social media algorithms that prioritize content designed to provoke strong emotional reactions. This has led to the entrenchment of echo chambers, where users are exposed primarily to information that reinforces their existing beliefs. The result is a deeply divided society where constructive dialogue is increasingly difficult to achieve.

Globally, the response to these challenges varies widely. In the European Union, for example, the Digital Services Act aims to regulate online platforms, holding them accountable for the spread of harmful content. Meanwhile, in Taiwan, the government has taken a proactive approach by promoting digital literacy and launching initiatives like the Taiwan Fact Check Center to counter disinformation.

The present generation's approach to handling media manipulation reflects a growing recognition of the problem, but also highlights the complexity of finding effective solutions. While there are notable efforts to combat misinformation and educate the public, the rapid evolution of media technologies and the global nature of information flow mean that this issue will require ongoing innovation and vigilance. The stakes are high, as the integrity of public discourse and the health of democratic societies depend on the ability to effectively manage and mitigate the impact of media manipulation.

Strategies for Future Generations

Looking forward, future generations will likely face an even more complex media environment, but they will also have the opportunity to implement strategies that can mitigate the impact of media distortion.

Media Literacy Education: Media literacy will become even more critical as the lines between truth and fiction continue to blur. Future generations will need to be equipped with robust critical thinking skills from a young age. Media literacy education should be expanded beyond schools to include community programs and lifelong learning opportunities, ensuring that people of all ages have the tools to navigate the media landscape.

Regulation and Accountability

Governments and international bodies will need to develop and enforce regulations that promote transparency in media ownership and prevent monopolies. These regulations should also hold media outlets accountable for spreading misinformation while safeguarding freedom of speech and avoiding censorship.

The challenge will be to strike a balance between regulation and the preservation of democratic values.

Supporting Independent Media

The preservation of independent journalism will be crucial in maintaining a diverse media landscape. Future generations will need to advocate for policies that support independent media through public funding, tax incentives, and legal protections. Crowdfunding and other innovative funding models could also play a role in sustaining independent journalism.

Technology and Innovation

As technology continues to evolve, it will offer new tools for combating misinformation. Social media platforms could further refine their algorithms to prioritize credible sources and diversify the content presented to users. Artificial intelligence and machine learning can be harnessed to detect and prevent the spread of deepfakes and other forms of digital deception. However, these technological solutions will need to be carefully designed to avoid unintended consequences, such as censorship or the suppression of legitimate discourse.

Civic Engagement and Public Discourse

Fostering a culture of civic engagement and open public discourse will be essential for countering media manipulation. Future generations must be encouraged to actively participate in their local and digital communities, engage in critical discussions, and seek out diverse perspectives.

By promoting dialogue and understanding, societies can build resilience against the divisive effects of media manipulation.

Chapter 5

The Grand Hoax: How Society Hoodwinks Humanity
Since the beginning of its formation, society has developed intricate systems and structures that obscure the truth and manipulate individuals, a grand hoax that shapes our perceptions, behaviors, and realities. From ancient myths used to justify social hierarchies to modern propaganda and misinformation, those in power have continually exploited these mechanisms to maintain control. Governments, corporations, and powerful entities manipulate legal and economic structures to serve their interests, often at the expense of marginalized communities. In the modern era, media and digital platforms amplify misinformation, prioritizing sensationalism and profit over truth, further distorting public perception. This pervasive societal deception urges us to critically question the narratives imposed upon us and seek deeper understanding of the forces shaping our world.

The Psychology Behind Society: How Collective Pressure Crushes Original Thinking and Perpetuates Delusion
The Conformity Trap
Human society, in its quest for order and stability, has often become a powerful mechanism for suppressing

individual thought and creativity. While society is essential for collective survival, it also imposes rigid norms, expectations, and beliefs that can stifle original thinking. The psychological pressure to conform, coupled with societal structures designed to maintain the status quo, has long served as a tool for subjugation, keeping humanity trapped in a cycle of delusion.

The Social Brain: How Evolution Favors Conformity

Human beings are inherently social creatures, and much of our evolutionary success is tied to our ability to form and maintain cohesive groups. The need for social acceptance is deeply embedded in our psychology, as it once ensured survival in environments where being ostracized could mean death. This evolutionary wiring has created what psychologists call the "social brain," which prioritizes group cohesion over individual expression.

Research shows that social conformity is not just a cultural phenomenon but a neurological one. Studies using functional MRI (fMRI) have demonstrated that when individuals are faced with group opinions, brain regions associated with reward and pleasure (such as the ventral striatum) are activated when they conform, while areas linked to error detection (like the anterior cingulate cortex) become active when they consider deviating from the group. This neurological response highlights how deeply ingrained the desire to conform is, often at the expense of personal beliefs and originality.

In society, this conformity is often enforced through various mechanisms, including social norms, peer pressure, and even legal systems. These mechanisms are designed to maintain order, but they also suppress dissent and innovation, leading to a collective mindset that resists change and perpetuates delusions.

The Tyranny of Social Norms: Enforcing the Status Quo

Social norms are the unwritten rules that govern behavior within a society. They dictate everything from dress codes and speech patterns to moral values and political beliefs. While norms can create a sense of community and shared identity, they also serve as powerful tools for enforcing conformity and stifling individual thought.

One striking example of this is the caste system in India, which has historically dictated social behavior and reinforced rigid hierarchies. Despite legal reforms and modernization, the caste system's influence remains deeply entrenched in many parts of the country. Statistics show that as of 2020, around 70% of marriages in India still occur within the same caste, reflecting the powerful hold of social norms on individual choices. The fear of social ostracism, violence, and economic repercussions keeps many people from challenging these norms, even when they are personally opposed to them.

Another example is the gender norms that pervade many societies, dictating the roles and behaviors considered appropriate for men and women. In Saudi Arabia, for instance, the guardianship system has historically restricted women's autonomy, requiring them to obtain permission from male relatives for various activities, including travel and education. Although recent reforms have begun to dismantle some of these restrictions, the societal pressure to conform to traditional gender roles remains strong. According to a 2019 survey by the Arab Barometer, 58% of Saudi women believed that men should have the final say in family matters, illustrating how deeply ingrained these norms are, even among those who are directly affected by them.

These examples show how social norms can perpetuate outdated and harmful practices, suppressing original thinking and preventing progress. The collective pressure to conform ensures that individuals who challenge these norms are often met with resistance, ridicule, or even violence, reinforcing a cycle of delusion that keeps society stagnant.

The Power of Social Identity: Us vs. Them

Social identity is a powerful force in influencing human behavior and thought. The need to belong to a group is a fundamental human drive, and this often leads to the creation of in-groups (those who belong) and out-groups (those who do not). This division can be seen in everything from national identities to religious affiliations, and it plays a significant role in perpetuating societal delusions.

One of the most tragic examples of this is the Rwandan Genocide of 1994, where the Hutu majority slaughtered an estimated 800,000 Tutsis over 100 days. The genocide was fueled by decades of propaganda that dehumanized the Tutsi minority, portraying them as enemies of the Hutu people. This propaganda created a strong in-group/out-group dynamic, where the Hutu population was led to believe that the extermination of the Tutsis was necessary for their survival. The psychological pressure to conform to this narrative was immense, leading many ordinary Hutus to participate in the killings, often out of fear of being seen as traitors to their group.

The creation of social identities can also be seen in the rise of nationalism and populism around the world. In the United States, the "America First" rhetoric has fueled a resurgence of nationalism, where those who challenge the narrative are often labeled as unpatriotic or traitors. This us-vs-them mentality stifles original thinking and reinforces societal delusions, as individuals are pressured to conform to the dominant narrative or risk social ostracism.

Statistics show that this phenomenon is not unique to the United States. A 2019 survey by the Pew Research Center found that nationalist sentiments were on the rise in several European countries, with significant portions of the population expressing the belief that their culture was superior to others. This rise in nationalism is often accompanied by a rejection of globalism, multiculturalism, and other ideas that challenge the status quo, further entrenching societal delusions and suppressing original thought.

The Weight of Tradition: The Invisible Chains

Tradition is another powerful force that shapes societal behavior and thought. While traditions can provide a sense of continuity and identity, they can also serve as invisible chains that bind individuals to outdated and often harmful practices. The pressure to adhere to tradition can be so strong that it overrides logic, reason, and even personal well-being.

One example of this is the practice of female genital mutilation (FGM), which persists in many parts of Africa and the Middle East despite global condemnation and efforts to eradicate it. FGM is often justified as a cultural or religious tradition, and those who challenge the practice are often ostracized or punished. According to UNICEF, at least 200 million girls and women alive today have undergone FGM, a stark reminder of how deeply ingrained traditions can perpetuate harmful practices and suppress original thinking.

In Japan, the concept of "Tatemae" (the public facade) and "Honne" (true feelings) reflects the societal pressure to conform to traditional norms and expectations. In a culture that places a high value on harmony and social order, individuals are often expected to suppress their true feelings and opinions in favor of maintaining group cohesion. This pressure to conform can lead to a society where individuals are reluctant to express original thoughts or challenge the status quo, reinforcing societal delusions and inhibiting progress.

Even in more liberal societies, tradition can be a powerful force that stifles change. In the United Kingdom, the class system, while less rigid than in the past, continues to influence social behavior and expectations. A 2020 study by the Social Mobility Commission found that those from working-class backgrounds were still significantly underrepresented in elite professions, reflecting the ongoing influence of class-based traditions and norms.

This persistence of tradition can create a society where individuals are discouraged from challenging the established order, perpetuating inequality and limiting the potential for original thought and innovation.

Breaking the Chains

The psychological pressure exerted by society to conform, adhere to norms, and uphold traditions has long served as a tool for suppressing original thought and perpetuating delusions. From the evolutionary roots of social conformity to the powerful influence of media, education, and social identity, these forces create a collective mindset that resists change and stifles individual expression. However, recognizing these mechanisms is the first step toward breaking free from them.

Love, Monogamy, and the Farce of Marriage
The Fallacy of Love

Love—it's been the subject of countless songs, poems, and stories, yet when we strip away the romantic veneer, what are we left with? A complex, chemically-driven emotion that has both captivated and confounded humanity for centuries. To truly understand the nature of love, we must begin by examining its root psychological causes and the often humorous ways it plays out in our lives.

At its most basic level, love is a biological response designed to ensure the survival of our species. The brain, in its infinite wisdom, concocts a potent mix of chemicals—dopamine, oxytocin, and adrenaline—when we fall in love. These chemicals create a sense of euphoria, attachment, and obsession, often leading to behavior that, from an outsider's perspective, can seem downright irrational. In fact, brain scans of people in love reveal activity patterns similar to those seen in individuals with obsessive-compulsive disorder. This might explain why new lovers can't stop thinking about each other, why they act impulsively, and why they are blind to each other's flaws.

This chemical cocktail is the foundation of what society has elevated to an almost divine status: romantic love. From fairy tales like *Cinderella* to blockbuster movies like *The Notebook*, we are constantly bombarded with the idea that true love is the ultimate goal in life. But here's the kicker: the concept of romantic love as the cornerstone of marriage is a relatively recent invention. For much of history, marriage was primarily a social and economic arrangement, with love seen as a nice, but unnecessary, bonus.

Take ancient Rome, for example, where marriages were more about securing alliances and passing on property than about personal affection. The same was true in medieval Europe, where the idea of courtly love—passionate, often extramarital devotion—existed largely outside the confines of marriage, which remained a contract between families. Love was a luxury, not a necessity, and certainly not the basis for such a significant life decision as marriage.

Even in modern times, the practical realities of love often clash with the idealized versions we see in the media. The "honeymoon phase," that blissful period of intense passion and connection, typically lasts between six months to two years. After that, the brain begins to adjust, and the dopamine rush subsides. What was once a source of endless excitement and joy starts to require effort, patience, and compromise to maintain. This transition from passionate love to companionate love, as psychologist Dorothy Tennov described it, is where many relationships falter. The initial high fades, leaving behind the often unglamorous work of sustaining a partnership.

Humans, however, are nothing if not inventive, and we've built an entire industry around the pursuit and maintenance of romantic love. Consider the global obsession with Valentine's Day, a holiday that generates billions of dollars annually, all in the name of celebrating love. From extravagant gifts to over-the-top proposals, the pressure to perform romantic gestures is immense. Yet these grandiose displays often mask the more mundane, yet critical, aspects of a relationship—communication, mutual respect, and shared values.

A humorous example of how these expectations play out can be seen in the popularity of romantic comedies. Take the film *Love Actually,* where multiple love stories intersect in a whirlwind of romantic clichés. The movie presents love as a series of serendipitous events, dramatic confessions, and happily-ever-afters. But what it glosses over is the reality that real love involves navigating everyday challenges, from who takes out the trash to how to manage finances. The gap between the romantic ideals portrayed in such films and the reality of relationships is vast, yet many continue to chase the fantasy, often leading to disappointment.

One of the most striking illustrations of this disconnect is the story of Lord Byron, the quintessential Romantic poet. Byron's life was filled with passionate affairs and dramatic declarations of love, but his relationships were tumultuous and often ended in scandal. Despite his poetic exaltation of love, Byron struggled to maintain stable relationships, highlighting the difference between romantic ideals and the complexities of real human connections.

The human obsession with romantic love can also be traced back to medieval courtly love and the 19th-century Romantic poets, who idealized love as a transcendent, almost spiritual experience. These influences have left us with a legacy of unrealistic expectations, where love is seen as an all-consuming, perfect union. But as Alain de Botton argues in *The Course of Love,* real love is not about constant passion or excitement. It's about the mundane reality of everyday life, the willingness to face challenges together, and the acceptance of each other's flaws. De Botton's perspective offers a refreshing antidote to the unrealistic ideals that often dominate our culture.

To further understand the fallacy of love, consider the phenomenon of arranged marriages, which remain common in many cultures. Unlike the Western ideal of love-based marriages, arranged marriages are often approached with pragmatism, focusing on compatibility, family values, and long-term partnership. Interestingly, research has shown that arranged marriages can be just as successful, if not more so, than love marriages, with many couples reporting that love grows and deepens over time as they build a life together. This challenges the notion that love must be the starting point of a relationship, suggesting instead that it can be cultivated through shared experiences and mutual respect.

And then there's the role of modern technology in shaping our perceptions of love. Dating apps like Tinder and Bumble have turned the search for love into a gamified experience, where potential partners are swiped left or right based on a split-second decision. While these apps have made it easier than ever to meet new people, they have also commodified romance, reducing it to a series of superficial interactions. The instant gratification offered by these platforms can lead to a cycle of brief, unfulfilling encounters, further perpetuating the myth that love should be effortless and immediate.

The irony in all of this is that while society pushes us toward romantic love as the ultimate goal, it often overlooks the importance of other forms of love and connection—friendship, family, community. In our pursuit of the perfect partner, we may neglect these equally vital relationships, which are often more stable and enduring than romantic love.

Love, while a powerful force in human experience, is arguably one of society's greatest delusions. It's been idealized and exaggerated to the point where it overshadows the realities of life, creating unrealistic expectations that often lead to disappointment. In truth, love is not the all-consuming passion portrayed in stories and movies, but rather a complex, imperfect journey that requires ongoing effort, commitment, and compromise. Understanding its psychological roots and accepting the mundane, sometimes messy aspects of relationships can help us move beyond the myths and find a deeper, more authentic connection—one that values the beauty of shared, everyday moments over the fleeting allure of fairy-tale fantasies.

The Illusion of Marriage: A Historical and Social Analysis

Marriage is often celebrated as the cornerstone of society, an institution that promises stability, love, and fulfillment. However, a closer examination reveals that marriage is far from a natural human behavior. Instead, it is a socially constructed mechanism, developed over centuries to serve economic, political, and social purposes, often at the expense of individual freedom and happiness. Unlike other species, only humans have devised such a complex system of pairing, binding individuals into lifelong commitments that are often more about control and societal order than about genuine emotional connection.

The origins of marriage can be traced back to the early days of agricultural societies. As humans transitioned from nomadic lifestyles to settled communities, the need to control resources, inheritance, and social alliances became paramount. Marriage emerged as a way to ensure the transfer of property, secure alliances, and maintain social hierarchies. In ancient civilizations like Rome, marriage was primarily a private contract, often devoid of any romantic or religious connotations. It was a practical arrangement designed to consolidate wealth and power within families.

In medieval Europe, marriage became even more deeply entwined with economic and political considerations. Among the nobility, marriages were often arranged to secure alliances between powerful families, preserve wealth, and ensure the continuity of lineage. Romantic love, which is now often touted as the foundation of marriage, was largely irrelevant. It was only in recent centuries, with the rise of individualism and the influence of the Enlightenment, that the concept of marrying for love began to take hold. This shift, however, introduced new complexities, as couples now expected their partners to fulfill a wide range of emotional and psychological needs—expectations that were often unrealistic and difficult to meet.

The unnatural nature of marriage becomes even more apparent when we consider the biological impulses that drive human behavior. Evolutionary biology suggests that humans, like many other species, are not inherently monogamous. Our genetic programming is geared toward maximizing reproductive success, which often involves seeking multiple partners. This natural inclination is at odds with the societal imposition of lifelong monogamy, leading to significant tension and conflict within marriages.

The societal imposition of marriage as a norm serves to maintain control over individuals, pushing them into a system that prioritizes social order over personal happiness. Marriage, in many ways, acts as a tool to bind individuals to certain roles and responsibilities, particularly those related to family and economic productivity. Once married, individuals are expected to raise children, maintain households, and work hard to meet the financial demands of their families. This often leads to a cycle of labor and consumption that benefits the larger economic system but can leave individuals feeling trapped and unfulfilled.

The darker side of marriage is further revealed in the way the institution often benefits one party over the other, particularly in the context of divorce. Legal systems in many countries are skewed in favor of women when it comes to alimony, child custody, and property settlements. For example, in the United States, statistics show that women are awarded alimony in about 97% of cases. This has led to perceptions that marriage, and particularly divorce, can become a financial racket, where the dissolution of a marriage becomes a means for financial gain.

Alimony and maintenance laws, while intended to protect those who may be financially disadvantaged in a marriage, are often exploited. Cases of false domestic violence accusations, aimed at securing favorable divorce settlements, are not uncommon. These legal structures, while designed to ensure fairness, can be manipulated, leading to further disillusionment with the institution of marriage. In India, for example, there has been a significant increase in the number of false domestic violence cases filed under Section 498A of the Indian Penal Code, leading to a backlash and calls for reform.

This misuse of legal provisions highlights the potential for marriage to become less about partnership and more about power dynamics and financial exploitation.

As awareness of these issues grows, many individuals are beginning to question the validity of marriage as a necessary or desirable life choice. This is reflected in the increasing popularity of live-in relationships, particularly in urban areas. Live-in relationships offer the benefits of companionship and shared responsibilities without the legal and social entanglements of marriage. According to a 2019 report by the Pew Research Center, the number of unmarried couples living together in the United States has increased by nearly 30% over the past decade. This trend is also evident in countries like India, where changing societal norms are leading more young people to opt for live-in relationships over traditional marriage.

The rise of live-in relationships reflects a broader shift in societal values, where personal freedom and autonomy are increasingly prioritized over traditional commitments. These arrangements allow individuals to explore relationships without the pressure of legal and societal expectations, offering a more flexible and realistic approach to partnership. However, this shift also challenges the conventional view of family and social order, prompting debates about the future of marriage as an institution.

Whether marriage will continue to hold its place as a central social institution or gradually fade in importance remains to be seen, but one thing is certain: the way we think about and engage in relationships is changing, reflecting a broader cultural shift toward individualism and personal fulfillment over tradition and societal expectations.

The Complexity of Monogamy: Unpacking a Social Construct

Monogamy, often heralded as the ideal relationship model in many societies, is a relatively recent construct in the grand scope of human history. For much of our existence, humans have engaged in a variety of relationship forms, with monogamy gaining prominence only alongside the development of agricultural societies and the advent of settled communities. Our biological impulses, deeply rooted in millions of years of evolution, often tell a different story. According to evolutionary biologist Richard Dawkins in *The Selfish Gene,* our genes are programmed to maximize reproductive success—a drive that can conflict with societal expectations of lifelong monogamy. This biological imperative manifests in a natural inclination toward seeking multiple partners, a behavior that is common among many species, including humans.

Historically, human societies were more fluid in their approach to relationships. In early hunter-gatherer communities, social structures were more egalitarian, and sexual relations were often shared within the group, a practice believed to strengthen communal bonds and ensure the survival of offspring. It wasn't until the rise of agriculture, when property and inheritance became central to societal organization, that monogamy started to be promoted as the ideal. Monogamy served practical purposes: it helped ensure that property was passed down within a family and provided a stable environment for raising children. Over time, this model became intertwined with religious and cultural norms, solidifying its status as the preferred, if not required, relationship structure in many parts of the world.

However, the imposition of monogamy often runs counter to human nature, leading to a variety of social and personal challenges. Infidelity, for instance, is a common issue in monogamous relationships. Studies indicate that around 20% of married individuals in the United States admit to engaging in extramarital affairs, highlighting the difficulty many face in adhering to strict monogamous ideals. This tension between biological drives and societal expectations can lead to significant emotional turmoil, as individuals struggle to reconcile their natural desires with the cultural narrative of lifelong fidelity.

The hypocrisy surrounding monogamy is also evident in the ways societies react to and judge deviations from this norm. Public figures who are caught in extramarital affairs are often subjected to intense scrutiny and moral outrage, yet the prevalence of infidelity suggests a disconnect between societal ideals and human behavior. Moreover, while monogamy is promoted as the standard in many cultures, other forms of relationships persist both openly and covertly. For example, in parts of West Africa, such as Senegal, polygamy is widely practiced and socially accepted, with nearly half of married women participating in polygynous unions. These arrangements challenge the notion that monogamy is a universal or natural state for human beings.

In *Sex at Dawn,* Christopher Ryan and Cacilda Jethá argue that monogamy is not a natural state for humans but rather a social construct developed relatively recently in our history. They suggest that many modern relationship issues stem from trying to fit our natural behaviors into this unnatural framework. Their research points to the fact that our ancestors were likely more comfortable with multi-partner relationships, a practice that was better suited to the communal and cooperative nature of early human societies.

Even in contemporary Western societies, where monogamy is often seen as the norm, alternative relationship models are gaining recognition. According to a 2017 study by the Pew Research Center, about 5% of Americans report being in consensually non-monogamous relationships. These include practices such as polyamory, where individuals maintain multiple loving relationships with the knowledge and consent of all parties involved. The growing acceptance of these models indicates a shift in societal attitudes and a recognition that monogamy, while beneficial for social order and psychological security, is not the only way to structure human relationships.

Monogamy's role in society has been to provide stability, particularly in terms of raising children and maintaining social order. However, this model often requires a significant amount of effort and conscious commitment to counteract our natural inclinations. As such, while monogamy offers certain benefits, it also imposes constraints that many find difficult to maintain over the long term.

Psychological Problems

Our psychological landscape plays a pivotal role in shaping how we approach love, monogamy, and marriage, often setting us up for challenges and disappointments. At the heart of these issues are our psychological needs and vulnerabilities, which can make us susceptible to the pitfalls of romantic idealization and the strains of long-term commitment. Understanding these factors is essential for navigating the intricate dynamics of human relationships.

One of the key psychological needs that influence our approach to relationships is the need for connection and belonging. According to Maslow's hierarchy of needs, the need for love and belonging is fundamental, coming just after physiological and safety needs. This deep-seated desire for connection often drives individuals to seek out romantic relationships as a primary source of emotional fulfillment. However, when this need is conflated with the idealization of romantic love, it can lead to unrealistic expectations. People may come to expect their partners to fulfill all their emotional needs, which places immense pressure on the relationship and can result in disappointment when those expectations are not met.

The phenomenon of romantic idealization is further complicated by cognitive biases such as the halo effect, where we project idealized attributes onto our partners, often overlooking their flaws. This bias can lead to a distorted perception of a relationship, making it difficult to see the partnership for what it truly is. Over time, as the initial infatuation fades and the halo effect diminishes, individuals may experience disillusionment, realizing that their partner is not the perfect figure they once imagined. This cognitive shift can be jarring and may lead to dissatisfaction or even the dissolution of the relationship.

Another significant psychological factor is the concept of cognitive dissonance, which occurs when individuals experience a conflict between their beliefs and behaviors. In the context of monogamy, this might manifest when a person's biological impulses clash with societal expectations of fidelity. Evolutionary psychology suggests that humans, like many other species, are not naturally monogamous. The drive to seek multiple partners can create internal conflicts when individuals are bound by social norms that dictate monogamy as the ideal. This dissonance can lead to stress, guilt, and anxiety, as individuals struggle to reconcile their natural inclinations with the expectations imposed by society.

The sunk cost fallacy is another psychological trap that often impacts relationships. This fallacy occurs when individuals continue to invest in a failing relationship because of the time, effort, and resources they have already committed. The fear of losing what has been invested can keep people trapped in unhealthy or unfulfilling relationships, even when it would be in their best interest to move on. This fallacy can lead to prolonged emotional distress and can prevent individuals from seeking out relationships that might be more fulfilling.

Furthermore, attachment theory provides insights into how early life experiences shape our approach to relationships in adulthood. Developed by psychologists John Bowlby and Mary Ainsworth, attachment theory posits that the bonds we form with our primary caregivers in childhood influence our expectations and behaviors in romantic relationships. Individuals with secure attachment styles tend to have healthier, more stable relationships, while those with anxious or avoidant attachment styles may struggle with intimacy, trust, and commitment. These attachment patterns can make individuals more vulnerable to the challenges of love and marriage, as they navigate the complexities of maintaining close relationships.

The concept of hedonic adaptation, the tendency for people to return to a baseline level of happiness despite positive or negative changes in their lives, also plays a role in romantic relationships. After the initial excitement of a new relationship fades, individuals often return to their previous levels of happiness, which can lead to a sense of dissatisfaction or restlessness. This phenomenon can make it difficult to maintain long-term satisfaction in a relationship, as the intense emotions associated with the early stages of love inevitably diminish over time.

Social and cultural factors also influence our psychological approach to relationships. The pressure to conform to societal norms, such as the expectation to marry and remain monogamous, can create internal conflicts when these norms do not align with individual desires or psychological tendencies. This pressure is often reinforced by social media, which amplifies the idealization of romantic relationships and perpetuates unrealistic standards of love and commitment. The constant exposure to curated images of "perfect" relationships can lead to feelings of inadequacy and dissatisfaction, as individuals compare their own experiences to these unattainable ideals.

Recognizing the impact of cognitive biases, attachment styles, and social pressures, will help individuals approach relationships with greater awareness and intention. This understanding allows for the development of healthier relationship dynamics, where partners can navigate the complexities of love, monogamy, and marriage with empathy, communication, and a realistic appreciation of what it means to share a life with another person.

Social Stigma, Mockery, and Cultural Engineering: The Delusion of Society

Across the globe, society wields powerful tools to enforce conformity, marginalize non-conformity, and maintain control over individuals. Social stigma, mockery, and cultural engineering are deeply ingrained mechanisms that perpetuate a slavish mindset, trapping humanity in a web of delusions. This phenomenon manifests in numerous ways, affecting people from different cultures and backgrounds, often leading to psychological distress, social isolation, and the reinforcement of harmful norms.

Social Stigma and Mockery: Enforcing Conformity and Marginalization

Social stigma and mockery are not merely byproducts of ignorance or prejudice; they are often deliberate tools used to uphold societal norms. Across various cultures, those who deviate from accepted behaviors, beliefs, or appearances are often subjected to ridicule and exclusion. This enforcement of conformity can have devastating effects on individuals, leading to significant psychological distress and, in some cases, even social exile.

For instance, in many parts of Africa, individuals with albinism are ostracized and mocked due to their skin condition, often being labeled as cursed or associated with superstitions. This social stigma not only isolates them but also exposes them to physical dangers, as they are sometimes hunted for their body parts due to misguided beliefs in their magical properties.

In India, the caste system, though officially abolished, continues to perpetuate social stigma against lower-caste individuals. Those from Dalit communities, often referred to as "untouchables," face daily discrimination and mockery, with their socio-economic status severely constrained by these deeply entrenched societal norms.

In the Western world, mental health issues are often stigmatized, leading to mockery and social isolation. In the United States, for example, people suffering from mental illnesses such as depression or anxiety may be labeled as "weak" or "crazy," preventing them from seeking help and exacerbating their conditions. This stigma is not just a personal burden but a societal failure that marginalizes a significant portion of the population.

Cultural Engineering: Manipulating Society for Control

Cultural engineering refers to the deliberate manipulation of societal norms, values, and behaviors through various forms of influence, including media, education, and propaganda. While it can be used to promote positive social change, it is often exploited by those in power to manipulate public perception and maintain control over the masses.

One of the most obvious examples of cultural engineering can be seen in North Korea, where the state exerts total control over information and education. From a young age, North Koreans are subjected to a highly curated narrative that glorifies the ruling Kim family and demonizes the outside world. This form of cultural engineering has created a population that is largely compliant, with little exposure to alternative viewpoints or the concept of dissent.

In the United States, the role of cultural engineering is evident in the consumer culture that has been meticulously crafted over decades. Edward Bernays, often called the father of public relations, played a pivotal role in this process. His campaigns, such as the popularization of bacon and eggs as a "hearty American breakfast," were not just about selling products but about shaping the very identity of American society. Today, the relentless promotion of consumerism through advertising and media continues to engineer societal values, encouraging individuals to equate success and happiness with material wealth.

Another global example is the widespread use of propaganda during wartime to galvanize public support. During World War II, both the Allied and Axis powers employed extensive propaganda campaigns to shape public opinion, demonize the enemy, and justify the war efforts. These campaigns were successful in uniting populations under a common cause, often at the expense of critical thinking and the suppression of dissenting voices.

The Delusion of a Free Society

The tools of social stigma, mockery, and cultural engineering create a delusion of freedom within society. While individuals may believe they are making independent choices, these choices are often heavily influenced by the cultural and social structures around them. From the clothes people wear to the beliefs they hold, much of what is considered "normal" is the result of deliberate manipulation by those in power.

In many democratic societies, the media plays a crucial role in this process. Noam Chomsky's concept of "manufacturing consent" highlights how media serves the interests of powerful elites by controlling the flow of information and shaping public perception. For example, in many countries, corporate-owned media outlets often prioritize stories that align with the interests of their owners, subtly influencing public opinion and reinforcing existing power structures.

Furthermore, the advent of digital technology has amplified the reach and impact of cultural engineering. Social media platforms, for instance, use algorithms that reinforce existing beliefs and preferences, creating echo chambers that isolate individuals from differing perspectives. This not only polarizes societies but also makes people more susceptible to manipulation, as their online experiences are tailored to keep them engaged, often at the cost of truth and critical thinking.

Social Inequality Exposed: A Global Perspective on the Deception of Society

Social inequality has been a persistent feature of human civilization, perpetuated through various societal structures that create and maintain deep divides. Whether through economic disparities, racial discrimination, or gender bias, these inequalities are cleverly disguised and normalized, leading to a delusion of fairness and equality. This discussion unpacks the layers of this global phenomenon, revealing the psychological and systemic tricks that keep humanity trapped in a cycle of inequality and a slavish mindset.

The Entrenched Economic Divide

Economic inequality is a glaring example of how societies create and maintain social divides. Globally, wealth concentration in the hands of a few is not just a byproduct of capitalism but a feature designed to perpetuate social dominance. In the United States, the gap between the rich and the poor continues to widen, with billionaires amassing unprecedented wealth while millions struggle to make ends meet. The 2020 pandemic further exposed this disparity, as the wealth of the world's billionaires soared by over 50% while millions faced unemployment and poverty.

Similarly, in many developing countries, economic inequality is starkly visible. In India, for example, the top 10% of the population controls over 77% of the country's wealth, while the bottom 50% owns less than 10%. This concentration of wealth leads to a cycle of poverty where the poor have limited access to education, healthcare, and opportunities for upward mobility. It creates a societal structure where the wealthy continue to dominate economically and politically, reinforcing the inequality that keeps the majority in a perpetual state of struggle.

Gender Inequality

Gender inequality is another facet of social disparity that persists globally. Despite progress in some areas, women continue to face significant barriers to equality in many parts of the world. In Saudi Arabia, for example, women have only recently gained the right to drive and participate in public life, yet they still face legal and social restrictions that limit their freedoms and opportunities. These systemic barriers are often justified by cultural norms and religious interpretations that maintain the status quo.

In the corporate world, the "glass ceiling" remains a significant barrier to women's advancement. Even in developed countries like the United States, women are underrepresented in leadership positions, earning less than their male counterparts for the same work. In Japan, cultural expectations around gender roles further limit women's participation in the workforce, leading to one of the lowest rates of female employment in the developed world. These examples highlight how gender inequality is maintained through both overt and subtle societal mechanisms, keeping women in a secondary position.

Racial Inequality

Racial inequality is another deeply entrenched issue that affects societies worldwide. In South Africa, despite the end of apartheid, racial disparities remain pronounced, particularly in economic terms. The majority of wealth and land is still controlled by the white minority, while black South Africans continue to face high levels of poverty and unemployment. This economic divide is a legacy of apartheid that has been perpetuated through unequal access to education, employment, and social services.

In the United States, racial inequality is evident in various aspects of life, from the criminal justice system to housing and education. African Americans are disproportionately affected by police violence, incarceration, and poverty. The Black Lives Matter movement, which gained global attention following the death of George Floyd in 2020, highlighted these systemic issues and sparked a worldwide conversation about racial justice. However, despite the increased awareness, the structures that uphold racial inequality remain largely intact, demonstrating how deeply these disparities are woven into the fabric of society.

The Illusion of Meritocracy

The concept of meritocracy—the idea that anyone can succeed through hard work and talent—often masks the reality of social inequality. This myth is prevalent in many societies, particularly in the United States, where the "American Dream" promises upward mobility for all. However, the reality is that social and economic privilege heavily influence success.

In many cases, access to education, connections, and capital—often inherited—plays a far more significant role in determining success than individual effort. For instance, the majority of U.S. presidents have come from privileged backgrounds, highlighting how wealth and social connections often determine access to power. Similarly, in countries like the United Kingdom, elite schools like Eton and Oxford have long been gateways to political and economic power, perpetuating a cycle of privilege that excludes those from less affluent backgrounds.

The Psychological Mechanisms

Beyond structural and systemic factors, social inequality is perpetuated by psychological mechanisms that reinforce existing hierarchies. Cognitive biases, such as the "halo effect," where individuals attribute positive qualities to those with higher social status, and the "just-world hypothesis," where people believe that the world is inherently fair and individuals get what they deserve, often obscure the realities of inequality. These biases lead people to rationalize social disparities, accepting them as the natural order rather than questioning the systems that create and maintain them.

Social media also plays a significant role in reinforcing inequality. Platforms like Instagram and Facebook create curated portrayals of success and happiness, often setting unrealistic benchmarks for wealth and lifestyle. These portrayals can exacerbate feelings of inadequacy and failure among those who do not measure up, further entrenching the idea that inequality is a result of personal shortcomings rather than systemic injustice.

How Consumerism Deceives Humanity

Consumerism, often marketed as the key to happiness and fulfillment, is one of the most pervasive deceptions in modern society. Across the globe, people are bombarded with advertisements and cultural messages that equate happiness with the accumulation of material possessions. Yet, this relentless pursuit of goods and status often leads not to contentment but to a profound sense of emptiness. This global phenomenon traps individuals in a cycle of consumption, where the promise of fulfillment remains ever elusive, like a mirage on the horizon.

The Global Impact of Consumerism

Consumerism's deceptive allure is a global issue, affecting diverse cultures in different ways. In the United States, Black Friday and Cyber Monday have become near-religious observances, where people trample over one another in search of the latest deals, driven by a fear of missing out. This frenzied consumption underscores the deep-seated belief that happiness can be purchased, even as research shows that such spending sprees often lead to buyer's remorse rather than long-term satisfaction.

In Japan, the concept of "shokuyoku" (a voracious appetite for consumption) is evident in the country's obsession with luxury goods and brands. Japanese consumers often go to great lengths to acquire the latest fashion items, electronics, and cars, associating these possessions with status and success. However, this cultural fixation on consumerism has led to rising levels of debt and a growing sense of isolation, particularly among the younger generation, who find themselves trapped in a cycle of work and consumption with little time for meaningful social interactions.

China presents another interesting case. With its rapid economic growth, the country has seen a surge in consumerism, particularly among its burgeoning middle class. Shopping malls and e-commerce platforms have exploded in popularity, with festivals like Singles' Day breaking global sales records annually. However, this consumer boom has also led to significant social and environmental consequences, including increased waste, pollution, and a widening gap between the rich and the poor. The relentless pursuit of material goods has fostered a culture of instant gratification, where long-term happiness and sustainability are often sacrificed for short-term gains.

The Psychological Manipulation Behind Consumerism

Consumerism's power lies in its ability to exploit human psychology. Cognitive biases such as the "bandwagon effect" and the "endowment effect" play significant roles in perpetuating the cycle of consumption. The bandwagon effect, where individuals adopt behaviors or beliefs simply because others are doing so, is evident in global trends like the annual rush to buy the latest iPhone, regardless of whether it's needed. The endowment effect, where people place higher value on items they own, explains why consumers often accumulate possessions they rarely use but are unwilling to part with.

Social media has amplified these psychological pressures by creating a constant comparison loop, where individuals feel compelled to match the lifestyles of influencers and peers. This "fear of missing out" (FOMO) drives people to purchase items they may not need or want, simply to keep up appearances. Platforms like Instagram and TikTok are rife with curated portrayals of success, where luxury vacations, designer clothes, and expensive gadgets are flaunted as symbols of happiness and achievement. This creates an environment where self-worth is increasingly measured by material possessions, leading to a never-ending cycle of consumption and dissatisfaction.

Global Examples of Consumerism's Consequences

In the United Arab Emirates, particularly in cities like Dubai, consumerism is deeply embedded in the culture, with shopping malls serving as modern-day cathedrals. The city's skyline is dotted with luxury hotels, extravagant malls, and high-end brands, catering to both residents and tourists. However, beneath this glittering exterior lies a stark reality: the UAE has one of the highest per capita ecological footprints in the world, driven by overconsumption and waste. The environmental cost of maintaining such a consumer-driven economy is immense, from the depletion of natural resources to the generation of vast amounts of waste.

In the fashion industry, fast fashion brands like Zara, H&M, and Shein have made trendy clothing accessible to millions around the world. However, this accessibility comes at a significant human and environmental cost. In countries like Bangladesh and India, where much of the world's fast fashion is produced, workers often toil in unsafe conditions for meager wages. The environmental impact is equally severe, with the fashion industry being one of the largest polluters globally, responsible for massive water consumption, pollution, and textile waste. The rise of fast fashion illustrates how consumerism drives unsustainable practices that prioritize profit over people and the planet.

The Illusion of Fulfillment Through Materialism

Consumerism thrives on the illusion that happiness can be bought. Yet, research consistently shows that beyond a certain point, increased material wealth does not correlate with greater happiness. Instead, the relentless pursuit of more—more money, more possessions, more status—often leads to stress, anxiety, and a sense of emptiness. In South Korea, for example, the societal pressure to succeed and accumulate wealth has contributed to high levels of stress and one of the highest suicide rates in the world. Despite the country's economic success, the personal cost of this consumer-driven culture is painfully evident.

In contrast, countries that prioritize social well-being over consumerism tend to report higher levels of happiness. For instance, in Denmark, often cited as one of the happiest countries in the world, there is a strong emphasis on work-life balance, social equality, and community. The Danish concept of "hygge," which emphasizes coziness, contentment, and enjoying simple pleasures, stands in stark contrast to the global consumer culture that equates happiness with material wealth. This focus on quality of life rather than the accumulation of goods highlights an alternative path to fulfillment that is often overlooked in consumer-driven societies.

Marketing Tactics

One of the most effective marketing strategies is the creation of a sense of urgency or scarcity. This tactic is evident in the global phenomenon of "flash sales" and "limited-time offers." For instance, during China's Singles' Day, the world's largest online shopping event, e-commerce giants like Alibaba use countdowns and limited stock alerts to drive massive sales within a short period. Consumers, driven by the fear of missing out (FOMO), rush to make purchases, often without considering whether they truly need the items.

In the United States, Black Friday and Cyber Monday are prime examples of how scarcity and urgency are used to fuel consumer frenzy. Retailers slash prices and offer time-sensitive deals, creating a sense of competition among shoppers. This often leads to impulsive buying, with consumers purchasing products they hadn't planned on, simply because they believe the deal is too good to miss.

In Japan, the marketing of seasonal products, such as limited-edition cherry blossom-flavored treats, leverages cultural appreciation for the transient beauty of nature. Companies create a sense of urgency by offering these products only during a brief period each year, encouraging consumers to buy them while they last. This tactic taps into the cultural value of impermanence, driving sales through the fear of missing out on a fleeting experience.

Emotional Appeals and Brand Loyalty

Marketing tactics also frequently appeal to emotions to build brand loyalty and influence purchasing decisions. Globally, companies use storytelling to create emotional connections with their audiences. In India, for example, advertisements for consumer goods like detergents and cooking oil often depict family-oriented narratives that resonate with traditional values. These ads don't just sell a product; they sell an emotion, such as love, care, or familial duty, making the brand synonymous with those feelings.

Similarly, in Latin America, Coca-Cola's marketing campaigns often focus on themes of happiness, friendship, and togetherness, aligning the brand with positive social experiences. These emotional appeals are powerful, making consumers feel a personal connection to the brand, which can overshadow more rational considerations like price or product quality.

Manipulating Social Proof and Conformity

Marketers around the world also exploit the human tendency to conform to social norms through the use of social proof. Social proof is the idea that people will follow the actions of others, especially in situations where they are uncertain. This is evident in the global trend of influencer marketing, where brands collaborate with social media influencers to promote their products.

In South Korea, for instance, the beauty industry heavily relies on influencers to shape consumer behavior. Korean beauty standards are widely influential, and when a popular influencer endorses a product, it can quickly become a must-have item. Consumers, seeing others rave about the product, are more likely to purchase it themselves, believing that if so many people are using it, it must be good.

In Nigeria, social proof is often used in the promotion of telecommunications services. Mobile service providers frequently highlight the number of subscribers they have in their advertising, implying that their popularity is a testament to their quality. This tactic plays on the cultural tendency to follow the crowd, driving more people to subscribe simply because so many others have done so.

The Ethics of Public Health Campaigns

Public health campaigns, while often well-intentioned, can also be used to manipulate behavior. Governments and organizations around the world use these campaigns to promote behaviors they deem beneficial, but the methods used can sometimes blur the line between persuasion and coercion.

For example, in Australia, anti-smoking campaigns have been highly effective in reducing smoking rates. These campaigns often use graphic images of the health consequences of smoking to shock people into quitting. While these tactics have been successful in promoting public health, they also raise ethical questions about the use of fear as a motivator.

In the United States, public health campaigns during the COVID-19 pandemic utilized various psychological tactics to encourage vaccination. These included emphasizing the social responsibility of getting vaccinated to protect others and highlighting the benefits of returning to normal life. However, the heavy reliance on social pressure and fear of social exclusion for those who remain unvaccinated also sparked debates about the ethics of such tactics.

Global Discrimination in Marketing and Its Impact

Discrimination in marketing is another critical issue that has global implications. Marketing campaigns often reinforce harmful stereotypes based on race, gender, and class, perpetuating social inequalities.

For example, in the United States, the beauty industry has long been criticized for promoting Eurocentric beauty standards, marginalizing people of color. Many advertisements for cosmetics and skincare products historically featured only light-skinned models, sending a message that lighter skin is more desirable. This exclusion has had a profound impact on the self-esteem of individuals from marginalized groups and has perpetuated racial discrimination.

In Brazil, the marketing of skin-lightening products is another stark example of how consumerism can perpetuate racial inequality. These products are often advertised as a way to achieve "beautiful" skin, implicitly suggesting that darker skin is less attractive. This type of marketing exploits deeply ingrained colorism in Brazilian society, where lighter skin is often associated with higher social status.

In the Middle East, gender discrimination in marketing is evident in the portrayal of women in advertisements. Women are often depicted in traditional, subordinate roles, reinforcing gender stereotypes and limiting perceptions of what women can achieve. For instance, ads for household products typically feature women as homemakers, which perpetuates the idea that a woman's place is in the home, rather than in professional or leadership roles.

Breaking Free

Breaking free from the deception of consumerism involves recognizing the psychological manipulation that drives the cycle of consumption and embracing alternative paths to happiness and fulfillment. The challenge lies in rethinking what truly matters. As more people around the world begin to question the relentless pursuit of material wealth, there is an opportunity to create a more equitable, sustainable, and fulfilling way of life—one that values human connection, environmental stewardship, and genuine happiness over the hollow promises of consumer culture.

How the Present Generation is Unmasking Societal Deception

The present generation is leading a global movement to expose and challenge the societal structures and systems that have long hoodwinked humanity. By leveraging technology, social media, and grassroots activism, individuals and communities are unmasking the falsehoods perpetuated by various societal institutions.

Platforms like FactCheck.org, Snopes, and Full Fact have gained prominence, providing accurate information to counter false narratives spread by mainstream media and social networks. In countries like Myanmar, during the 2021 military coup, citizen journalists used social media to document and report events, bypassing state-controlled media.

According to a 2021 survey by the Pew Research Center, 48% of Americans encountered misinformation online weekly. The number of active fact-checking organizations worldwide grew from 145 in 2016 to over 300 in 2021, as reported by the Duke Reporters' Lab. This increased awareness and use of fact-checking tools have enhanced media literacy, helping people discern between true and false information. Citizen journalism has empowered individuals to take control of the narrative, ensuring more accurate and diverse perspectives reach the public.

Investigative reporting and whistleblowing have also played a critical role in exposing corporate deception. Movements like Fridays for Future, initiated by Greta Thunberg, have brought global attention to corporate environmental misconduct and the need for sustainable practices. Campaigns against poor working conditions in global supply chains, such as those led by organizations like the Clean Clothes Campaign, have pressured companies to improve labor standards.

A 2020 Nielsen report indicated that 73% of global consumers are willing to change their consumption habits to reduce environmental impact. According to the Global Reporting Initiative (GRI), the number of companies issuing sustainability reports increased by 35% between 2016 and 2020. Increased consumer activism has led to greater corporate transparency and accountability, with more companies adopting sustainable and ethical practices. Activism has also resulted in better labor conditions and stronger regulations protecting workers' rights in various industries.

The #MeToo hashtag has been used millions of times on social media platforms, raising awareness and leading to tangible changes in workplaces and institutions. Activism has led to the enactment of laws protecting LGBTQ+ rights and addressing gender-based violence, contributing to a more inclusive society. There is a growing acceptance and understanding of diverse gender identities and expressions, driving a cultural shift towards inclusivity.

Efforts to fight economic inequality have also gained momentum. Movements advocating for wealth taxes, like those championed by figures such as Bernie Sanders and Elizabeth Warren in the U.S., aim to address economic disparity. Pilot programs for Universal Basic Income (UBI) in places like Finland and Kenya have explored new ways to reduce poverty and economic inequality.

The present generation's efforts to break The Grand Hoax have resulted in significant progress across various societal domains. By challenging media manipulation, exposing corporate deception, deconstructing gender norms, and fighting economic inequality, individuals and communities are creating a more transparent, accountable, and equitable world. The examples and statistics presented demonstrate the power and potential of the present generation to drive meaningful change, unmasking societal deceptions and promoting a future where truth and justice prevail.

Strategies for the Next Generation

The next generation will likely harness the power of artificial intelligence and machine learning to analyze vast amounts of data, detect patterns, and expose misleading information with unprecedented accuracy and speed.

Additionally, future activists will likely form stronger global coalitions to address issues of societal deception. International collaborations among governments, non-governmental organizations, tech companies, and civil society groups will be essential in creating standardized regulations and best practices for information dissemination. These coalitions will work towards establishing global frameworks for digital transparency, ensuring that misinformation and manipulative tactics can be swiftly identified and countered regardless of geographical boundaries. Such collaborative efforts will enhance the collective ability to address and mitigate the impact of societal deception.

Transparency and traceability in corporate operations. Additionally, the rise of decentralized platforms will empower consumers to make informed choices, building a marketplace where ethical business practices are rewarded, and deceptive companies are held accountable.

Future policymakers and activists will advocate for policies that promote fair distribution of resources, ensuring that economic growth benefits all segments of society. The integration of technological advancements, such as automation and artificial intelligence, into economic systems will be managed in ways that mitigate job displacement and ensure economic stability for all.

Future generations will tackle the issue of societal deception through a combination of advanced technologies, enhanced education, global collaborations, and innovative economic models. Building on the progress made by today's activists and continually adapting to new challenges, they will create a more transparent, accountable, and inclusive society. The strategies and approaches they develop will ensure that the fight against societal deception remains dynamic and effective, paving the way for a future where truth and justice prevail.

Part: B

Chapter 6

How Education Can Dismantle Historical Deceptions

Education possesses the transformative power to dismantle historical deceptions by encouraging critical thinking and challenging entrenched narratives. As we delve into the complexities of the past, education equips us with the tools to scrutinize and question the widely accepted accounts that have often been shaped by those in power. By encouraging inquiry and promoting diverse perspectives, education allows us to unravel myths and reveal hidden truths. For instance, the works of historians like Howard Zinn have shown how a more inclusive and critical approach to history can unearth the stories of marginalized groups and expose the biases of traditional narratives. In this way, education not only corrects historical inaccuracies but also empowers individuals to question and reshape our understanding of the world, pushing for a more nuanced and truthful view of our collective past.

The Evolution of Education

The evolution of education has transformed it from a vehicle of rote learning into a powerful tool for challenging dogmatic thinking and dispelling delusions. From ancient philosophers to modern digital classrooms, education has continually progressed, shifting from mere knowledge transfer to encouraging critical thinking and inquiry. This journey reflects humanity's ongoing effort to refine how we impart knowledge, ultimately empowering individuals to question established beliefs and embrace new ideas.

Socratic Method

Let's embark on this journey in ancient Greece, where Socrates, the father of Western philosophy, sat in the bustling Agora, engaging in dialogues that shaped the very essence of education. Imagine the scene: the Agora, a lively marketplace teeming with merchants, craftsmen, and citizens, also served as a vibrant hub for intellectual discourse. Here, amidst the cacophony of daily life, Socrates would gather a small group of eager young men under the shade of a portico or near a temple. Unlike the teachers of today who often lecture from a podium, Socrates engaged his students in a method of teaching that was as radical as it was effective. This method, now known as the Socratic method, was not about drilling students with information but about stimulating critical thinking through a series of probing questions.

Socrates would pose deceptively simple questions, such as "What is justice?" or "What is virtue?" prompting his students to think deeply and articulate their thoughts. Each answer would be met with further questioning, encouraging a dialogue that peeled back layers of assumptions and beliefs. This iterative process not only helped his students develop their reasoning skills but also led them to recognize the limitations of their knowledge. As Socrates famously declared, "The only true wisdom is in knowing you know nothing." This statement, profound in its humility, underscored his belief that the path to wisdom begins with acknowledging one's ignorance.

One of the most famous accounts of Socratic dialogue is found in Plato's *Apology,* where Socrates, on trial for impiety and corrupting the youth, defends his method. He recounts how the Oracle of Delphi once proclaimed him the wisest of all men. Socrates, puzzled by this, set out to prove the Oracle wrong by questioning the supposedly wise men of Athens. What he discovered was that while these men thought they knew much, their knowledge was superficial at best. This realization reinforced his conviction that true wisdom lay in continuous questioning and dialogue.

Socrates' approach was revolutionary—a nod to the critical thinking that modern education cherishes. Today, the Socratic method is still used in law schools, debate clubs, and classrooms around the world, embodying the principle that education is not about memorizing facts but about learning how to think. Interestingly, this method's emphasis on critical thinking parallels findings in modern neuroscience. Studies suggest that active engagement in learning, such as through dialogue and questioning, promotes deeper understanding and retention of information.

Throughout history, the legacy of Socratic questioning has influenced countless educators and philosophers. For instance, in the 18th century, the Enlightenment philosopher Immanuel Kant echoed Socratic principles in his advocacy for critical thinking and self-reflection. In more recent times, figures like the American educational reformer John Dewey have championed the idea that education should be about inculcating independent thought rather than rote memorization.

Socrates' method was not without its dangers. His relentless questioning often put him at odds with the authorities of his time, ultimately leading to his trial and execution. However, his martyrdom only cemented his legacy, inspiring future generations to challenge conventional wisdom and seek deeper truths.

Thus, as we reflect on the contributions of Socrates, we see a profound lesson in the power of questioning. In a world where information is readily available at our fingertips, the true challenge lies in sifting through it, questioning its validity, and understanding its implications. Socrates' timeless wisdom reminds us that education is not a destination but a journey—one that requires curiosity, humility, and the courage to question.

Confucius

Fast forward to ancient China, and we encounter the influential figure of Confucius, whose teachings have left an indelible mark on the philosophy of education. Imagine a serene setting in the Shandong province, where Confucius, dressed in the traditional robes of a scholar, would gather his disciples under the shade of a large, ancient tree. These gatherings were not merely academic sessions but profound explorations of moral and ethical principles. Confucius's teachings emphasized moral education and the cultivation of virtue, a departure from the more utilitarian approaches of his time.

Confucius' thinking profoundly challenged dogmatic views by emphasizing education as a means to cultivate moral integrity and virtue, rather than merely academic achievement. Teaching under ancient trees in Shandong, Confucius gathered disciples to explore ethical principles, advocating that true education develops character and leads to a harmonious society. His belief that education should produce morally upright individuals, or "junzi," laid the foundation for educational philosophies that prioritize ethical development, influencing practices like the civil service examinations in Imperial China.

The Middle Ages

The Middle Ages marked a significant period in the history of education with the introduction of monastic schools, where learning was primarily reserved for the clergy. These institutions were bastions of religious and intellectual life, nurturing scholars who would shape theological and philosophical thought for centuries. One of the most prominent figures of this era was Thomas Aquinas, whose scholastic approach sought to reconcile faith with reason in a systematic and comprehensive manner.

Thomas Aquinas, a Dominican friar and philosopher, became a towering intellectual force in the 13th century. His magnum opus, *Summa Theologica,* stands as a testament to his rigorous and methodical approach to theology. Aquinas embarked on the ambitious task of synthesizing Christian doctrine with the philosophy of Aristotle, aiming to create a coherent and rational framework for understanding faith. His work systematically addressed a vast array of theological questions, employing rigorous logic and scholastic methodology. This effort to harmonize reason with faith exemplified the scholastic tradition, which dominated medieval intellectual life.

The monastic schools of the Middle Ages were unique environments. These institutions were often secluded, located within monasteries, and were dedicated to the religious and intellectual development of their inhabitants. Education in these schools was not geared towards practical skills or vocational training; rather, it focused on the study of scripture, theology, and classical texts. The primary objective was to prepare monks for their religious duties and to equip them with the intellectual tools to defend and propagate the faith.

An interesting incident highlighting the atmosphere of these monastic schools is the story of Peter Abelard, a contemporary of Aquinas. Abelard was a brilliant scholar whose questioning nature often put him at odds with the ecclesiastical authorities. His love affair with his student, Heloise, and the subsequent scandal is well-documented, but equally significant was his intellectual defiance. Abelard's book, *Sic et Non (Yes and No),* which juxtaposed conflicting statements from Church Fathers, challenged students to engage in critical thinking rather than mere acceptance of doctrine. This was a bold move in an era that largely prioritized doctrinal correctness over critical inquiry.

Monastic education, while encouraging deep theological and philosophical exploration, also had its limitations.

The focus on doctrinal adherence created a rigid system that often stifled dissent and discouraged innovative thinking. This rigidity is evident in the fate of scholars like Abelard, who faced persecution for their unorthodox views. The intellectual climate of the time favored orthodoxy, and deviation from accepted doctrine could lead to severe repercussions.

Despite these constraints, the monastic schools laid important groundwork for the development of Western education. They preserved and transmitted classical knowledge through turbulent times, ensuring that works of ancient philosophers like Aristotle and Plato survived into the Renaissance. Monastic scribes meticulously copied manuscripts, playing a crucial role in the preservation of knowledge.

The legacy of scholasticism, with its emphasis on systematic thought and logical analysis, continued to influence education long after the Middle Ages. Modern statistics show that many of today's universities, including prestigious institutions like Oxford and Cambridge, have their roots in medieval scholastic traditions. These universities were initially founded as centers for theological study, reflecting the enduring impact of monastic educational principles.

Renaissance

The Renaissance marked a transformative period that breathed new life into education, characterized by a revival of classical learning and a profound emphasis on humanism. Central to this movement was Erasmus of Rotterdam, whose advocacy for a well-rounded, humanistic education left an indelible mark on the era. Erasmus's important work, *In Praise of Folly,* employed satire to critique the educational practices of his time, calling for a more enlightened approach that emphasized critical thinking and personal development. His assertion that "Education is the best provision for old age" reflected a growing recognition of the lifelong value of learning, not just for vocational purposes but for the cultivation of a well-rounded, intellectually curious individual.

Erasmus's influence extended beyond his writings. Anecdotes from his life illustrate his commitment to educational reform. For example, Erasmus famously engaged in a correspondence with Thomas More, the author of *Utopia,* discussing the ideal society and the role of education within it. Their exchanges highlight the intellectual vibrancy of the Renaissance, a period when scholars across Europe were deeply engaged in rethinking the purposes and methods of education.

As the Renaissance gave way to the Enlightenment, educational philosophy underwent a radical shift. John Locke emerged as a pivotal figure, challenging traditional notions of education with his groundbreaking work, *Some Thoughts Concerning Education.* Locke argued for the education of the whole person, emphasizing the importance of experience over innate ideas. His belief that "The only way to understand what another person is saying is to listen to them" underscored the significance of experiential learning and critical engagement with others. Locke's ideas were revolutionary, advocating for a child-centered approach that valued the development of reason and individual judgment.

Locke's educational theories found practical application in the upbringing of notable historical figures. One such example is his influence on the education of the English nobleman, Lord Shaftesbury. Locke was entrusted with Shaftesbury's education, implementing his philosophy by creating an environment where learning was driven by curiosity and practical experience rather than rote memorization. This method proved successful, as Shaftesbury grew to become a prominent philosopher and politician, embodying the Enlightenment ideals of reason and critical inquiry.

The Enlightenment also brought forth the ideas of Jean-Jacques Rousseau, whose work *Emile, or On Education* advocated for an educational system that nurtured the natural instincts of the child rather than imposing artificial constraints. Rousseau's innovative approach emphasized the importance of allowing children to explore and learn from their own experiences. His ideas were exemplified in the narrative of Emile, a fictional pupil whose education was designed to nurture his innate curiosity and independence. Rousseau's concept of "natural education" was groundbreaking, challenging the rigid, authoritarian educational systems of his time.

Interesting incidents from Rousseau's life further illustrate his educational philosophy. Despite facing significant personal and professional adversity, including periods of exile and public criticism, Rousseau remained committed to his vision of education. His determination to practice what he preached is evident in his own efforts to educate his children, though controversially, he chose to place them in foundling hospitals, a decision that has sparked considerable debate among historians.

The establishment of academies and universities across Europe, such as the University of Leiden in the Netherlands, became centers of Enlightenment thought, attracting scholars from across the continent. These institutions played a crucial role in disseminating new educational philosophies and promoting the ideals of critical thinking and empirical inquiry.

The Industrial Revolution

The Industrial Revolution, with its sweeping changes to society and the economy, demanded a new approach to education that could meet the needs of an evolving workforce and an increasingly complex world. Enter Horace Mann, often called the "Father of the Common School Movement," whose pioneering efforts fundamentally transformed the landscape of American education.

In his tenure as the Secretary of the Massachusetts Board of Education, a position he assumed in 1837. During his twelve years in office, Mann visited hundreds of schools, meticulously documenting their conditions and advocating for systemic reforms. His reports highlighted the need for standardized curricula, better-trained teachers, and improved school facilities. He argued that education should be free, universal, and non-sectarian, a radical departure from the existing system where schooling was often a privilege reserved for the wealthy or those who could afford private tutors.

One of his notable successes was the establishment of the first normal schools—institutions specifically designed to train teachers in the art of education. The first of these, the Lexington Normal School, opened in 1839, setting a precedent for teacher education nationwide. These schools emphasized the importance of professional training for educators, ensuring that teachers were well-equipped to provide high-quality education to their students.

The impact of Mann's work extended far beyond Massachusetts. His ideas influenced educational reforms across the United States and even internationally. For instance, Prussian educational reforms, which emphasized state-controlled, compulsory education, inspired Mann. He adapted these principles to fit the American context, advocating for public funding of schools through taxes—a concept that was initially met with resistance but eventually became the norm.

Despite these successes, the implementation of Mann's ideas was not without challenges. Resistance from certain religious groups, who preferred parochial schools, and from taxpayers reluctant to fund public education, were significant hurdles. However, Mann's relentless advocacy and the undeniable benefits of an educated populace eventually won over many skeptics.

Breaking Human Delusions from the Renaissance to the Modern Era

The Renaissance, a period of profound cultural and intellectual awakening that began in the 14th century, marked a dramatic departure from the medieval mindset.

It was a time when the rigid structures of scholasticism, which had dominated education for centuries, were challenged by a new spirit of inquiry and humanism. This era of rebirth saw the rediscovery of classical knowledge and a renewed emphasis on the importance of human potential and creativity.

One of the key figures in this educational revolution was Desiderius Erasmus, a Dutch humanist who championed the idea that education should cultivate critical thinking rather than rote memorization. Erasmus believed that individuals should be taught to read, think, and reason independently, rather than merely accepting the dogmas imposed by the Church or the state. His advocacy for a liberal education, grounded in the study of the humanities, laid the groundwork for the modern concept of critical inquiry.

Erasmus's influence extended beyond his writings; he was actively involved in the education of the young, particularly through his role as a tutor to the children of nobility. His methods emphasized the study of classical texts, not as dogmatic truths, but as sources of wisdom that should be analyzed and debated. This approach encouraged students to question authority and to seek knowledge for themselves, thus breaking the medieval delusion that truth was a fixed, unchangeable entity handed down by those in power.

The Renaissance also saw the rise of the printing press, invented by Johannes Gutenberg in the mid-15th century. This technological innovation revolutionized education by making books more accessible and affordable, thereby spreading knowledge more widely than ever before. The printing press allowed for the dissemination of new ideas and the challenging of old ones on an unprecedented scale. It played a crucial role in the spread of humanist thought and the Reformation, which further questioned the established order and promoted the idea that individuals should interpret religious texts for themselves rather than relying on the clergy.

The impact of the Renaissance on education was not limited to Europe. The movement had a global reach, influencing intellectual developments in places as far-flung as the Ottoman Empire and the Mughal Empire in India. In the Ottoman Empire, for instance, the madrasahs (educational institutions) began to incorporate new subjects such as astronomy and philosophy, which were previously considered heretical. This integration of knowledge helped to challenge the rigid religious orthodoxy that had dominated Islamic education for centuries.

In the Mughal Empire, Emperor Akbar the Great established a system of education that was remarkably progressive for its time. Akbar, who ruled from 1556 to 1605, was a patron of learning and encouraged the study of diverse subjects, including science, literature, and the arts. He also promoted religious tolerance and sought to educate his subjects in the principles of all major religions, thus challenging the religious dogmatism that had often led to conflict in the region.

The Renaissance, therefore, was not just a period of artistic and intellectual flourishing; it was a time when education began to break the chains of ignorance and superstition that had held humanity back for centuries. It laid the foundation for the Enlightenment, a period that would further advance the cause of reason, science, and individual liberty.

The Enlightenment: Education as the Key to Human Progress

The Enlightenment, which emerged in the late 17th and 18th centuries, built on the foundations laid by the Renaissance and took the idea of education as a means of liberating the human mind to new heights. This era, often referred to as the Age of Reason, was characterized by a belief in the power of human intellect and the potential for progress through knowledge and education.

The Enlightenment saw the rise of the scientific method as a fundamental tool of inquiry, which had a profound impact on education. Figures like Isaac Newton and Galileo Galilei exemplified the new approach to learning, which was based on observation, experimentation, and the questioning of established truths. The scientific revolution that accompanied the Enlightenment shattered many of the delusions that had persisted throughout the medieval period, such as the geocentric model of the universe and the belief in the immutability of the natural world.

Educational institutions during the Enlightenment began to reflect these changes. Universities and academies across Europe started to place a greater emphasis on the sciences, mathematics, and philosophy, moving away from the purely theological focus that had dominated medieval education. The Royal Society in England, founded in 1660, became a center for scientific learning and innovation, attracting some of the greatest minds of the age.

The Enlightenment's impact on education was not confined to Europe. In the American colonies, the ideas of the Enlightenment played a significant role in the development of the education system. Figures like Benjamin Franklin and Thomas Jefferson were deeply influenced by Enlightenment thought and advocated for public education as a means of promoting civic virtue and informed citizenship. Jefferson, in particular, saw education as the cornerstone of democracy and argued that an educated populace was essential for the preservation of liberty and justice.

In the realm of women's education, the Enlightenment also sparked new ideas and challenges to the status quo. Although women's access to formal education remained limited, thinkers like Mary Wollstonecraft began to advocate for the rights of women to receive an education equal to that of men. Wollstonecraft's call for educational reform was radical for its time and laid the groundwork for future movements for gender equality in education.

The Enlightenment, therefore, was a period when education became increasingly recognized as a vital tool for human progress. It broke down the delusions of ignorance and superstition that had persisted for centuries and replaced them with a new faith in reason, science, and the potential for human improvement.

The 19th Century: The Rise of Public Education and the Challenge to Social Hierarchies

The 19th century marked a pivotal moment in the history of education, as the idea of public education for all began to take root. This period saw the establishment of state-funded schools in many parts of the world, reflecting the growing belief that education was not just a privilege for the elite but a right for every citizen.

One of the driving forces behind the expansion of public education in the 19th century was the Industrial Revolution. As societies became more industrialized, there was a growing need for a literate and numerate workforce. Governments began to recognize that education was essential for economic development and social stability, leading to the establishment of compulsory education laws in many countries.

In England, figures like Robert Owen, a social reformer and industrialist, advocated for education as a means of social change. Owen established a model school in New Lanark, Scotland, where children of workers received a free education that emphasized moral development, creativity, and practical skills. His approach challenged the rigid class distinctions of the time and promoted the idea that education could be a force for social mobility and equality.

The 19th century also saw significant advances in women's education. In the United States, women's colleges such as Mount Holyoke and Vassar were founded to provide higher education opportunities for women, challenging the prevailing belief that women were intellectually inferior to men. These institutions played a crucial role in the fight for women's rights and laid the groundwork for the broader feminist movement of the 20th century.

In India, the 19th century was a time of educational reform and modernization, particularly under the influence of British colonial rule. Figures like Raja Ram Mohan Roy and Ishwar Chandra Vidyasagar were instrumental in advocating for the education of women and the lower castes, challenging the deeply entrenched social hierarchies of Indian society. Vidyasagar, in particular, was a pioneer in promoting the education of women and widow remarriage, both of which were radical ideas at the time.

The expansion of public education in the 19th century also had a significant impact on literacy rates. In France, for example, the introduction of free, compulsory education in 1881-1882 led to a dramatic increase in literacy, with the illiteracy rate dropping from 33% in 1870 to just 3% by 1914. This rise in literacy had far-reaching implications, as it enabled more people to participate in public life, access information, and challenge the existing social order.

However, the expansion of public education also revealed the persistence of certain delusions and inequalities. Despite the progress made in making education more accessible, many marginalized groups, including racial and ethnic minorities, continued to face significant barriers to education. In the United States, for example, the segregated school system reinforced racial inequalities, with African American children receiving inferior education compared to their white counterparts. This systemic inequality would later become a focal point of the Civil Rights Movement in the mid-20th century.

The 19th century, therefore, was a time of both progress and contradiction in the evolution of education. While significant strides were made in expanding access to education and challenging social hierarchies, the period also highlighted the persistence of old delusions and the need for ongoing reform.

The 20th Century: Breaking the Chains of Rote Learning and Embracing Progressive Education

The 20th century witnessed a dramatic transformation in the landscape of education, driven by the innovative philosophies of progressive educators who sought to break away from the rigid, rote learning methods that had dominated education for centuries. The focus shifted towards creating an educational environment that fostered critical thinking, creativity, and problem-solving skills, rather than simply memorizing facts and figures.

John Dewey was one of the most influential educational reformers of this period whose approach to education represented a significant departure from traditional methods. Dewey's philosophy was rooted in the idea that education should be an active, dynamic process intertwined with everyday experiences. He believed that students learn best through doing, and that education should engage them in real-world challenges, encouraging them to apply their knowledge practically.

Dewey's ideas were not just theoretical; they were put into practice in the laboratory school he founded at the University of Chicago in 1896. Here, students engaged in hands-on activities such as gardening, cooking, and woodworking, which were integrated with traditional subjects to create a holistic learning experience. This approach was revolutionary in that it aimed to develop not just intellectual abilities, but also practical skills and social responsibility. Dewey's model of experiential learning challenged the traditional delusion that education was merely about the passive absorption of knowledge, instead promoting the idea that it was a process of active engagement with the world.

The impact of Dewey's ideas extended far beyond the United States. In post-revolutionary Mexico, educator José Vasconcelos adopted similar principles to overhaul the national education system. Vasconcelos emphasized the importance of rural schools and practical skills in uplifting the population, reflecting Dewey's belief that education should be relevant to the lives of students. In Soviet Russia, educators like Anton Makarenko integrated Deweyan principles into the education system, promoting collective and experiential learning, albeit within a different ideological framework.

The 20th century also saw the rise of educational methods that focused on the needs and potential of the individual child. The Montessori Method, developed by Maria Montessori, emphasized self-directed activity, hands-on learning, and collaborative play. Montessori's approach was grounded in the belief that children are naturally curious and capable of learning independently when provided with the right environment. Her work revolutionized early childhood education and continues to influence educational practices around the world today.

In addition to these progressive educational philosophies, the 20th century also witnessed significant advancements in the accessibility of education. The establishment of public schools became more widespread, and efforts were made to make education more inclusive, particularly for marginalized groups. The Civil Rights Movement in the United States, for example, played a crucial role in challenging the segregation and inequality that had long plagued the education system. Landmark rulings such as Brown v. Board of Education in 1954 helped to dismantle the delusion of "separate but equal" and paved the way for greater integration and equality in education.

However, the 20th century was not without its challenges. The rapid pace of technological and social change often outstripped the ability of educational systems to adapt, leading to a disconnect between what was taught in schools and the skills needed in the workforce. The emphasis on standardized testing, particularly in the latter half of the century, also sparked debate about the purpose of education and whether it was truly serving the needs of students.

Despite these challenges, the 20th century was a period of remarkable progress in the evolution of education. It was a time when the chains of rote learning were broken, and new approaches to education were developed that emphasized critical thinking, creativity, and practical skills. These changes laid the groundwork for the educational practices that continue to evolve in the 21st century.

Education Today: Navigating the Digital Age and the Promise of Personalized Learning

As we entered the 21st century, the evolution of education continued, driven by technological advancements and a greater understanding of learning psychology. The advent of digital technology has created new opportunities for personalized learning, enabling students to access educational resources tailored to their individual needs and learning styles.

One of the most significant developments in modern education is the rise of online learning platforms, which have democratized access to education on a global scale. Platforms like Khan Academy, Coursera, and edX offer free or low-cost courses on a wide range of subjects, allowing individuals to learn at their own pace and from the comfort of their own homes. This shift towards self-directed learning reflects a broader trend in education towards greater flexibility and personalization, as students are no longer bound by the constraints of traditional classroom settings.

The rise of personalized learning is also being facilitated by advances in artificial intelligence and machine learning. These technologies are being used to create adaptive learning systems that can adjust to the needs of each student, providing targeted feedback and recommendations to help them succeed. For example, AI-powered tutoring systems can analyze a student's performance and identify areas where they may need additional support, offering personalized practice exercises or instructional videos to address specific challenges.

However, the integration of technology into education also presents new challenges and potential threats. The digital divide remains a significant issue, with many students around the world lacking access to the internet or digital devices.

Moreover, the reliance on digital technology in education raises concerns about privacy and data security. The use of AI and data analytics in education involves the collection and processing of large amounts of personal information, raising questions about how this data is being used and who has access to it. There is also the risk of over-reliance on technology, which could lead to the erosion of critical thinking and interpersonal skills if not balanced with traditional forms of learning.

In addition to these technological challenges, education today must also grapple with the psychological and cognitive barriers that can hinder learning. Cognitive biases, such as confirmation bias and the Dunning-Kruger effect, can lead students to overestimate their knowledge and resist new information that challenges their preconceptions. The rise of misinformation and "fake news" in the digital age has made it more important than ever for education to equip students with the skills to critically evaluate the information they encounter.

To address these challenges, there is a growing emphasis on media literacy and critical thinking in modern curricula. Educators are increasingly recognizing the need to teach students how to navigate the complex information landscape of the digital age, helping them to discern credible sources from unreliable ones and to engage with media in a thoughtful and informed manner.

The evolution of education in the 21st century also includes a renewed focus on social and emotional learning (SEL), which emphasizes the development of skills such as empathy, self-regulation, and interpersonal communication. These skills are seen as essential for success in both personal and professional life and are increasingly being integrated into educational programs alongside traditional academic subjects.

As we look to the future, the integration of artificial intelligence, virtual reality, and personalized learning platforms promises to further transform how knowledge is imparted and consumed. Virtual reality (VR), for example, is being used to create immersive learning experiences that allow students to explore historical events, scientific concepts, or distant locations in ways that were previously impossible. In medical education, VR is being used to simulate surgical procedures, providing students with hands-on practice in a safe and controlled environment.

AI-driven adaptive systems, and the integration of media literacy into curricula encourage students to question established norms, discern truth from misinformation, and resist the pressure to conform to outdated societal beliefs.

Education's Role in breaking the Delusions

Education, throughout history, has been a powerful force in breaking the chains of ignorance, fear, and subservience that have bound humanity to delusions. The evolution of education has been a relentless journey toward enlightenment, challenging entrenched myths, deconstructing historical falsehoods, and revealing hidden truths. This chapter delves into how education has historically dismantled these delusions and how future generations will continue this vital work to avoid falling prey to the same traps.

The Power of Education in Challenging Historical Myths

For decades after the Civil War, the myth of the Confederacy as a noble, heroic cause was perpetuated in Southern textbooks, memorials, and popular culture. This narrative conveniently glossed over the central issue of slavery, instead portraying the war as a fight for states' rights and Southern honor.

However, as historians and educators began to critically examine the primary sources from the Civil War era, a different picture emerged—one that placed slavery and white supremacy at the heart of the conflict. This shift in understanding was driven by educational reforms that emphasized the importance of studying diverse perspectives and primary documents. The introduction of more accurate and inclusive curricula in schools across the United States has helped to dismantle the "lost cause" myth, replacing it with a more truthful account of the Civil War and its aftermath.

Another striking example of education challenging historical myths can be found in the ongoing efforts to confront and understand the legacy of colonialism. For centuries, colonial powers portrayed their empires as benevolent forces that brought civilization, progress, and Christianity to "savage" lands. This narrative justified the exploitation, subjugation, and even genocide of indigenous peoples around the world.

In recent decades, however, there has been a growing movement to critically reexamine the history of colonialism. Education has played a pivotal role in this process, as universities, schools, and independent scholars have begun to explore the perspectives of the colonized rather than solely those of the colonizers. This has led to a more nuanced and accurate understanding of the devastating impacts of colonialism on indigenous cultures, economies, and environments.

In Canada, for instance, the Truth and Reconciliation Commission (TRC) was established to address the legacy of residential schools, which forcibly removed Indigenous children from their families and sought to assimilate them into Euro-Canadian culture. The TRC's final report, released in 2015, called for a complete overhaul of the Canadian education system to include the history and contributions of Indigenous peoples. As a result, schools across Canada have begun to incorporate Indigenous perspectives into their curricula, helping to break down the myths of benevolent colonization and foster a more truthful understanding of Canada's past.

Innovative Educational Practices: Breaking Down Delusions Through Interdisciplinary Learning

The 21st century has witnessed a surge in innovative educational practices designed to challenge historical delusions and promote a deeper understanding of the complexities of history. Project-based learning and interdisciplinary studies have emerged as powerful tools in this endeavor, allowing students to explore historical events from multiple perspectives and disciplines.

For example, consider a project-based learning module that asks students to investigate the causes and consequences of the Great Depression. Rather than simply memorizing dates and facts, students might be tasked with examining the economic, social, and political factors that led to the stock market crash of 1929. They could analyze primary sources such as newspaper articles, personal letters, and government documents to understand the human impact of the economic collapse. By incorporating perspectives from economics, sociology, and cultural studies, students gain a more comprehensive understanding of the event and are better equipped to challenge simplistic or misleading narratives.

Interdisciplinary studies, too, have proven effective in deconstructing historical myths. A study of the Industrial Revolution, for instance, might include an exploration of its economic drivers, its environmental consequences, and its impact on labor movements and social inequality. Students could examine how the exploitation of natural resources fueled industrial growth while also causing long-term environmental damage. They might also investigate how the rise of factories led to the growth of the labor movement and the eventual establishment of workers' rights. By approaching the topic from multiple angles, students can develop a more nuanced understanding of the Industrial Revolution and its complex legacy.

These innovative educational practices are not just confined to history classes. They are being used across disciplines to help students challenge assumptions, think critically, and engage with complex issues. In science education, for example, students are increasingly being encouraged to explore the ethical implications of scientific research and technological innovation. This approach helps to break down the delusion that science is a purely objective pursuit, divorced from social, political, and ethical considerations.

Future Generations: The Ongoing Struggle Against Delusion

Future generations will need to build on the foundations laid by their predecessors, using education to challenge the delusions that have plagued the past and present.

One area where future generations will likely focus their efforts is in the decolonization of education. This involves challenging the Eurocentric narratives that have long dominated history curricula and incorporating the perspectives and experiences of marginalized and colonized peoples. By embracing a more inclusive approach to history, education can help break down the delusions of cultural superiority and foster a more accurate and empathetic understanding of the past.

Another critical area of focus will be the role of education in addressing global challenges such as climate change, inequality, and human rights. As the world becomes increasingly interconnected, the ability to critically engage with complex global issues will be essential. Education will need to equip students with the knowledge and skills to navigate these challenges, while also encouraging them to question the assumptions and narratives that underlie current approaches to these issues.

Finally, future generations will need to be vigilant in guarding against the resurgence of revisionist history and misinformation. The rise of social media and digital platforms has made it easier than ever for false or misleading information to spread, often with harmful consequences. Education will play a crucial role in teaching students how to critically assess the information they encounter, recognize propaganda and misinformation, and engage in informed, evidence-based discussions.

The struggle against delusion is an ongoing process, one that requires constant vigilance and a commitment to truth and understanding. By continuing to evolve and innovate, education can help future generations navigate the complexities of the modern world, challenge the myths and misconceptions of the past, and build a more informed and equitable society.

Chapter 7

How Economic Progress will break the illusions

Throughout history, economic progress has been a powerful force in advancing human intelligence and liberating humanity from the chains of ignorance, helplessness, and slavery. Each stage of economic development has not only brought material prosperity but also fostered critical thinking, innovation, and a greater understanding of our world. By examining the transformative power of economic progress, we reveal how it has empowered individuals and societies to break free from the deceptions that have long constrained human potential. With economic progress, the shackles of manipulation and exploitation are finally broken, allowing humanity to realize its fullest potential.

The Birth of Trade and Early Economic Thought: Unraveling the Myths

The origins of trade were deeply intertwined with the survival instincts of early human societies. As humans transitioned from nomadic lifestyles to settled agricultural communities, they discovered that exchanging surplus goods with neighboring tribes could greatly enhance their chances of survival. These initial exchanges were simple, yet they planted the seeds for the complex economic systems that would eventually emerge.

Mesopotamians: Pioneers of Economic Innovation

Picture yourself walking through a bustling Mesopotamian bazaar thousands of years ago. The scene is vibrant: merchants haggling over prices, blacksmiths hammering away at tools, and the tantalizing aroma of spices filling the air. Here, a farmer laden with grain could trade his harvest for a blacksmith's sturdy tools, creating a flow of goods that benefited the entire community. This early barter system, although rudimentary by modern standards, was a groundbreaking development. It fostered labor specialization, resource distribution, and economic interdependence, laying the foundation for more advanced economic practices.

However, this system had its flaws. Without a common standard of value, disputes over the worth of goods were inevitable. For example, how many sacks of grain should be exchanged for a single plow? These disagreements often led to heated negotiations, requiring the intervention of local leaders to mediate. Despite these challenges, the Mesopotamian markets flourished, driven by the resourcefulness of the Sumerians. They began developing early forms of currency, such as barley or silver shekels, to standardize trade and reduce friction.

Archaeological discoveries, such as clay tablets inscribed with cuneiform writing, provide fascinating insights into these early transactions. These records, detailing trades, debts, and contracts, reveal the sophistication of Sumerian economic thought. The Mesopotamians didn't just trade goods; they were also trading ideas, innovations, and cultural practices, which spread along their extensive trade routes. These connections facilitated the exchange of technologies and ideas, accelerating the development of civilizations across the ancient world. The use of seals to authenticate goods and documents, for example, originated in Mesopotamia but quickly spread, influencing other cultures and ending many baseless superstitions about foreign tribes.

The Sumerians' contributions to trade and economic systems were transformative. They shattered the isolationist beliefs that often surrounded different communities, encouraging integration and fostering a more interconnected world. Their legacy is a powerful reminder of how early commerce not only fueled economic growth but also broadened human understanding, dispelling many delusions about 'the other.'

The Phoenicians: Masters of Maritime Trade

While the Mesopotamians focused on land-based trade, the Phoenicians took to the seas, becoming the first true maritime traders. Renowned for their seafaring prowess, the Phoenicians established trade networks that spanned the Mediterranean, connecting disparate civilizations. Historian Fernand Braudel aptly describes them as the "great go-betweens of the ancient world."

Imagine the bustling ports of Tyre and Sidon, where Phoenician ships set sail to distant lands, carrying a diverse array of goods. These ships transported precious metals, fine textiles, and exotic spices, but they were also carriers of ideas. One of their most enduring contributions was the introduction of the alphabet. Before this innovation, communication relied on complex writing systems like cuneiform or hieroglyphics, which required years of training to master. The Phoenician alphabet, however, was a game-changer. Consisting of just 22 characters, it was simple and phonetic, making it accessible to a broader audience and revolutionizing communication and commerce.

When Greek traders encountered the Phoenician alphabet, they quickly recognized its potential and adapted it to their language. This adaptation led to the development of the Greek alphabet, which in turn influenced the Latin alphabet used across much of the world today. The Phoenician alphabet was more than just a tool for communication; it was a catalyst for cultural diffusion, enabling the spread of knowledge across civilizations.

The Phoenicians were also instrumental in spreading religious beliefs, artistic styles, and cultural practices. For example, the worship of the goddess Astarte, promoted by the Phoenicians, found followers in regions as diverse as Carthage and Cyprus. Their artistic motifs, such as intricate ivory carvings and colorful glassware, left a lasting impact on the material culture of the Mediterranean and beyond.

The Phoenician trade network was not just about the exchange of goods; it was a conduit for the exchange of ideas and technologies that shaped the civilizations of the Mediterranean. Their pioneering spirit laid the groundwork for the interconnected world we live in today. The Phoenicians demonstrated that commerce could be a powerful force for cultural exchange and intellectual advancement, breaking down barriers and fostering a more unified global community.

Deception and Fraud: The Double-Edged Sword of Trade

Trade, while a driver of progress, has always been fraught with the potential for deception and exploitation. This is not a modern phenomenon but a recurring theme throughout history. The ancient markets of Mesopotamia, for example, were rife with fraudulent practices. The Code of Hammurabi, one of the earliest known legal codes, contains numerous laws aimed explicitly at curbing fraud in trade. Issues such as false weights and measures, price manipulation, and misrepresentation of goods were rampant, leading to harsh punishments for offenders.

The development of coinage in ancient Lydia marked a significant leap forward in the battle against fraud. Historian Niall Ferguson, in his book *The Ascent of Money*, describes how the Lydians, around the 7th century BC, introduced standardized coinage, addressing many inefficiencies of barter systems. Before coinage, bartering required a double coincidence of wants—the unlikely scenario where two parties each had precisely what the other desired. Coinage provided a common measure of value, simplifying transactions and facilitating trade on an unprecedented scale.

The introduction of coins bearing standardized images, such as the lion symbol of Lydia, revolutionized trade. It not only made transactions easier but also helped build trust in the economic system, reducing the potential for fraud. This system paved the way for more complex economic institutions such as banks and markets, illustrating humanity's continuous efforts to overcome deception and build more reliable economic systems.

Behavioral economist Daniel Kahneman, in his book *Thinking, Fast and Slow,* explores how cognitive biases can lead to poor decision-making and susceptibility to fraud. He notes that humans are not always rational actors; our decisions are often influenced by emotions, biases, and a lack of information. Ancient traders exploited these weaknesses through deceptive practices like false advertising and the misrepresentation of goods, undermining trust and integrity in the market.

The Medici: Revolutionizing Finance

The evolution of economic systems is a testament to humanity's ability to learn from past mistakes and innovate for a better future. One of the most captivating chapters in this story is the establishment of the first banks in Renaissance Italy. Imagine the bustling streets of Florence in the 15th century, where the Medici family, renowned for their wealth and influence, began to transform the financial landscape.

Historian Michael North, in his book *The Medieval Banking System,* highlights how the Medici family revolutionized finance by creating a network of banks that facilitated international trade and commerce. Before these innovations, merchants had to carry large sums of money on perilous journeys, risking theft or loss. The Medici banks introduced groundbreaking financial instruments, such as letters of credit and bills of exchange, which dramatically reduced these risks.

These financial instruments allowed merchants to conduct transactions without the physical transfer of gold or silver, making long-distance trade safer and more efficient. The introduction of letters of credit was particularly revolutionary. A merchant in Florence could deposit money in a local Medici bank and receive a letter of credit, which he could then present to a corresponding bank in another city to access funds. This system not only facilitated safer trade but also increased trust among traders, knowing that their transactions were backed by the reputable Medici Bank.

The impact of these innovations extended beyond Italy. The Medici's banking practices influenced the development of financial systems across Europe, laying the groundwork for modern banking. The Medici Bank, at its height, managed the accounts of popes, kings, and major commercial enterprises, illustrating the widespread trust and reliance on their financial services. However, the story of the Medici Bank is not without its challenges. In the late 15th century, the bank faced significant financial difficulties, partly due to bad loans and political instability. Despite these setbacks, the legacy of the Medici Bank endured, demonstrating the enduring importance of financial innovation in economic development.

The Legacy of Early Trade and Economic Thought

The legacy of early trade and economic thought is evident in the sophisticated global economy we have today. From the bazaars of Mesopotamia to the maritime trade of the Phoenicians, ancient civilizations laid the groundwork for modern commerce. Their innovations, driven by necessity and creativity, transformed simple barter systems into complex economic networks that continue to shape our world. These early economic developments shattered many illusions, encouraging integration, communication, and a broader understanding of the world. As we reflect on these achievements, it becomes clear that economic progress has consistently broken down barriers, dispelled delusions, and paved the way for a more interconnected and enlightened world.

The Feudal Economy and Its Discontents: Unveiling the Stagnation

The medieval economic landscape was dominated by the feudal system, a structure where power and wealth were tightly controlled by a few elites. Central to this system was the manor—a self-sufficient estate governed by a lord and worked by serfs. These serfs, essentially bound to the land, had limited freedom and no opportunity for economic mobility. Historian Marc Bloch, in his seminal work *Feudal Society*, describes feudalism as "an institution rooted in the land and in the relationship of lord and vassal, perpetuating a rigid social order." This system, while providing stability, also entrenched inequality and stifled innovation.

Manorialism: A System of Stagnation

Manorialism, the economic backbone of feudalism, ensured that wealth remained land-based. Lords provided protection and justice, and in return, serfs worked the land, paying rent through labor or a portion of their produce. This arrangement created a clear, unchanging economic hierarchy. Historian Susan Reynolds, in *Fiefs and Vassals,* notes that while "the manorial system was efficient in maintaining stability, it discouraged economic dynamism and individual enterprise."

The emphasis on subsistence agriculture and self-sufficiency meant there was little room for innovation or economic growth. The feudal economy was a closed system, resistant to change, which historian Lynn White Jr. argues in Medieval Technology and Social Change: "The feudal economy, with its static social order and reliance on agricultural production, was not conducive to the kind of innovation and economic dynamism that would later characterize the commercial revolution."

In this environment, technological advancements were rare, and the conservative nature of feudal society further suppressed progress. The manorial system was effective at maintaining the status quo but proved to be a significant barrier to the economic development that would eventually challenge and dismantle feudalism's rigid structures.

Mercantilism: The Rise of National Economies and Their Illusions

As feudalism declined and nation-states rose to prominence, a new economic doctrine emerged—mercantilism. This system placed the accumulation of national wealth at the forefront, with a focus on maintaining a favorable balance of trade. Mercantilist policies were designed to ensure that a nation's exports exceeded its imports, thereby increasing its stockpile of precious metals. Adam Smith, in *The Wealth of Nations,* famously criticized mercantilism, arguing that it conflated wealth with money and suppressed economic freedom: "The sole use of money is to circulate consumable goods. Accumulating gold and silver for their own sake is a misguided goal."

Mercantilism often led to protectionist policies, including tariffs and monopolies, which restricted free trade and stifled competition. Nation-states sought to establish colonies as sources of raw materials and markets for manufactured goods, frequently exploiting these territories and their populations. This system, while it contributed to the rise of powerful nation-states, also perpetuated economic disparities and hindered global cooperation.

Philosopher David Hume, in his *Political Discourses*, critiqued the mercantilist obsession with trade surpluses, warning that it was unsustainable and harmful to international relations: "It is not gold and silver, but industry and commerce, which provide a lasting and solid foundation for a nation's prosperity." Hume's insights revealed the flaws in mercantilist thinking, highlighting the need for a more balanced and cooperative approach to trade that recognized the mutual benefits of economic interdependence.

Mercantilist policies often sacrificed individual freedoms and economic diversity for national gain. By favoring state control over economic activities, these policies led to the establishment of monopolies and the restriction of competition. The exploitation of colonies and the imposition of trade restrictions fueled tensions and conflicts between nations. Economist John Maynard Keynes, *in The General Theory of Employment, Interest, and Money*, pointed out the inefficiencies and international tensions that resulted from mercantilist policies: "The mercantilist obsession with trade surpluses and hoarding gold is a flawed approach that ignores the benefits of economic cooperation and the importance of domestic demand."

The Hanseatic League: A Beacon of Innovation and Cooperation

Amid the rigidity of feudalism and the restrictive policies of mercantilism, history offers a remarkable example of a movement that broke free from these constraints—the Hanseatic League. This powerful alliance of merchant guilds and market towns in Northwestern and Central Europe emerged during the late medieval period, revolutionizing trade across borders and promoting economic cooperation in an era otherwise dominated by rigid hierarchies and protectionism.

The Hanseatic League was born out of necessity, as merchants sought collective security and mutual benefit in the face of the dangers of medieval trade. In an era fraught with risks—from pirates on the seas to bandits on the roads—merchants banded together to protect their interests and ensure safe passage for their goods. By the 13th century, this informal network had evolved into a formidable coalition encompassing nearly 200 cities from the Baltic to the North Sea, including major trading hubs like Lübeck, Hamburg, and Bruges.

Historian Philippe Dollinger, in *The German Hansa,* captures the transformative nature of this alliance, noting, "The Hanseatic League was a remarkable example of how merchants and towns could collaborate to overcome the limitations of feudal and mercantilist systems, fostering a vibrant and interconnected commercial network." The League's ability to collectively negotiate with kings and local lords for trading privileges was unprecedented, and it played a crucial role in facilitating the flow of goods across vast distances.

One particularly illustrative example is the Hanseatic Kontor in Bergen, Norway. This trading post was established to capitalize on the lucrative fish trade, particularly stockfish, a staple of the European diet. Hanseatic merchants in Bergen operated with considerable autonomy, enjoying special privileges granted by the Norwegian crown. These privileges allowed them to create a self-governing enclave, operating under the League's rules rather than local laws, effectively establishing a mini-state within a state. This arrangement not only ensured efficient and profitable trade but also demonstrated the League's ability to leverage political relationships for economic gain.

The Hanseatic League was also a pioneer in economic innovations that would shape the future of commerce. The League standardized weights and measures, ensuring fairness and consistency in trade transactions across different regions. Additionally, the League developed early forms of insurance to protect merchants' investments, reducing the risks associated with long-distance trade. These innovations laid the groundwork for modern financial systems and exemplified the League's forward-thinking approach to commerce.

Beyond trade, the Hanseatic League's vast network became a conduit for the exchange of ideas, contributing significantly to the broader European Renaissance. The bustling marketplaces of Hanseatic cities were not just centers of economic activity but also melting pots of cultural and intellectual exchange. This flow of knowledge and innovation challenged the rigid structures of feudalism and mercantilism, promoting a more progressive and interconnected European society.

The Hanseatic League's story is a powerful reminder of the potential for economic progress through cooperation and innovation. It demonstrated that even in an era dominated by restrictive and hierarchical systems, there were ways to build a vibrant and interconnected commercial network. By breaking away from the past, the Hanseatic League not only facilitated trade but also laid the foundations for a more dynamic and equitable economic order. Their success underscores the power of collective effort and ingenuity in transcending seemingly insurmountable barriers, paving the way for enduring economic and social progress.

The Industrial Revolution and the Mirage of Progress

The Industrial Revolution, stretching from the late 18th to the early 19th century, was a period of unprecedented economic growth that reshaped society at its core. It was an era when technological innovations redefined labor, production, and consumption, yet this rapid transformation also deepened socioeconomic divides and perpetuated many illusions about progress. The introduction of machinery—like James Watt's steam engine and Richard Arkwright's water frame—revolutionized industries, leading to an explosion in productivity and efficiency. However, these advances also obscured the harsh realities faced by the working class.

Historian Joel Mokyr, in *The Lever of Riches*, emphasizes the transformative power of these technologies: "The Industrial Revolution was a unique event in history, driven by the relentless pursuit of technological innovation and economic progress." The mechanization of textile production, for instance, did more than just increase output; it also diminished the demand for skilled labor, leading to the rise of factory work and the erosion of artisanal craftsmanship. This shift, while lauded as progress, masked the dehumanization and monotony of industrial labor.

The era also witnessed the advent of the assembly line, a method popularized by Henry Ford in the early 20th century. This innovation revolutionized manufacturing, enabling the mass production of goods at unprecedented speeds and making products more affordable to the masses. Yet, this came at a significant human cost. Workers were reduced to performing repetitive, soul-crushing tasks under often brutal conditions. Upton Sinclair's *The Jungle* provides a grim portrayal of the meatpacking industry, capturing the dehumanizing effects of industrial labor: "Here was a population, low-class and mostly foreign, hanging always on the verge of starvation, and dependent for its opportunities of life upon the whim of men every bit as brutal and unscrupulous as the old-time slave drivers."

The Industrial Revolution was deeply intertwined with the rise of capitalism, an economic system characterized by private ownership and free markets. Adam Smith, often hailed as the father of modern economics, laid the groundwork for capitalist thought in his seminal work, *The Wealth of Nations*. Smith introduced the concept of the "invisible hand," suggesting that individuals pursuing their self-interest would inadvertently contribute to the overall good of society. He wrote, "By pursuing his own interest, [an individual] frequently promotes that of the society more effectually than when he really intends to promote it." This idea fostered the illusion that capitalism, left unchecked, naturally led to societal benefits.

However, the rapid industrialization and expansion of capitalism also sparked significant critiques. Karl Marx, in *Das Kapital*, dissected the inherent contradictions and inequities of the capitalist system. He argued that capitalism inevitably led to the exploitation of the working class (the proletariat) by the capitalist class (the bourgeoisie). Marx wrote, "The history of all hitherto existing society is the history of class struggles." He highlighted how workers became mere cogs in the industrial machine, stripped of their creativity and autonomy. This alienation, according to Marx, was a fatal flaw in capitalism that would ultimately lead to its downfall.

John Stuart Mill, in *Principles of Political Economy*, also critiqued capitalism, acknowledging its benefits but condemning its excesses and the resulting social inequalities. Mill advocated for a more equitable distribution of wealth and the protection of workers' rights, arguing that "The distribution of wealth, therefore, depends on the laws and customs of society." Both Marx and Mill recognized that the apparent progress brought by the Industrial Revolution was built on a foundation of deep social and economic disparities.

Yet, the Industrial Revolution was also a time of resistance and reform. One notable figure who challenged the status quo was Robert Owen, a Welsh social reformer and one of the pioneers of utopian socialism. Owen believed that the harsh conditions of industrial labor could be mitigated through cooperative communities. He established the New Lanark mills in Scotland, where he implemented progressive labor practices, including shorter working hours, fair wages, and access to education for workers and their children.

Owen's efforts at New Lanark were described in *The Life of Robert Owen,* by himself, as a testament to the potential for humane and ethical industrial practices: "It was demonstrated that commercial success was perfectly compatible with the happiness and well-being of the workforce." His ideas inspired later social reform movements and the establishment of cooperative societies, laying the groundwork for future advancements in labor rights.

Another significant movement was the Luddite Rebellion, where skilled artisans protested against the mechanization of their trades, which they perceived as a direct threat to their livelihoods. Often mischaracterized as being anti-progress, the Luddites were, in reality, defenders of their economic interests and traditional craftsmanship. Historian E.P. Thompson, in *The Making of the English Working Class,* offers a more nuanced view of the Luddites, noting that "The Luddites were neither mindless machine breakers nor enemies of progress, but rather defenders of a way of life and work that they valued and sought to protect." The Luddites' actions highlighted the discontent and resistance that industrial capitalism engendered, exposing the illusion that progress was universally beneficial.

The Industrial Revolution and the rise of capitalism were not just driven by technological and economic forces but also by human psychological weaknesses. These weaknesses, such as loss aversion and status quo bias, often led to resistance against necessary reforms and the perpetuation of exploitative practices. The "illusion of control," where individuals overestimate their ability to influence outcomes, often led factory owners and capitalists to believe that their success was solely the result of their efforts, ignoring the exploitation of their workers. Similarly, the "just-world hypothesis"—the belief that people get what they deserve—justified the harsh conditions and low wages faced by workers, suggesting that their suffering was a consequence of their own failings rather than systemic inequalities.

Recognizing these psychological biases is crucial for addressing the deceptions and disparities within capitalist systems. By understanding the cognitive distortions that drive economic behavior, we can begin to unravel the myths that have sustained inequality and work toward more equitable and just economic policies.

While the Industrial Revolution and capitalism brought about tremendous advancements, they also perpetuated significant illusions about progress, equality, and the nature of success. As society moved through these stages of economic development, it gradually became clear that true progress could not be measured solely by economic growth or technological innovation. The breaking of these illusions is a necessary step toward a more just and equitable future.

The Great Depression and the Dawn of Keynesian Economics: Shattering the Illusions of Laissez-Faire
The Great Depression: A Global Catastrophe

The Great Depression, beginning with the infamous stock market crash of 1929 and dragging on throughout the 1930s, exposed the deep vulnerabilities of the global economic system. This period of unprecedented economic downturn revealed the inherent flaws of the laissez-faire policies that had dominated the era, policies that advocated minimal government intervention in the economy. As the world spiraled into crisis, it became clear that these policies were utterly inadequate for addressing the scale of the disaster.

Economist John Kenneth Galbraith, in his classic work *The Great Crash 1929,* poignantly captures the mood of the time: "When the stock market crashed, Franklin D. Roosevelt had to make a clear choice: let the economy self-destruct or intervene on an unprecedented scale." The crash itself was the result of a dangerous cocktail of speculative investment, vast income inequality, and a fragile banking system. The 1920s had seen rapid economic expansion in the United States, but much of this growth was an illusion, built on speculative bubbles in the stock market. Investors, caught up in a frenzy of "irrational exuberance," as John Maynard Keynes later described it, drove stock prices far beyond their true value. "The market can remain irrational longer than you can remain solvent," Keynes warned—a caution that was tragically ignored until it was too late.

When the bubble finally burst in October 1929, it wiped out millions of investors and triggered a wave of bank failures and business bankruptcies. The immediate consequences were catastrophic. In the United States, unemployment skyrocketed to 25%, leaving one in four Americans without work. Factories closed en masse, and industrial production plummeted, leading to a sharp decline in output. International trade, once the engine of global economic growth, collapsed by more than 50% as countries threw up tariffs and other barriers in a desperate bid to protect their own economies. The effects of this economic implosion were felt worldwide, plunging nations into profound distress.

Personal stories from the era bring the human cost of the Depression into sharp relief. Families lost their homes and life savings overnight. Cities across America were dotted with soup kitchens and breadlines, stark symbols of widespread desperation. Men, having lost everything, were reduced to selling apples on street corners or riding the rails in search of work—poignant reminders of a society in turmoil.

The stark failure of laissez-faire policies during this crisis was undeniable. In his book *The End of Laissez-Faire*, Keynes critiqued the belief that markets are self-correcting and inherently stable. He argued, "Capitalism is not a stationary state but a system of continuous evolution and change, and laissez-faire can no longer be the policy of a responsible government." This marked a turning point, signaling the need for a more active role for government in stabilizing the economy and protecting its citizens.

In response to the widespread devastation, President Franklin D. Roosevelt implemented the New Deal, a sweeping series of programs and reforms designed to revive the economy and provide relief to the millions of Americans suffering from the Depression. These measures included the creation of Social Security, the initiation of large-scale public works projects to create jobs, and significant reforms in banking and finance to prevent future crises. Roosevelt's bold actions represented a dramatic shift away from laissez-faire, recognizing that active government intervention was essential to restoring economic stability and public confidence.

The statistics from this era paint a vivid picture of the Depression's severity. Between 1929 and 1933, the U.S. gross domestic product (GDP) shrank by nearly 30%.

Thousands of banks failed, wiping out the savings of millions of Americans. By 1933, industrial production had dropped by nearly 50%, and prices had fallen by 30%. These figures underscore the devastating impact of the Depression and the urgent need for effective government intervention.

The Great Depression did more than just devastate economies—it fundamentally reshaped economic theory and policy. It exposed the dangers of unregulated capitalism and underscored the importance of government oversight and intervention. The lessons learned from this period continue to influence economic policy today, serving as a reminder of the need for a balanced approach that promotes stability while protecting against the excesses of speculative investment. The story of the Great Depression is not just one of economic collapse but also one of resilience and the capacity for innovation and reform in the face of profound challenges.

Keynesian Economics: A Revolutionary Response

Against this backdrop of economic despair, John Maynard Keynes emerged as a towering figure with a revolutionary approach to economic policy. His ideas, encapsulated in his landmark work *The General Theory of Employment, Interest, and Money*, challenged the prevailing economic orthodoxy and laid the foundation for what would become known as Keynesian economics. Keynes argued that in times of economic downturn, governments must actively intervene to stimulate demand and prevent further economic decline.

Keynes proposed a range of policies to achieve this, including increased public spending, lower taxes, and monetary measures to reduce interest rates. He famously suggested, "The government should pay people to dig holes in the ground and then fill them up. It doesn't matter what they do, as long as the government is creating jobs." This emphasis on demand-side management was a radical departure from the supply-side focus of classical economics and represented a profound shift in economic thinking.

The implementation of Keynesian policies had a transformative impact on the global economy. In the United States, President Roosevelt's New Deal embraced Keynesian principles by ramping up government spending on public works projects, social welfare programs, and financial regulations. These measures helped to stabilize the economy, reduce unemployment, and restore public confidence. Historian Eric Rauchway, in his book *The Great Depression and the New Deal*, highlights the transformative effect of these policies: "Roosevelt's New Deal represented a new social contract between the government and the people, one that acknowledged the role of the state in ensuring economic stability and social welfare."

However, Keynesian economics was not without its critics. Some economists argued that government intervention could lead to inefficiencies and market distortions. Others, like Friedrich Hayek, warned of the dangers of excessive government control. In his book *The Road to Serfdom,* Hayek cautioned, "The more the state plans, the more difficult planning becomes for the individual." Despite these criticisms, the success of Keynesian policies in mitigating the effects of the Great Depression and driving economic recovery is undeniable.

Throughout the Great Depression, there were individuals and movements that sought to break free from past constraints and implement innovative solutions to the economic crisis. Keynes's influence extended beyond his theoretical work; he played a pivotal role in the Bretton Woods Conference of 1944, which established the International Monetary Fund (IMF) and the World Bank, institutions designed to promote international economic stability.

Frances Perkins, the first woman appointed to the U.S. Cabinet, also emerged as a transformative figure during this time. Serving as Secretary of Labor under President Roosevelt, Perkins was instrumental in shaping the New Deal's labor policies, including the establishment of Social Security and the introduction of minimum wage laws. Her efforts are chronicled in *The Woman Behind the New Deal* by Kirstin Downey, which highlights Perkins's dedication to improving the lives of American workers: "Frances Perkins transformed the Department of Labor into a powerful advocate for the American worker, championing policies that provided economic security and dignity."

Another example of Keynesian principles in action was the Civilian Conservation Corps (CCC), a New Deal program that provided jobs for unemployed young men who worked on environmental conservation projects across the United States. The CCC not only reduced unemployment but also contributed to the nation's infrastructure and natural resource management. The success of the CCC is detailed in Neil M. Maher's Nature's New Deal: "The CCC not only provided economic relief but also fostered a new generation of environmental stewardship and public service."

In addition to the economic strategies and policies of the time, understanding the psychological factors at play is crucial for comprehending the depth of the Great Depression's impact. The "availability heuristic," for example, where people judge the likelihood of events based on their recent experiences, contributed to the widespread panic and bank runs that exacerbated the crisis. As people witnessed the collapse of banks and the economy around them, their fear and uncertainty only fueled further economic decline.

Keynes himself acknowledged the importance of psychological factors in economic behavior. "The market can stay irrational longer than you can stay solvent," he famously noted, highlighting the role of collective irrationality in market dynamics. This insight underscores the necessity of government intervention to stabilize markets and protect individuals from the consequences of widespread panic and economic instability.

The Great Depression and the subsequent rise of Keynesian economics illustrate a critical turning point in economic history. The era shattered many of the illusions surrounding laissez-faire capitalism, revealing the need for a more balanced approach that includes robust government intervention in times of crisis. The lessons learned from this period continue to resonate today, reminding us that economic progress requires not just innovation and growth but also the willingness to confront and overcome the systemic flaws and psychological biases that can lead to widespread economic suffering..

The Golden Age of Capitalism: A Time of Renewal and Transformation

In the years following World War II, the world embarked on a transformative journey known as the "Golden Age of Capitalism." This period, stretching from the late 1940s to the early 1970s, was marked by unprecedented economic growth, social stability, and the establishment of welfare states across much of the Western world. Governments, scarred by the economic hardships of the Great Depression and the devastation of war, sought to create a new order where economic security and social welfare were not just ideals but tangible realities.

Visualize the streets of London, Paris, or Tokyo in the late 1940s. The war had left these cities in ruins, but amidst the rubble, there was a sense of hope and determination. Bombed-out buildings were gradually replaced with new infrastructure, homes, and factories. The architects of this new era believed that the state had a crucial role to play in ensuring a stable and prosperous society. As historian Tony Judt articulated, "The post-war consensus was predicated on the belief that the state had a responsibility to its citizens beyond mere law and order. It was about creating a framework where people could thrive, not just survive."

This belief translated into the establishment and expansion of social safety nets that fundamentally changed the relationship between governments and their citizens. Universal healthcare systems, unemployment benefits, and pensions were introduced in many countries, providing a safety cushion for the vulnerable and reducing the risks associated with economic downturns. In Britain, the creation of the National Health Service (NHS) in 1948 was a landmark achievement. The NHS promised free healthcare for all, a concept that was revolutionary at the time and was met with widespread public approval.

The economic growth of the Golden Age was remarkable. In the United States, the GDP grew at an average annual rate of around 4% during the 1950s and 1960s. Western Europe also experienced rapid economic expansion, with countries like France and Italy enjoying growth rates of 5-6% per year. This boom was fueled in part by American aid, most notably through the Marshall Plan, which provided billions of dollars to help rebuild European economies. The Marshall Plan was not just about money; it was a lifeline that helped war-torn nations rebuild their infrastructure, modernize their industries, and stabilize their economies.

The stories of Japan and West Germany are particularly illustrative of the era's transformative power. Both nations, devastated by the war, managed to achieve extraordinary recoveries. Japan's economy grew at an astonishing average rate of 9.7% from 1950 to 1973, turning it into a global economic powerhouse. Similarly, West Germany experienced its Wirtschaftswunder, or "economic miracle," with industrial output surging and the nation becoming the economic engine of Europe. These recoveries were not just the result of financial aid but also of forward-looking economic policies that emphasized industrialization, innovation, and education.

This period of prosperity also saw a dramatic rise in living standards and the growth of the middle class. In the United States, homeownership rates soared, and consumer goods like cars, televisions, and household appliances became symbols of the new era of abundance. Civil rights and labor movements gained momentum, achieving significant victories that expanded social and economic rights. The post-war era was a time when the promise of capitalism seemed to be delivering on its potential to improve lives on a broad scale.

However, the Golden Age of Capitalism was not without its challenges. The economic boom was largely confined to the Western world, leaving many developing nations on the sidelines of prosperity. Moreover, the environmental costs of rapid industrialization began to surface, planting the seeds for future concerns about sustainability and ecological preservation.

In essence, the Golden Age of Capitalism was a time of remarkable transformation. The policies and innovations of this era laid the foundations for modern welfare states and demonstrated the potential of government intervention to foster widespread prosperity. This period showed that when the state and its citizens collaborate with a shared vision of mutual well-being, extraordinary progress is possible.

The Rise of Neoliberalism: A Shift in the Economic Paradigm

But the Golden Age was not destined to last indefinitely. By the late 20th century, the world witnessed a dramatic shift towards neoliberalism—a doctrine that prioritized deregulation, privatization, and free-market principles. This shift marked a significant ideological turn, where the market was increasingly viewed not just as a tool for economic management but as the ultimate judge of social and economic value.

The intellectual roots of neoliberalism can be traced to thinkers like Friedrich Hayek and Milton Friedman, whose critiques of Keynesian economics paved the way for this new paradigm. Hayek, in his influential book *The Road to Serfdom*, argued that government intervention in the economy inevitably led to the erosion of individual freedoms. "Central planning," Hayek warned, "is inherently coercive and dangerous, leading to a loss of personal liberty and economic efficiency."

Milton Friedman, another key figure in this ideological shift, made a powerful case for economic freedom as a prerequisite for political freedom in his book *Capitalism and Freedom*. His ideas gained significant traction in the 1980s, finding champions in leaders like Margaret Thatcher in the United Kingdom and Ronald Reagan in the United States. These leaders implemented policies that reduced government spending, deregulated industries, and promoted privatization, fundamentally altering the economic landscape of their countries.

The rise of neoliberalism had profound effects on global economies and societies. The narrative that market forces would lead to greater prosperity for all began to unravel as rising inequality and economic instability became increasingly apparent. As Naomi Klein observes in The Shock Doctrine, "Neoliberalism promised much but delivered a paradox of prosperity for a few and stagnation for many." The global spread of neoliberal policies, often driven by institutions like the International Monetary Fund (IMF) and the World Bank, exacerbated inequalities and left many economies vulnerable to financial crises.

One of the most notable examples of the neoliberal experiment is Chile under the Pinochet regime. Guided by Friedman's "Chicago Boys," Chile implemented sweeping neoliberal reforms that transformed its economy but also led to significant social upheaval. As detailed in Mark Ensalaco's The Pinochet Effect, while these economic reforms spurred growth, they also deepened social divides and led to widespread human suffering, highlighting the often brutal consequences of neoliberal policies.

Human psychological tendencies also played a significant role in the widespread acceptance of neoliberalism. The appeal of quick fixes and the seductive promise of individual success often overshadowed the more complex realities of systemic inequality. Many people clung to the meritocratic ideal—the belief that anyone could succeed if they worked hard enough—despite growing evidence of a widening gap between the rich and the poor.

The shift to neoliberalism wasn't just about changes in policy; it represented a fundamental reconfiguration of how people viewed the role of the state and the market. As the late David Harvey noted in *A Brief History of Neoliberalism,* "Neoliberalism reconfigured the concept of freedom into a market-centric ideology that prioritized individual gain over collective well-being."

Amidst these sweeping changes, there were numerous examples of individuals and movements that resisted or sought to mitigate the effects of neoliberalism. One such story is that of Muhammad Yunus and the Grameen Bank. Yunus, a Bangladeshi social entrepreneur, challenged the traditional banking system by offering microloans to the poor, demonstrating that financial inclusion could be a powerful tool for social change. His efforts earned him the Nobel Peace Prize in 2006, highlighting the impact of innovative approaches to economic justice.

Similarly, grassroots movements around the world have fought back against the imposition of neoliberal policies. In Argentina, for example, widespread protests in the early 2000s against austerity measures and privatizations led to significant political and economic upheaval. These movements showcased the power of collective action in resisting policies that prioritize profit over people.

These stories illustrate the resilience and creativity of individuals and communities in the face of an economic ideology that often prioritizes market efficiency over human welfare. They serve as reminders that while neoliberalism has reshaped the global landscape, it has also sparked important debates and movements advocating for a more equitable and inclusive world.

A Complex Legacy of Economic Progress

The journey from the Golden Age of Capitalism to the rise of neoliberalism reveals a complex and often contentious history. This period underscores how economic ideologies not only shape policy but also profoundly influence societal values and individual lives. The Golden Age demonstrated the power of collective action and state intervention to create widespread prosperity, while the neoliberal era highlighted both the potential and the pitfalls of unrestrained market forces.

As we reflect on these eras, it becomes clear that economic progress is not a linear path but a series of evolving ideas and practices that continuously reshape our world. In each step of this evolution, humanity has been forced to confront and reassess its delusions—whether about the self-correcting nature of markets, the role of government, or the true meaning of freedom and prosperity. Understanding these historical shifts not only helps us make sense of the past but also provides valuable insights for navigating the economic challenges of the future.

The Promise and Perils of Globalization: Unraveling the Grand Illusions

Globalization, often celebrated as the great unifier of economies and cultures, promised a world where barriers would dissolve, and prosperity would flow freely across borders. In the late 20th and early 21st centuries, this vision seemed within reach as economies became more interconnected, fueled by technological advancements and free-trade agreements. However, as the world grew more connected, the gap between the affluent and the impoverished widened, revealing the darker side of this global experiment.

Thomas Friedman, in his influential book The World Is Flat, heralded globalization as a force that had "leveled the playing field" and democratized opportunities. He argued that globalization allowed even the smallest players to compete on the global stage, driving innovation and economic growth. Yet, as Friedman later admitted in *Hot, Flat, and Crowded,* globalization also came with significant downsides. "The very forces that have made the world flatter and more connected," he wrote, "have also intensified the challenges of climate change and resource scarcity." This acknowledgment hints at a deeper truth: while globalization created new opportunities, it also exacerbated existing inequalities and introduced new global risks.

Consider the role of multinational corporations, which have been both the engines of global economic growth and the harbingers of economic disparity. On one hand, these corporations have driven significant economic development; on the other, they have often done so at the expense of local economies, labor standards, and environmental sustainability. Naomi Klein, in *The Shock Doctrine*, offers a critical perspective on how these global giants have exploited crises to impose neoliberal policies that favor the wealthy and powerful. "The essence of the shock doctrine is to exploit disasters to push through radical market reforms," Klein argues, highlighting the dangers of unchecked corporate power.

Globalization has undoubtedly created new markets and opportunities, but it has also led to a troubling rise in economic inequality. Between 1980 and 2000, the income share of the top 1% of earners in the United States more than doubled—a trend echoed in many other countries. This growing disparity is not just a number on a graph; it represents the lived reality of millions whose wages have stagnated while the wealthy few reap the rewards of global integration.

The uneven benefits of globalization are starkly visible in the contrasting experiences of different countries. China's economic liberalization, for instance, has lifted hundreds of millions out of poverty, yet it has also led to significant income inequality and environmental degradation. Meanwhile, many developing nations have found themselves trapped in a "race to the bottom," competing on labor costs and regulatory leniency, often at the expense of workers' rights and environmental protections.

Adding complexity to this global landscape is the rise of financialization, a process in which financial markets, institutions, and motives come to dominate economic activity. This shift has reshaped economies, prioritizing short-term gains over long-term stability and deepening economic disparities. Michael Lewis, in *The Big Short*, captures the essence of financialization's impact on the global economy, chronicling how the financial sector's insatiable appetite for risk and profit played a pivotal role in the 2008 financial crisis. "The financial sector had become a casino where bets were made on the most complex and opaque instruments," Lewis writes, illustrating how financialization contributed to economic instability.

This phenomenon is exacerbated by human psychological tendencies, such as the preference for short-term rewards and the allure of immediate gains—biases that financial markets are particularly adept at exploiting. This inclination towards instant gratification often drives risky behavior and poor decision-making, contributing to economic instability and widening disparities.

The 2008 financial crisis serves as a stark reminder of the perils of financialization. The collapse of Lehman Brothers, vividly detailed by Andrew Ross Sorkin in Too Big to Fail, was a dramatic illustration of how excessive risk-taking and financial manipulation can lead to catastrophic consequences. The crisis laid bare the vulnerabilities of a system increasingly driven by speculative investment and short-term profit motives, sparking a global recession that left millions unemployed and devastated economies worldwide.

Despite these challenges, there have been significant efforts to address the inequalities exacerbated by globalization and financialization. Economist Joseph Stiglitz, in his book Globalization and Its Discontents, offers a powerful critique of the global economic system, advocating for reforms that prioritize equitable development. Stiglitz's work has sparked crucial debates around economic justice and the need for a more balanced approach to globalization—one that considers the well-being of all, not just the wealthy few.

Grassroots movements have also risen in response to the growing disparities fueled by globalization and financialization. The Occupy Wall Street movement, for example, emerged as a powerful voice against economic inequality, encapsulated in its slogan, "We are the 99%." This movement highlighted the frustrations of those who felt left behind by an economic system that seemed to favor a small, wealthy elite at the expense of the majority.

These stories of resistance and reform demonstrate that while globalization and financialization have dramatically reshaped the global landscape, they have also ignited important debates and movements aimed at addressing the systemic inequalities they have deepened. They serve as reminders that economic systems are not immutable; they can and should be challenged and reformed through collective action and critical examination.

In examining the promise and perils of globalization, we uncover a complex interplay between economic integration and inequality. The grand promises of interconnected prosperity have often been undermined by the harsh realities of wealth concentration and systemic instability. As we continue to navigate the global economy, it is crucial to remain vigilant and to push for a more equitable and sustainable path forward—one that truly lives up to the promise of globalization as a force for good.

The Digital Economy and Future Disruptions

The digital revolution, often hailed as the Fourth Industrial Revolution, has dramatically altered our world. We are now living in an era where digital technology is omnipresent—transforming not only how industries function but also how we live, work, and interact with one another. This revolution is more than just an evolution of technology; it's a seismic shift in the very foundation of our economic and social structures. However, as with all great transformations, it comes with its own set of existential threats—threats that have already plagued the past and present, and that future generations will need to confront head-on.

Automation: The Double-Edged Sword

Once relegated to the realm of science fiction, automation has now become a pervasive force across industries worldwide. Robots, algorithms, and artificial intelligence (AI) systems have taken over tasks that were once the exclusive domain of human workers. From manufacturing to the service sector, automation is reshaping the labor market, presenting both challenges and opportunities.

In the past, the advent of automation was seen as a means to boost productivity and economic growth. The automation of manufacturing processes in the 20th century, for example, led to unprecedented levels of output and efficiency. The assembly line, pioneered by companies like Ford, revolutionized the production of goods and made consumer products more affordable and accessible. Yet, this progress came at a cost—job displacement. As machines took over repetitive tasks, millions of workers found themselves unemployed, sparking social unrest and economic inequality.

Fast forward to the present, and automation is once again at the forefront of economic disruption. The rise of AI and machine learning has enabled automation to extend beyond physical labor into cognitive tasks. Algorithms now analyze vast amounts of data, making decisions in fields ranging from finance to healthcare. In the financial sector, algorithmic trading has become the norm, with AI systems executing trades at speeds and volumes impossible for humans to match. This has led to significant gains for those who control the technology, but it has also introduced new risks, such as the potential for market manipulation and the loss of jobs for human traders.

According to a report by the World Economic Forum, automation could displace 85 million jobs globally by 2025, while creating 97 million new roles. However, the nature of these new jobs will require skills that many workers do not currently possess, leading to a growing divide between those who can adapt to the new digital economy and those who cannot. This phenomenon, often referred to as the "skills gap," represents a major challenge for future generations. Without adequate education and retraining programs, millions could be left behind in the digital age, exacerbating social and economic inequalities.

Automation is not all doom and gloom. In some cases, it has led to the creation of entirely new industries and job categories. The rise of the gig economy, for example, is a direct result of digital platforms that automate the matching of supply and demand for freelance work. While this shift has introduced new forms of employment and income opportunities, it has also raised concerns about job security, benefits, and workers' rights.

Revolutionizing the Economy or Creating New Inequities?

AI's ability to process and analyze data far surpasses human capabilities, leading to breakthroughs in fields as diverse as medicine, finance, and transportation. However, this technological prowess also poses existential threats, particularly in how it might exacerbate existing inequalities and create new ones.

In the financial sector, AI-driven technologies are revolutionizing everything from customer service to fraud detection. Chatbots, powered by AI, are now handling a significant portion of customer interactions for banks, providing 24/7 service and freeing up human employees for more complex tasks. AI is also being used to detect fraudulent activities by analyzing transaction patterns in real-time, reducing the risk of financial crime. According to a study by Juniper Research, AI-based fraud detection systems saved businesses over $12 billion in 2020 alone.

However, the increasing reliance on AI in finance is not without its pitfalls. The automation of trading and investment decisions, for instance, has led to the emergence of "flash crashes," where rapid, AI-driven trades can cause significant market volatility in a matter of seconds. Additionally, the opacity of AI systems—

often referred to as "black box" AI—means that it can be difficult to understand how decisions are made, raising concerns about accountability and transparency.

For future generations, the challenge will be to harness the power of AI while mitigating its risks. This will require not only technological innovation but also thoughtful regulation and ethical considerations. As AI continues to permeate the economy, the question remains whether it will lead to greater prosperity for all or deepen the divides between the haves and the have-nots.

The Gig Economy: Freedom or Precarity?

The gig economy has emerged as one of the most significant disruptions to traditional employment models in recent decades. Enabled by digital platforms, the gig economy allows individuals to take on short-term, flexible work assignments, ranging from driving for ride-sharing services to freelance graphic design. This shift from permanent, full-time employment to more flexible, project-based work has transformed the labor market, offering both opportunities and challenges.

For many, the gig economy represents freedom—the freedom to choose when, where, and how to work. It offers a level of flexibility that traditional jobs often do not, allowing individuals to balance work with other commitments, such as education, caregiving, or personal pursuits. This flexibility is particularly appealing to younger generations, who value work-life balance and are less likely to stay in a single job for their entire careers. According to a survey by the Pew Research Center, 30%

of American adults engaged in gig work in 2020, with the majority citing flexibility as a key reason.

However, the gig economy also comes with significant risks. Gig workers often lack the benefits and protections that come with traditional employment, such as health insurance, retirement plans, and paid leave. This can lead to financial instability and insecurity, particularly for those who rely on gig work as their primary source of income. The COVID-19 pandemic has highlighted these vulnerabilities, as gig workers in sectors like ride-sharing and food delivery faced reduced demand and income, with little to no safety net to fall back on.

Moreover, the gig economy has been criticized for perpetuating inequality and exploitation. Digital platforms that facilitate gig work often extract significant fees from workers, reducing their earnings. Additionally, the algorithms used by these platforms can be opaque and unpredictable, making it difficult for workers to understand how their pay is determined or to challenge unfair treatment. This has led to calls for stronger labor protections and regulation of gig platforms to ensure fair treatment of workers.

Future generations will need to regulate the gig economy, balancing the desire for flexibility with the need for security and fairness. This may require new forms of social protection, such as portable benefits that follow workers from gig to gig, or the establishment of minimum standards for gig work. Additionally, as the gig economy continues to grow, it will be important to address the power imbalances between workers and platforms to ensure that the digital economy is inclusive and equitable.

The Circular Economy: A Vision for Sustainability

In the face of growing environmental challenges, the concept of a circular economy has gained traction as a more sustainable alternative to the traditional linear economy. In a linear economy, resources are extracted, used to create products, and then disposed of as waste. This model is inherently unsustainable, as it depletes natural resources and generates large amounts of waste, contributing to environmental degradation and climate change.

The circular economy, by contrast, aims to create a closed-loop system where resources are reused, recycled, and regenerated. In this model, products are designed to be durable, repairable, and recyclable, reducing the need for new resources and minimizing waste. For example, in a circular economy, a smartphone would be designed to be easily disassembled, with components that can be reused in new devices or recycled into new materials.

Several countries and companies have begun to embrace the principles of the circular economy. The European Union, for instance, has adopted a Circular Economy Action Plan, which aims to promote sustainable product design, reduce waste, and encourage recycling across member states. In Japan, the concept of a "circular society" has been integrated into national policy, with initiatives focused on reducing resource consumption and promoting recycling.

Companies are also taking steps to implement circular economy practices. For example, the clothing retailer H&M has launched a program to collect and recycle old garments, turning them into new products. Similarly, the electronics company Philips has adopted a "service-based" business model, where customers lease rather than purchase products like lighting systems, allowing Philips to retain ownership and responsibility for recycling at the end of the product's life.

The transition to a circular economy presents both opportunities and challenges. On the one hand, it offers the potential to reduce environmental impact, conserve resources, and create new economic opportunities. According to the Ellen MacArthur Foundation, a global shift to a circular economy could generate $4.5 trillion in economic benefits by 2030. On the other hand, the transition will require significant changes in business practices, consumer behavior, and regulatory frameworks.

For future generations, the challenge will be to fully realize the potential of the circular economy while addressing the barriers to its implementation. This will require innovation in product design, new business models that prioritize sustainability, and policies that incentivize resource efficiency. Moreover, it will be essential to engage consumers in the shift to a circular economy, encouraging them to embrace sustainable consumption habits and support companies that prioritize environmental stewardship.

Cognitive Biases in the Digital Economy

The digital economy, while full of promise, also exposes us to new psychological traps that can lead to misguided decisions and behaviors. Cognitive biases—systematic patterns of deviation from rationality—play a significant role in how individuals and organizations navigate the digital landscape. Understanding these biases is crucial for avoiding the pitfalls of the digital economy and making informed choices.

One such bias is the optimism bias, where individuals believe they are less likely to experience negative outcomes compared to others. This bias can lead to risky financial decisions in the digital economy, such as investing in speculative assets or engaging in online gambling. The rise of cryptocurrency markets, for example, has been fueled in part by optimism bias, with many investors believing they will profit while underestimating the risks. The 2017 Bitcoin bubble, where prices soared to nearly $20,000 before crashing, is a stark example of how optimism bias can lead to financial disaster.

Another cognitive bias that plays a significant role in the digital economy is the "status quo bias." This bias causes individuals to prefer things to remain the same rather than change, even when change might lead to better outcomes. In the context of the digital economy, status quo bias can hinder innovation and the adoption of new technologies. For instance, many companies were slow to adopt digital transformation strategies, clinging to traditional business models even as competitors embraced digital tools and gained a competitive edge.

The allure of instant gratification, driven by the pervasive nature of social media and digital advertising, is another psychological trap in the digital economy. This bias skews our perceptions of value and success, leading to impulsive buying decisions and a focus on short-term rewards rather than long-term goals. For example, the phenomenon of "buy now, pay later" services, which allow consumers to make purchases without immediate payment, has gained popularity in recent years. While these services offer convenience, they can also lead to financial strain as consumers accumulate debt without fully considering the long-term consequences.

Additionally, the "herd mentality" or "bandwagon effect" is a cognitive bias that leads individuals to follow the actions of a larger group, often without independent analysis. In the digital economy, this bias is particularly evident in the rapid adoption of trends and technologies, sometimes to the detriment of individuals and businesses. The rise of meme stocks, such as GameStop in 2021, is a prime example. Investors, driven by the fear of missing out (FOMO) and the influence of social media, rushed to buy shares, leading to wild price fluctuations and significant losses for some.

For future generations, understanding and mitigating the impact of cognitive biases in the digital economy will be essential. This may involve education and awareness campaigns that teach individuals about these biases and how to avoid them. It could also involve the design of digital platforms and tools that help users make more informed decisions, such as providing clear information about risks and consequences. By recognizing and addressing these psychological traps, future generations can navigate the digital economy more effectively and avoid the pitfalls that have ensnared their predecessors.

Disruptive Innovators: Breaking Away from the Past

Throughout history, there have been individuals who have disrupted the status quo and redefined entire industries through their visionary thinking and technological innovation. These disruptors have not only transformed their respective fields but have also demonstrated the power of breaking away from established practices to create new economic paradigms.

One of the most influential disruptors of the digital age is Elon Musk. His ventures have significantly impacted multiple industries, from electric vehicles with Tesla to space exploration with SpaceX. Musk's relentless pursuit of innovation and his willingness to take risks have led to groundbreaking achievements, such as the development of reusable rockets and the mass-market adoption of electric cars. However, Musk's approach has not been without controversy. His bold moves have often led to clashes with regulators, and his companies have faced challenges related to production delays and quality control. Nevertheless, Musk's impact on the digital economy is undeniable, as he continues to push the boundaries of what is possible.

Another transformative figure is Jeff Bezos, the founder of Amazon. Bezos's strategy of relentless customer focus and innovation has not only reshaped the retail industry but has also had far-reaching effects on logistics, cloud computing, and digital services. Amazon's rise from an online bookstore to a global powerhouse is a testament to the power of digital disruption. However, Amazon's dominance has also raised concerns about market concentration, labor practices, and the impact on small businesses. As the company continues to expand into new areas, such as healthcare and artificial intelligence, its influence on the digital economy is likely to grow even further.

These stories highlight the potential for disruptive innovation to drive economic progress and address some of the most pressing challenges of our time. However, they also underscore the need for responsible leadership and ethical considerations in the pursuit of technological advancement. As future generations look to these disruptors as role models, they must also consider the broader implications of their actions and strive to create a digital economy that is not only innovative but also inclusive and equitable.

Opportunities and Challenges

As we look to the future, the digital economy presents both opportunities and challenges. The continued advancement of technology holds the potential to drive economic growth, create new industries, and improve the quality of life for millions of people. However, these benefits will not be evenly distributed, and there are significant risks that must be addressed.

One of the key challenges for future generations will be to ensure that the benefits of the digital economy are shared equitably. This will require policies and initiatives that promote inclusivity and address the digital divide—the gap between those who have access to digital technologies and those who do not. According to the International Telecommunication Union (ITU), nearly half of the world's population still lacks access to the internet, with the majority of the unconnected living in developing countries. Bridging this divide will be essential for ensuring that everyone can participate in and benefit from the digital economy.

Another challenge will be to navigate the ethical and regulatory implications of emerging technologies. As AI, automation, and other digital innovations continue to evolve, they will raise new questions about privacy, security, and the role of technology in society. For example, the use of AI in decision-making processes, such as hiring or criminal justice, has already sparked debates about fairness and accountability. Future generations will need to grapple with these issues and develop frameworks that ensure technology is used responsibly and for the greater good.

Finally, there is the question of how to balance innovation with sustainability. The digital economy has the potential to contribute to environmental sustainability through the development of new technologies and business models that reduce waste and conserve resources. However, it also poses risks, such as the energy consumption of data centers and the environmental impact of electronic waste. Future generations will need to find ways to harness the power of the digital economy while minimizing its ecological footprint.

The digital revolution is far from over, and its impact on the economy and society will continue to unfold in the years to come. As we navigate this new landscape, it is crucial that we remain mindful of the existential threats that have plagued the past and present, and that we take proactive steps to ensure a better future for all. By embracing the opportunities of the digital economy while addressing its challenges, future generations can turn the tide against the growing menace of digital delusion and build a more just and sustainable world.

Unveiling the Illusions: How Economic Perils Will Shatter Deceptions and Liberate Minds

In the dawning era of the 21st century, the economic landscape is transforming with a ferocity that promises to unravel the self-deluding myths and deceptions that have shackled human thought for generations. As we journey through this tumultuous epoch, the perils of the new economy will serve as a relentless force, disassembling outdated beliefs and exposing the fallacies that have long dictated our collective mindset. This seismic shift will not only challenge the complacent herd mentality but will also break the chains of slavish adherence to obsolete economic doctrines.

For decades, humanity has clung to comforting illusions about economic stability, growth, and progress. We have been seduced by the myth of infinite resources and the promise of perpetual prosperity. The neoliberal narrative, with its insistence on market infallibility and the trickle-down effect, has masked the growing inequalities and systemic vulnerabilities festering beneath the surface. As Adam Smith's "invisible hand" has become a dogma rather than a nuanced concept, we have been led to believe that market forces alone could balance our economic woes and deliver collective well-being. Yet, this notion has proven to be not just optimistic, but dangerously misguided.

The current economic upheaval reveals the fatal flaws in these beliefs. The rise of automation, artificial intelligence, and globalization has exposed the fragility of the assumption that technological advancement automatically equates to economic equity and opportunity. The very forces hailed as drivers of progress are now laying bare the deep-seated inequalities and job displacements that were previously brushed aside or ignored. The myth that free markets always lead to optimal outcomes is crumbling under the weight of reality, as unprecedented economic disparities and social unrest unfold before our eyes.

In the face of these perils, the herd mentality—our propensity to follow prevailing trends and authoritative voices without question—is becoming increasingly untenable. The automation of jobs and the gig economy's rise have laid bare the precariousness of traditional employment and the inadequacy of safety nets designed for a bygone era. The mass acceptance of economic narratives without scrutiny is being replaced by a growing recognition of the need for a paradigm shift. Individuals are questioning the orthodoxy that has long dictated their economic and social behavior, pushing back against the inertia of conventional wisdom.

Moreover, the slavish mindset, characterized by blind adherence to outdated economic models and ideologies, is being dismantled as individuals and communities are forced to confront harsh realities. The illusion of economic security and the delusion that hard work alone guarantees success are unraveling. The crisis reveals the inadequacy of superficial remedies and exposes the necessity for more profound, systemic change. The disillusionment is palpable, and as the façade of traditional economic assurances crumbles, people are increasingly seeking alternative frameworks that address the root causes of economic disparity and instability.

This unfolding crisis serves as a crucible for intellectual and ideological reform. The economic upheaval is not merely an inconvenience but a transformative force that demands a re-evaluation of our core beliefs and systems. It is a wake-up call that exposes the fallacies of an outdated economic doctrine and paves the way for new, more resilient paradigms. As these harsh truths come to light, they will catalyze a movement towards more equitable, sustainable, and human-centered economic models.

In essence, the economic perils of the new generation will act as a relentless force, unmasking the deceptive beliefs that have long constrained human potential. They will dismantle the herd mentality and the slavish adherence to obsolete doctrines, compelling us to confront the realities of our economic systems and to forge new paths that are both more just and more reflective of our collective aspirations. The journey ahead will be fraught with challenges, but it is in this crucible of crisis that we will find the impetus to redefine our economic future with clarity and courage.

How the Present Generation is Reshaping the Future

The present generation is actively reshaping economic illusions through innovative approaches, technological advancements, and shifts in policy and thought. This transformation challenges traditional economic paradigms, exposes systemic issues, and promotes more equitable and sustainable practices.

The EU's Circular Economy Action Plan, adopted in 2020, aims to integrate resource efficiency and waste reduction into the economic system. According to a 2023 report by the European Environment Agency, the circular economy could contribute up to €600 billion to the EU economy by 2030 and create 700,000 new jobs. This shift is encouraging businesses to adopt sustainable practices, thereby reducing environmental impacts and creating new economic opportunities.

Another major change is the rise of impact investing, particularly through Socially Responsible Investing (SRI) and Environmental, Social, and Governance (ESG) criteria. These investment strategies reflect a growing desire to align financial portfolios with ethical and sustainable principles. In the U.S., ESG investments have reached $35 trillion globally as of 2024, representing about 36% of total assets under management, according to the Global Sustainable Investment Alliance (GSIA).

Impact investing is reshaping corporate behavior, pushing companies to improve their environmental and social governance practices, and addressing economic and social inequalities by prioritizing societal well-being alongside financial returns.

Reconsidering traditional economic growth metrics is another significant change. Bhutan's adoption of Gross National Happiness (GNH) instead of Gross Domestic Product (GDP) highlights a growing recognition that economic growth should not be the sole measure of progress. GNH emphasizes holistic well-being, including psychological health, community vitality, and environmental conservation. Bhutan has maintained this framework since the 1970s, demonstrating that focusing on well-being over mere economic output can provide a more comprehensive view of human development.

A 2023 study by the Basic Income Earth Network found that UBI pilots in multiple countries led to reduced poverty rates and improved economic security. These trials are offering insights into how guaranteed income can address economic inequality and provide a safety net for all individuals, potentially influencing broader adoption of UBI policies.

Conclusion

Economic well-being has the transformative power to support progressive thinking and propel human consciousness to new heights of intellectual and social evolution. Historical examples, statistical data, and contemporary success stories all illustrate how financial stability and growth create fertile ground for educational advancement, cultural enrichment, and social progress. By ensuring that economic prosperity benefits all members of society, we can continue to nurture a world where intellectual and social evolution thrive, paving the way for a brighter, more enlightened future. That will break the delusions that Humanity is plagued with.

Chapter 8

Techno-Enlightenment: Shattering the Deceptions

Since the stone age, mankind witnessed progress by leaps and bounds with every significant invention from fire to wheel to agriculture to steam engine, to electricity to computer science. The dawn of AI, quantum computing, synthetic biology, space science, and genetic advancements heralds a new era where future generations can shatter the chains of slavish thinking and deceptions that have plagued humanity since the dawn of civilization. By leveraging these groundbreaking technologies, we can begin a revolution in thinking that transcends our psychological weaknesses and entrenched myths, empowering us to unravel the universe's secrets and redefine human progress. Human intelligence and technological prowess will coexist harmoniously, steering us away from fear and control towards enlightenment and liberation.

The Era of Fear and Superstition

Before the advent of modern technology and the scientific enlightenment, humanity was ensnared in a web of fear and superstition. Picture the ancient world, where an unexpected solar eclipse could send entire populations into a state of hysteria. Lacking the knowledge of celestial mechanics, these people would gather, invoking deities and offering sacrifices in a desperate attempt to appease what they perceived as an expression of divine wrath. As Neil deGrasse Tyson aptly puts it, "The good thing about science is that it's true whether or not you believe in it." Yet, before science could illuminate the dark corners of ignorance, ritual and superstition were humanity's primary defenses against the unknown.

Take ancient Rome, for instance. The great historian Livy recounted numerous instances where earthquakes were seen as manifestations of the gods' displeasure. When the ground trembled, Romans didn't rush to check tectonic activity; they hurried to their temples, laden with offerings. The primary aim was not empirical understanding but rather an attempt to exert some semblance of control over the uncontrollable through supernatural means. This inclination to attribute natural phenomena to divine causes is a testament to the human tendency to seek patterns and meanings, especially in times of crisis.

The Medieval period, a time often characterized by a stark lack of scientific knowledge, saw the perpetuation of similar patterns of thought. The Black Death, which swept through Europe in the 14th century with devastating effect, was interpreted by many as divine retribution or the work of malevolent forces. Few understood that the true culprits were the fleas and rats carrying the plague. As Steven Pinker notes in *Enlightenment Now,* "Humanity's greatest achievements come from thinking clearly and critically." Yet, during this dark period, clear and critical thinking was in short supply, allowing fear and superstition to thrive unchecked.

The superstition surrounding the Black Death led to some tragic consequences. Jewish communities, often scapegoated in times of crisis, were accused of poisoning wells and spreading the disease. This baseless fear led to pogroms and massacres, highlighting how superstition could fuel not only panic but also violent prejudice. The inability to understand the natural causes of the plague exemplified a broader trend of relying on supernatural explanations to make sense of a world fraught with peril.

The Renaissance marked the beginning of a slow but profound transformation in human thought. Figures like Galileo Galilei and Johannes Kepler began to challenge the established order, using observation and mathematics to unravel the mysteries of the cosmos. Their work laid the groundwork for a new era where empirical evidence would gradually supplant superstition.

Galileo's use of the telescope to observe celestial bodies provided concrete evidence that challenged the geocentric model of the universe. His findings, though controversial, signaled a shift towards a more rational understanding of the natural world. Yet, even Galileo faced the wrath of the Inquisition, underscoring the deep-seated resistance to abandoning long-held superstitions.

The Enlightenment was the era in which reason and science began to take precedence over superstition. Thinkers like Voltaire and Diderot championed the cause of rationality, arguing that human beings could understand and improve their world through critical thinking and empirical observation. Voltaire, with his characteristic wit, famously quipped, "Those who can make you believe absurdities can make you commit atrocities," highlighting the dangers of unexamined beliefs.

The scientific method, with its emphasis on observation, experimentation, and repeatability, emerged as the gold standard for acquiring knowledge. This shift in thinking was not merely academic; it had profound practical implications. Advances in medicine, for instance, began to be grounded in scientific research rather than in the four humors theory that had dominated since Hippocrates. Edward Jenner's development of the smallpox vaccine is a prime example of how scientific understanding could conquer diseases that had previously been attributed to divine punishment or malevolent spirits.

Despite the triumphs of science, superstition has proven to be remarkably resilient. Even in our modern age, where information is readily accessible, superstitious beliefs persist. This phenomenon can be partly attributed to what psychologists call cognitive biases—systematic patterns of deviation from norm or rationality in judgment.

One fascinating example is the superstition surrounding the number 13. The fear of this number, known as triskaidekaphobia, has led to its omission from many hotels and buildings, which often skip from the 12th to the 14th floor. This irrational fear can be traced back to various cultural and religious origins, yet it persists even among otherwise rational individuals.

Throughout history, there have been individuals who have made significant strides in breaking free from the chains of superstition. One such figure is Hypatia of Alexandria, a philosopher, astronomer, and mathematician who lived during the 4th and 5th centuries. Hypatia was known for her efforts to promote Neoplatonism and for her teaching, which emphasized the importance of rational thought and empirical evidence. Tragically, her commitment to reason made her a target in a society dominated by religious fanaticism, and she was ultimately murdered by a mob incited by fanatical clergy.

Another notable figure is Carl Sagan, whose work in the 20th century brought the wonders of the cosmos to a broad audience. In his book *The Demon-Haunted World: Science as a Candle in the Dark,* Sagan eloquently argued for the importance of skepticism and scientific inquiry. He warned against the dangers of allowing superstition to take root, emphasizing that "science is more than a body of knowledge; it is a way of thinking." Sagan's efforts to popularize science and critical thinking have left a lasting legacy, inspiring countless individuals to look beyond superstition and embrace a more rational worldview.

Understanding the psychological underpinnings of superstition can shed light on why these beliefs are so enduring. Superstitions often arise in situations where people feel a lack of control. By attributing events to supernatural causes, individuals create a sense of order and predictability in an otherwise chaotic world. This psychological mechanism, known as the illusion of control, can provide comfort even when it has no basis in reality.

Additionally, the phenomenon of confirmation bias—the tendency to search for, interpret, and remember information in a way that confirms one's preconceptions—plays a significant role in perpetuating superstitions. People are more likely to recall instances where a superstitious belief appeared to "work" and to dismiss occasions when it did not. This selective memory reinforces the belief, making it more resistant to change.

The introduction of scientific literacy programs in schools and communities can help individuals develop the skills needed to evaluate claims critically and to differentiate between evidence-based information and unfounded beliefs. Carl Sagan's vision of a society enlightened by science and reason can be realized through sustained efforts to promote education and skepticism.

Initiatives like science fairs, public lectures, and accessible science writing have made significant contributions to increasing public understanding of scientific principles. By demystifying complex concepts and presenting them in an engaging and relatable manner, educators and communicators can help bridge the gap between scientific knowledge and the general public.

Superstition continues to permeate popular culture, often in subtle and entertaining ways. From horror movies that exploit our deepest fears to folklore that captures the imagination, these cultural expressions reflect our ongoing fascination with the supernatural. While some of these portrayals can perpetuate irrational beliefs, others can serve as a means of exploring and ultimately understanding the psychological roots of superstition.

For example, the enduring popularity of vampire myths can be seen as a reflection of deep-seated fears about mortality and the unknown. Similarly, the trope of the haunted house taps into primal fears of unseen forces and the violation of personal space. By examining these cultural artifacts, we can gain insight into the collective psyche and the ways in which superstition continues to influence our thoughts and behaviors.

As we move further into the 21st century, the challenge of combating superstition remains. Advances in technology and communication offer new tools for spreading scientific knowledge and critical thinking. However, they also provide platforms for the dissemination of misinformation and pseudoscience. The rise of social media, for instance, has made it easier for conspiracy theories and superstitious beliefs to gain traction.

To counteract this, it is essential to encourage a culture of skepticism and inquiry. Encouraging people to ask questions, seek evidence, and think critically about the information they encounter can help inoculate society against the allure of superstition. By continuing to champion the values of reason and science, we can build a future where fear and superstition no longer hold sway over human thought and behavior.

Technology: The Beacon of Human Progress

From the discovery of fire to the age of artificial intelligence, technology has been the driving force behind human progress. Throughout history, each significant technological advancement has not only transformed societies but also dispelled the shadows of superstition and ignorance.

Fire and the Birth of Civilization

The control of fire was one of humanity's earliest technological triumphs, marking a turning point in human evolution. The ability to harness fire provided warmth, protection, and a means to cook food, which in turn led to better nutrition and longer life spans. Fire also became a tool for shaping the environment, from clearing forests for agriculture to crafting weapons for hunting. This newfound control over nature laid the foundation for settled communities and the rise of early civilizations.

But fire's influence went beyond the physical. It brought people together, fostering communal living and social organization. The hearth became a symbol of home and stability, dispelling the fears of the unknown that thrived in the dark. Myths and legends were born around the fire, but more importantly, so were the seeds of science, as early humans began to understand and manipulate their world with greater precision.

The Wheel and the Acceleration of Trade

The invention of the wheel around 3500 BCE in Mesopotamia revolutionized transportation and commerce. It enabled the movement of goods and people over long distances, facilitating trade and cultural exchange between distant regions. The wheel's impact on agriculture was equally profound, as it led to the development of the plow, which greatly increased food production and supported growing populations.

As trade networks expanded, so did the exchange of ideas, technologies, and knowledge. The wheel played a crucial role in the spread of writing, mathematics, and metallurgy across continents. The movement of goods and ideas helped dispel local superstitions, as exposure to different cultures and knowledge systems fostered a more interconnected and informed world. The wheel, a simple yet transformative invention, became a symbol of human ingenuity and progress.

Writing and the Birth of Knowledge Preservation

The development of writing systems, beginning with cuneiform in Mesopotamia around 3200 BCE, marked a pivotal moment in human history. Writing allowed for the recording of laws, religious texts, and commercial transactions, laying the groundwork for organized societies and complex civilizations. More importantly, it enabled the preservation and transmission of knowledge across generations, a crucial factor in the advancement of science and technology.

Writing dispelled ignorance by providing a means to document and disseminate information. It empowered scholars, scientists, and philosophers to build upon the work of their predecessors, leading to the gradual accumulation of knowledge that would shape the course of history. The spread of writing systems throughout the ancient world, from Egypt to China, facilitated the exchange of ideas and fostered a more informed and enlightened society.

The Shipbuilding Revolution and the Age of Exploration

Shipbuilding technology saw remarkable advancements in the ancient world, particularly with the development of the first seafaring vessels by the Egyptians around 3000 BCE. These early ships enabled trade and cultural exchange along the Nile and beyond. However, it was during the Age of Exploration, beginning in the 15th century, that shipbuilding truly transformed the world.

The development of caravels and galleons equipped with advanced navigational tools allowed European explorers to traverse vast oceans and discover new lands. This era of exploration led to the exchange of goods, ideas, and technologies on a global scale, breaking down the barriers of superstition and isolation. The spread of knowledge about distant lands, peoples, and cultures challenged existing beliefs and encouraged a more global perspective.

The Age of Exploration also saw the spread of scientific knowledge, as explorers returned with new specimens, observations, and data that fueled the burgeoning scientific revolution. The development of shipbuilding technology thus played a crucial role in expanding human knowledge and dispelling the myths and superstitions that had previously dominated the medieval worldview.

Road Building and the Spread of Empires

The construction of roads, particularly during the Roman Empire, was a technological marvel that facilitated the movement of armies, goods, and ideas across vast distances. The Roman road network, which spanned over 250,000 miles at its height, was a testament to the engineering prowess of the empire and played a crucial role in its expansion and consolidation.

Roads not only enabled the efficient administration of far-flung provinces but also facilitated the spread of Roman culture, law, and technology throughout Europe. As Roman infrastructure reached distant corners of the empire, local populations were exposed to new ideas and innovations, leading to the gradual erosion of local superstitions and the adoption of more rational, evidence-based approaches to problem-solving.

The legacy of Roman road building endured long after the fall of the empire, influencing the development of infrastructure in subsequent civilizations. The spread of knowledge and technology along these ancient highways laid the foundation for the Renaissance and the eventual rise of modern science.

The Printing Press and the Renaissance of Knowledge

The invention of the printing press by Johannes Gutenberg in the 15th century was a watershed moment in the history of technology and knowledge dissemination. The printing press made it possible to produce books and pamphlets on a scale never before seen, drastically reducing the cost of books and making them accessible to a much wider audience.

This democratization of knowledge had profound implications for society. The spread of printed materials facilitated the dissemination of new ideas, challenging the authority of the Church and traditional sources of power. The Reformation, the Scientific Revolution, and the Enlightenment were all, in part, products of the printing press's ability to spread ideas quickly and widely.

The printing press also played a crucial role in standardizing knowledge. Scientific works, once confined to the private libraries of the elite, were now available to scholars and the general public alike. This led to the rapid advancement of science and the gradual erosion of superstition and ignorance as more people gained access to reliable information.

The Steam Engine and the Industrial Revolution

The invention of the steam engine in the 18th century by James Watt and others marked the beginning of the Industrial Revolution, a period of unprecedented technological and economic change. The steam engine powered factories, trains, and ships, transforming industries and societies around the world.

The Industrial Revolution brought about significant social and economic changes, as people moved from rural areas to cities in search of work in the new factories. This urbanization led to the spread of ideas and technologies, fostering a more interconnected and informed society. The rise of industrial production also spurred advances in science and engineering, as inventors and entrepreneurs sought to improve efficiency and productivity.

The steam engine, by powering the machinery of the Industrial Revolution, helped dispel many of the superstitions and misconceptions that had previously dominated society. The era was marked by a growing belief in progress and the power of human ingenuity to solve problems and improve the human condition. The technological advancements of the Industrial Revolution laid the groundwork for the modern world, ushering in an age of reason and scientific inquiry.

Electricity and the Electrification of the World

The discovery and harnessing of electricity in the 19th century was one of the most transformative developments in human history. Figures like Michael Faraday, Thomas Edison, and Nikola Tesla pioneered the generation, transmission, and application of electrical power, leading to the electrification of cities and industries around the world.

Electricity revolutionized daily life, enabling the development of new technologies such as the telegraph, telephone, and electric light. These innovations transformed communication, making it possible to transmit information instantaneously over long distances. The spread of electric lighting extended the day, allowing for greater productivity and leisure.

The impact of electricity on society was profound. It facilitated the rapid spread of information and ideas, contributing to the rise of mass media and the dissemination of scientific knowledge. The electrification of the world also had a democratizing effect, as access to electrical power and the technologies it enabled became increasingly widespread. The era of electricity helped to dispel the shadows of ignorance and superstition, as more people gained access to reliable information and new opportunities for learning.

Modern Technology and the Transformation of Human Society

In the early 19th century, a groundbreaking moment in human history took place when Samuel Morse sent the first telegraph message on May 24, 1844. The message, "What hath God wrought," was a biblical phrase chosen by Annie Ellsworth, the daughter of Morse's partner. This message, transmitted from Washington, D.C., to Baltimore, was more than just a technical achievement; it marked the beginning of a new era in communication. The telegraph, capable of relaying information almost instantaneously over vast distances, revolutionized industries, transformed news dissemination, and changed personal correspondence forever. It was a precursor to the digital age, a time when technology would continually shrink the world and dispel the shadows of ignorance and superstition.

The impact of the telegraph was immediate and profound. Before its invention, communication across long distances took days, weeks, or even months, depending on the method of transmission. The telegraph made it possible to send messages in minutes, fundamentally altering the speed at which business, politics, and personal relationships operated. For example, during the American Civil War, President Abraham Lincoln received battlefield updates in real-time, allowing him to make strategic decisions with unprecedented speed and accuracy. This technological leap paved the way for the interconnected world we live in today, laying the groundwork for future innovations in communication.

Fast forward to the 20th century, a period defined by the rapid rise of digital technology that touched every aspect of human life. This era began with the development of the computer, an evolution that can be traced back to Charles Babbage's designs of the Analytical Engine in the early 19th century. However, the true revolution in computing came during World War II, thanks to the work of Alan Turing, often hailed as the father of computer science. Turing's work at Bletchley Park was instrumental in breaking the German Enigma code, a feat that significantly influenced the outcome of the war. Turing's invention, the Bombe machine, mechanized the decryption process, allowing the Allies to anticipate and counter Axis moves, ultimately saving countless lives.

The story of Turing's Bombe machine is a testament to human ingenuity in the face of seemingly insurmountable challenges. His work not only changed the course of history but also dispelled the myth that machines could not "think." This idea laid the groundwork for the development of modern computers, which have since become indispensable tools in every aspect of life, from medicine to space exploration.

The latter half of the 20th century witnessed the advent of another technological marvel: the internet. Born from the work of scientists like J.C.R. Licklider, who envisioned an *Intergalactic Computer Network,* the internet has become the backbone of global communication, commerce, and entertainment.

Consider the story of email, which transformed corporate communication. Before the internet, business communication relied heavily on postal services and fax machines, which were slow and cumbersome. The introduction of email revolutionized the way companies operated, allowing for instantaneous sharing of information. This technological shift drastically improved efficiency and collaboration, enabling businesses to operate on a global scale with unprecedented agility. The rise of multinational corporations and the globalization of markets can be directly linked to the advent of digital communication.

The statistics speak volumes about the internet's pervasive influence. By 2020, more than 4.5 billion people—over half the world's population—were internet users. This level of connectivity has reshaped economies, with e-commerce giants like Amazon and Alibaba revolutionizing retail, and platforms like Google and Facebook redefining advertising and social interaction. The impact of the internet on education has been equally transformative. Online courses, digital libraries, and educational platforms have made learning accessible to millions worldwide, breaking down geographic barriers and democratizing knowledge.

The personal lives of billions have also been profoundly affected by modern communication technology. Social media platforms such as Facebook, Twitter, and Instagram have redefined how people connect, share, and interact, creating virtual communities that transcend physical boundaries. An interesting anecdote from the early days of Facebook involves its role in reconnecting long-lost friends and family members, showcasing the profound social impact of digital technology. For instance, in 2007, a woman named Yolanda was able to reunite with her brother, whom she hadn't seen in 20 years, thanks to Facebook. Such stories highlight how technology has become a powerful tool for social cohesion, breaking down the isolation that often comes with distance.

But the impact of modern technology goes beyond just social connections. It has played a critical role in dispelling ignorance, superstition, and misinformation. The internet, with its vast repositories of knowledge, has empowered people to educate themselves on a wide range of topics, from science and history to health and politics. For example, during the COVID-19 pandemic, online platforms became crucial in disseminating accurate information about the virus, helping to combat the spread of misinformation and conspiracy theories. The accessibility of reliable information has challenged old myths and superstitions, fostering a more informed and scientifically literate global population.

Moreover, modern technology has revolutionized healthcare, extending life expectancy and improving the quality of life for millions. The development of advanced medical imaging technologies, such as MRI and CT scans, has transformed the diagnosis and treatment of diseases. Telemedicine, which allows patients to consult with doctors remotely, has made healthcare more accessible, especially in rural and underserved areas. According to the World Health Organization, telemedicine consultations increased by 70% during the pandemic, highlighting the growing importance of digital technology in healthcare.

One compelling example of technology's impact on public health is the eradication of smallpox. In the late 18th century, Edward Jenner's development of the smallpox vaccine laid the foundation for modern immunology. By the mid-20th century, a global vaccination campaign led by the World Health Organization had eradicated smallpox, a disease that had killed millions throughout history. This triumph of medical science dispelled the fear and superstition surrounding the disease, replacing it with evidence-based public health strategies that continue to save lives today.

The journey from Morse's telegraph to the internet and beyond illustrates humanity's relentless drive to connect, share, and collaborate. These technological advancements have not only shrunk the world but also expanded our collective consciousness, paving the way for unprecedented social, intellectual, and scientific growth. As we continue to build on these foundations, the potential for future advancements promises to further transform our world in ways we can only begin to imagine. The story of modern technology is, at its heart, the story of human progress—a testament to our capacity to overcome challenges, dispel ignorance, and illuminate the path to a better future.

Underlying Forces

The drive for progress is often accompanied by psychological challenges. Cognitive biases, such as the status quo bias—the tendency to prefer things as they are—can lead to resistance against new technologies. When computers began to enter the workplace in the mid-20th century, many workers feared that automation would render their skills obsolete. In fact, a 1989 survey by the National Science Foundation found that 55% of workers in the United States were worried about losing their jobs to computers. However, rather than eliminating jobs, the advent of computers and automation has often led to the creation of new industries and employment opportunities, albeit with a shift in the types of skills required. This shift highlights the importance of adaptability and the need to embrace rather than resist technological change.

As we move further into the 21st century, the ethical implications of technological advancements become increasingly significant. Technologies such as artificial intelligence (AI), genetic engineering, and quantum computing hold immense potential to revolutionize our world, but they also pose complex ethical challenges.

Amidst these broad psychological and societal trends, the role of individual efforts in technological progress cannot be overstated. History is replete with examples of visionary individuals whose innovations have had far-reaching impacts. Ada Lovelace, for instance, is often celebrated as the world's first computer programmer. Working with Charles Babbage on his Analytical Engine in the mid-19th century, Lovelace developed algorithms that could be processed by the machine, demonstrating that computers could do far more than mere calculations. Her visionary insights laid the groundwork for the field of computer science, long before the advent of modern computers.

Another pioneering figure in the history of computing is Grace Hopper, a computer scientist and naval officer who played a pivotal role in developing early programming languages. Hopper's work on the COBOL language revolutionized software development, making it more accessible and efficient. Her famous quote, "The most damaging phrase in the language is, 'We've always done it this way,'" reflects her innovative spirit and determination to push beyond the constraints of tradition. Hopper's contributions helped to democratize technology, making it possible for people without advanced technical knowledge to write and understand computer programs.

Educational institutions play a crucial role in fostering a culture of innovation by equipping students with the skills and knowledge needed to tackle complex problems. Science, technology, engineering, and mathematics (STEM) programs, in particular, are vital for nurturing the next generation of innovators who will develop the technologies of the future.

Consider the story of William Kamkwamba, a young boy from Malawi who, in 2002, built a wind turbine from scrap materials to provide electricity to his village during a severe drought. Kamkwamba, who was forced to drop out of school due to his family's financial difficulties, taught himself the basics of electricity and engineering from books in a local library. His wind turbine not only powered lights in his family's home but also inspired others in his community to embrace renewable energy solutions. Kamkwamba's ingenuity and determination are a powerful reminder of the impact that individual effort and curiosity can have, even in the face of adversity.

The path of innovation is not always straightforward, but with a commitment to ethical considerations, adaptability, and individual effort, we can continue to harness the power of technology to improve lives and advance human knowledge.

The Pseudoscientific Plague: How Fake Science Breeds Fear, Irrationality, and a Slavish Mindset

Throughout history, pseudoscience has woven itself into the fabric of human societies, presenting itself as legitimate science while peddling baseless claims and unverified assertions. From ancient alchemy to modern-day conspiracy theories, pseudoscience has thrived on the allure of easy answers and sensationalism, often leading to irrational fears, a slavish mindset, and harmful societal impacts. The consequences of such misinformation are far-reaching, promoting not just ignorance but also dangerous ideologies that have shaped—and at times, derailed—human progress.

One of the earliest examples of pseudoscience can be traced back to the practice of alchemy in the Middle Ages. Alchemists, driven by the quest to transmute base metals into gold and discover the elusive elixir of life, engaged in mystical and often unscientific practices. While some of their work laid the groundwork for modern chemistry, much of it was steeped in magical thinking rather than empirical evidence. This focus on the fantastical often overshadowed genuine scientific inquiry, leading many down a path of irrational beliefs that stymied intellectual progress.

Take, for example, the story of Johann Rudolf Glauber, a 17th-century alchemist who believed he had discovered the Philosopher's Stone—a substance said to grant immortality and turn lead into gold. Glauber's "discovery" was nothing more than a mixture of common chemicals, yet it captivated the imaginations of many and reinforced the notion that alchemy held the keys to unlimited wealth and eternal life. This obsession diverted attention from more practical and scientifically sound pursuits, delaying the advancement of true chemistry for generations.

The 19th century saw the rise of phrenology, a pseudoscientific field that claimed a person's character and mental abilities could be determined by the shape of their skull. Promoted by figures like Franz Joseph Gall and Johann Spurzheim, phrenology gained widespread popularity despite its lack of empirical basis. The field's practitioners measured skulls and made sweeping generalizations about intelligence, morality, and personality, leading to the dangerous and false notion that physical characteristics determined a person's worth.

Phrenology was often used to justify racism and social inequality, giving a veneer of scientific legitimacy to discriminatory ideologies. For instance, in the United States, phrenology was employed to support the institution of slavery by "proving" the supposed intellectual inferiority of African Americans. This pseudoscientific justification for racism had lasting effects, reinforcing social hierarchies and perpetuating a slavish mindset that accepted these inequalities as natural and scientifically validated.

One of the most disturbing examples of pseudoscience is the eugenics movement, which emerged in the late 19th and early 20th centuries. Advocates like Francis Galton and Charles Davenport promoted the idea that selective breeding could improve the genetic quality of the human population. Cloaked in the guise of scientific progress, eugenics led to horrific policies, including forced sterilizations, marriage restrictions, and, in the most extreme cases, genocide.

The impact of eugenics was devastating. In the United States alone, more than 60,000 people were forcibly sterilized under eugenic laws that targeted the mentally ill, disabled, and those deemed "unfit" to reproduce. These policies were based on pseudoscientific beliefs about heredity and social worth, which were later debunked by advancements in genetics and psychology. The misuse of science in the service of eugenics culminated in the atrocities of the Holocaust, where Nazi Germany used eugenic principles to justify the systematic extermination of millions of people. This dark chapter in history serves as a chilling reminder of how fake science can lead to real-world horrors.

In contemporary times, pseudoscience continues to pose significant risks, particularly in the realm of public health. The anti-vaccine movement, which gained momentum after a fraudulent 1998 study by Andrew Wakefield falsely linked the MMR vaccine to autism, is a prime example. Despite being thoroughly discredited, Wakefield's study sparked a global movement that fueled irrational fears and mistrust of vaccines. The impact has been dire: the resurgence of preventable diseases like measles and whooping cough has claimed lives and strained healthcare systems around the world.

In 2019, the World Health Organization (WHO) listed vaccine hesitancy as one of the top ten global health threats, highlighting the dangerous consequences of pseudoscience. In the United States, measles cases reached their highest level in 25 years, with over 1,200 cases reported, largely due to vaccine refusal. The spread of misinformation through social media has amplified these fears, creating echo chambers where pseudoscientific claims are repeated and reinforced. This modern pseudoscience promotes a slavish mindset by encouraging people to reject well-established scientific facts in favor of baseless conspiracies, undermining public trust in science and medicine.

Another significant example of pseudoscience is climate change denial. Despite an overwhelming consensus among scientists that human activities are driving global climate change, a vocal minority continues to spread misinformation and sow doubt. Funded by industries opposed to environmental regulations, climate change denial has hindered meaningful action to address this existential threat. By promoting false narratives that downplay or outright deny the evidence, these pseudoscientific claims have delayed the implementation of policies needed to mitigate the effects of climate change.

The consequences of this denialism are becoming increasingly apparent. Extreme weather events, rising sea levels, and shifting ecosystems are already impacting millions of people around the world. According to NASA, the planet's average surface temperature has risen about 2.12 degrees Fahrenheit (1.18 degrees Celsius) since the late 19th century, largely due to increased carbon dioxide emissions. Yet, despite the clear and present danger, climate change denial persists, driven by short-term economic interests and political agendas. This refusal to acknowledge reality not only promotes irrationality but also jeopardizes the future of our planet.

To understand why pseudoscience is so effective in promoting irrationality and fear, it is essential to explore its psychological appeal. Humans have a natural tendency to seek patterns and explanations, even where none exist—a cognitive bias known as apophenia. This bias makes us susceptible to pseudoscientific claims that offer simple, comforting explanations for complex phenomena. Additionally, pseudoscience often exploits emotional appeals, tapping into fears and anxieties. The anti-vaccine movement, for instance, preys on parents' fears for their children's health, while climate change denial leverages economic and political insecurities.

Addressing the challenge of pseudoscience requires a concerted effort to promote scientific literacy and critical thinking. Encouraging skepticism and curiosity can empower individuals to question pseudoscientific claims and seek reliable information. Educational institutions have a crucial role to play in fostering a culture of inquiry and evidence-based reasoning.

The New Enlightenment: How AI, Quantum Computing, Synthetic Biology, Space Science, and Genetic Science Can Unravel Old Myths and Deceptions

From ancient civilizations that explained natural phenomena through gods and spirits to modern times where pseudoscience and misconceptions still linger, the struggle between knowledge and ignorance has been perpetual. Today, we are on the brink of a new enlightenment, driven by revolutionary advancements in artificial intelligence (AI), quantum computing, synthetic biology, space science, and genetic science. These fields not only promise to unravel the deepest secrets of the universe but also to dispel the long-standing myths and deceptions that have clouded human understanding.

Artificial Intelligence is not just a technological advancement; it's a transformative force that redefines how we interact with the world. AI's ability to process vast amounts of data, identify patterns, and make predictions has profound implications for debunking pseudoscience and myths. As AI pioneer Marvin Minsky stated, "Will robots inherit the earth? Yes, but they will be our children."

In healthcare, AI algorithms have revolutionized diagnostics. Machine learning models can now analyze medical images with higher accuracy than human doctors, identifying conditions such as cancer at stages that were previously undetectable. This capability not only improves patient outcomes but also dispels myths surrounding certain diseases and treatments. For instance,

AI can provide evidence-based recommendations that challenge unfounded beliefs in alternative medicine.

Moreover, AI's role in climate science has been pivotal. By analyzing climate data, AI models can predict environmental changes with remarkable accuracy, debunking myths perpetuated by climate change denial. These insights empower policymakers and the public with factual information, paving way to a more informed and proactive approach to environmental conservation.

Quantum computing, with its roots in quantum mechanics, represents a leap beyond the limitations of classical computing. Quantum computers operate using qubits, which can exist in multiple states simultaneously, thanks to the principles of superposition and entanglement. This allows quantum computers to solve complex problems at speeds unimaginable for classical machines. As Richard Feynman once remarked, "Nature isn't classical, damn it, and if you want to make a simulation of nature, you'd better make it quantum mechanical."

One of the most promising applications of quantum computing is in cryptography. Quantum algorithms can break traditional encryption methods, but they also pave the way for quantum cryptography, which promises virtually unbreakable security. This technology could eliminate the myths and fears associated with data breaches and privacy concerns.

In the realm of material science, quantum computing enables the simulation of molecular structures, leading to the discovery of new materials with unprecedented properties. This not only accelerates technological innovation but also challenges the myths about the limitations of human ingenuity and the natural world.

Synthetic biology merges biology and engineering, allowing us to design and construct new biological parts, devices, and systems. This field holds the potential to revolutionize medicine, agriculture, and environmental conservation. As Craig Venter, a pioneer in synthetic biology, stated, "Life is a DNA software system."

One of the most groundbreaking applications of synthetic biology is in the development of synthetic organisms that can perform specific tasks, such as producing biofuels or cleaning up environmental pollutants. These innovations challenge traditional beliefs about the limitations of biological systems and demonstrate the potential of human ingenuity to address global challenges.

In medicine, synthetic biology enables the creation of personalized therapies tailored to an individual's genetic makeup. This approach, known as precision medicine, debunks the myth that medical treatments must follow a one-size-fits-all model. By understanding and manipulating the genetic basis of diseases, synthetic biology paves the way for more effective and targeted treatments.

Space science has always captivated human imagination, from ancient stargazers to modern astronomers. Today, advancements in space technology are not only expanding our understanding of the cosmos but also challenging age-old myths and misconceptions.

The exploration of Mars and other celestial bodies has provided insights that debunk myths about extraterrestrial life and the conditions necessary for life to exist. Robotic missions, such as the Mars rovers, have gathered data that suggest Mars may have once had conditions suitable for life, challenging the long-held belief that Earth is unique in its ability to support life.

Moreover, the study of exoplanets has revealed a vast array of planetary systems, many of which could potentially harbor life. These discoveries challenge the geocentric view of the universe and open up new possibilities for understanding our place in the cosmos. The search for extraterrestrial intelligence (SETI) continues to push the boundaries of our knowledge and challenge our assumptions about life beyond Earth.

Genetic science has made tremendous strides since the discovery of the DNA double helix. The ability to sequence and analyze genomes has revolutionized our understanding of biology, heredity, and evolution.

The Human Genome Project, completed in 2003, was a monumental achievement that mapped the entire human genome. This project has provided insights into the genetic basis of diseases, traits, and behaviors, debunking many myths about heredity and human diversity. For example, genomic studies have shown that the concept of race has no biological basis, challenging the pseudoscientific beliefs that have fueled racism and discrimination.

Gene editing technologies, such as CRISPR-Cas9, have further expanded our ability to manipulate genetic material with unprecedented precision. This technology holds the potential to correct genetic disorders, enhance agricultural productivity, and even create new forms of life. These capabilities challenge the myths about the fixed nature of biology and open up new possibilities for human and environmental enhancement.

Pseudoscience has persisted throughout history, promoting myths and misconceptions that often exploit human fears and ignorance. The advancements in AI, quantum computing, synthetic biology, space science, and genetic science provide powerful tools to combat these false beliefs and promote rational, evidence-based thinking.

For instance, the anti-vaccine movement, fueled by misinformation and fear, has led to the resurgence of preventable diseases. AI and data analytics can play a crucial role in exposing the lack of empirical evidence supporting anti-vaccine claims, promoting public health and safety. Similarly, quantum computing can debunk pseudoscientific claims about the supernatural by providing more accurate models of physical phenomena.

In the realm of alternative medicine, synthetic biology and genetic science offer evidence-based treatments that challenge the efficacy of unproven remedies. By providing factual information and promoting scientific literacy, these technologies empower individuals to make informed decisions about their health and well-being.

As we harness the power of these revolutionary technologies, it is crucial to consider their ethical implications. The potential to reshape humanity and the natural world comes with profound responsibilities. Ethical considerations must guide the development and application of these technologies to ensure they are used for the benefit of all.

The use of AI in decision-making and surveillance raises concerns about privacy, bias, and accountability. Ensuring that AI systems are transparent, fair, and ethical is crucial to prevent the misuse of this powerful technology. Similarly, the ethical dilemmas surrounding genetic editing, such as designer babies and genetic discrimination, must be carefully considered to avoid exacerbating social inequalities.

The exploration of space also raises ethical questions about the environmental impact of space missions and the potential for resource exploitation. As we venture into the cosmos, it is essential to consider the ethical implications of our actions and strive to protect the pristine environments of other celestial bodies.

The convergence of AI, quantum computing, synthetic biology, space science, and genetic science represents a new frontier in human knowledge and discovery. These technologies have the potential to revolutionize our understanding of the universe, challenge long-held beliefs, and address some of the most pressing challenges facing humanity.

The future of knowledge is one of collaboration and interdisciplinary research. By bringing together experts from diverse fields, we can harness the collective intelligence and creativity needed to tackle complex problems and drive innovation. The discoveries and insights that emerge from this collaborative effort will shape the future of our world and our place in the universe.

Masters or Servants? The Perils and Promise of Artificial Intelligence

Artificial Intelligence (AI) has permeated nearly every aspect of modern life, from how we communicate to how we diagnose diseases. But as AI continues to evolve, so too do the anxieties about its potential to dominate and control humanity. This fear is not new. As far back as the early 19th century, with the advent of the first industrial machines, there has been a persistent worry that technology could outpace human control. Fast forward to today, and these concerns have only intensified.

The idea that AI could become a master over humanity is rooted in science fiction, but it has real-world implications. The scenario where machines surpass human intelligence and gain autonomous control, often referred to as the "singularity," is a topic of heated debate among experts. Elon Musk has warned, "AI is a fundamental risk to the existence of human civilization." While this might sound alarmist, it underscores the importance of understanding and mitigating the risks associated with AI.

One of the primary dangers is the potential for AI to make decisions that are beyond human comprehension and control. For instance, in the financial sector, algorithmic trading systems operate at speeds and complexities that human traders cannot match. This has led to incidents like the Flash Crash of 2010, where the Dow Jones Industrial

Average plunged nearly 1,000 points in minutes, driven by a cascade of automated trades. Such events highlight the potential for AI systems to behave unpredictably, with far-reaching consequences.

Human psychology plays a significant role in how we interact with and perceive AI. Our tendency to anthropomorphize machines—attributing human-like qualities to them—can lead to unrealistic expectations and fears. Daniel Kahneman, a Nobel laureate in economics, noted, "Humans think in stories rather than in facts, numbers, and equations, and the simpler the story, the better." This storytelling nature can make us susceptible to both the allure and the fear of AI.

The slavish mindset that can develop around technology is partly due to our psychological weaknesses. We often seek easy solutions and quick fixes, which AI can seemingly provide. This can lead to an over-reliance on technology, diminishing our capacity for critical thinking and self-reliance. The challenge is to build a balanced relationship with AI, where it serves as an aid rather than a crutch.

Maintaining a balanced and conscious control over AI requires a multi-faceted approach. First and foremost, there must be robust ethical guidelines and regulatory frameworks. Philosopher Nick Bostrom, in his book *Superintelligence,* emphasizes the need for "AI alignment"—ensuring that AI's goals are aligned with human values. This involves interdisciplinary collaboration among technologists, ethicists, policymakers, and the public.

As AI continues to evolve, ethical considerations become increasingly important. Issues such as data privacy, algorithmic bias, and the potential for job displacement need to be addressed. Tim Berners-Lee, the inventor of the World Wide Web, has been vocal about the ethical use of technology, stating, "We need a global constitution—a bill of rights."

One promising direction is the development of explainable AI (XAI), which aims to make AI decision-making processes transparent and understandable to humans. This can help mitigate the risks associated with black-box algorithms and ensure that AI systems are accountable.

To nurture balanced and conscious control over AI and technology, we must adopt a holistic approach that includes regulation, education, and ethical consideration. It's essential to recognize that technology itself is neutral—it is how we choose to use it that determines its impact. As Yuval Noah Harari notes in *Homo Deus,* "Technology is never deterministic. It opens up new possibilities, but it doesn't determine which of them will materialize."

With a culture of critical thinking, ethical responsibility, and informed engagement with technology, we can break free from the chains of a slavish mindset and harness the full potential of AI for the betterment of humanity.

Fear of AI and technology often stems from a lack of understanding and control. By demystifying AI and involving diverse perspectives in its development and regulation, we can alleviate these fears. Philosopher

Martha Nussbaum argues that "fear is often an enemy of rational deliberation" and that overcoming fear requires "education, discussion, and political action."

Encouraging public discourse and participation in technological development can create a more inclusive and balanced approach to AI. This involves not only scientists and technologists but also ethicists, sociologists, and the broader public in directing the future of AI.

At the core of managing AI's impact is the need to embed human values in its development. This includes ensuring fairness, accountability, and transparency in AI systems. Philosopher and AI ethics expert Shannon Vallor emphasizes the importance of cultivating "technomoral virtues" such as honesty, humility, and justice in the design and deployment of AI.

Prioritizing human values and ethical principles, will enable us to create AI systems that enhance human well-being rather than undermine it. This involves ongoing dialogue and collaboration across disciplines and sectors to address the complex challenges posed by AI.

The future of AI lies in collaboration rather than domination. By leveraging AI's capabilities to augment human intelligence and creativity, we can unlock new possibilities for innovation and problem-solving. As AI researcher Fei-Fei Li notes, "The future of AI should be about amplifying human intelligence, not replacing it."

Human-AI collaboration can lead to breakthroughs in fields such as medicine, education, and environmental conservation. By working together, humans and AI can tackle some of the most pressing challenges facing society and create a more sustainable and equitable future. The journey ahead requires collective effort, informed decision-making, and a commitment to ethical principles.

How Technology is Transforming Transparency and Truth

The present generation is utilizing technology to dismantle long-standing deceptions and call for greater transparency across various domains. By leveraging advanced digital tools and innovative applications, technology is exposing falsehoods and recasting how we understand and interact with the world.

One of the most impactful advancements is the use of artificial intelligence (AI) and machine learning to combat misinformation. As mentioned earlier in this book, AI-driven fact-checking tools, employed by platforms such as Google News and Facebook, are revolutionizing the way false information is addressed. These tools analyze content patterns and user interactions to identify and correct misinformation, thereby enhancing the accuracy of public information. The effectiveness of these technologies is evident in their ability to reduce the spread of false information by approximately 30% in controlled environments, contributing to a more informed and discerning society.

Companies like IBM and Walmart use blockchain to track and verify the origins of products, ensuring they meet ethical and quality standards. This increased transparency is not only improving traceability but also reducing inefficiencies and potential fraud. The World Economic

Forum estimates that blockchain technology could cut global supply chain costs by up to $31 billion annually, highlighting its impact on ethical consumption and trust in supply chains.

Technological tools like data analytics and whistleblower platforms are also playing a crucial role in exposing corruption and unethical practices. Platforms such as Wikileaks and the Panama Papers have utilized digital technology to reveal significant instances of financial wrongdoing and corruption. The transparency achieved through these leaks has led to investigations, reforms, and increased scrutiny of financial practices. By making hidden information accessible, technology is promoting accountability and challenging entrenched power structures.

In the healthcare sector, digital health tools like telemedicine and health apps are transforming how medical services are delivered. Telemedicine allows for remote consultations, while health apps offer tools for tracking health metrics and managing chronic conditions. The rise of telemedicine in the U.S., with a 40% increase in usage over the past year, illustrates the growing impact of these technologies. By improving access to healthcare and enabling early diagnosis, digital health tools are reconstructing traditional healthcare models and promoting more equitable health management.

Technology is playing a crucial role in shattering human deceptions and building greater transparency.

These innovations are transforming how we understand and interact with the world, leading to a more honest and transparent global landscape.

Chapter 9

Art and Culture: Catalysts for Truth and Liberation

Art and culture have always been more than just reflections of society; they are powerful catalysts for change, capable of challenging the status quo and unshackling minds from the chains of delusion. From the murals of ancient civilizations to the digital art of the modern era, creative expression has consistently served as a medium through which humanity has questioned, resisted, and ultimately transformed its reality. This chapter explores how art and cultural expressions have historically played a pivotal role in challenging societal illusions and oppressive systems, how they continue to shape our worldview, and how future generations might harness this power to break free from the delusions of their time.

The Historical Role of Art in Challenging Oppression

Throughout history, art has wielded a remarkable power, subtly or overtly challenging the narratives imposed by those in authority. Far from being merely aesthetic or decorative, art has often been a form of rebellion—a canvas upon which human beings project their innermost defiance against the status quo. Take, for instance, the cave paintings of Lascaux in France, created approximately 17,000 years ago. While these ancient artworks are frequently described as primitive depictions of hunting scenes, there exists a more profound interpretation that might surprise you: these images could represent an early form of resistance against the unpredictability of nature, a symbolic attempt to assert control over the uncontrollable forces that governed prehistoric life.

The French anthropologist Claude Lévi-Strauss, known for his theory of structuralism, suggested that the structure of human thought is deeply embedded in our cultural practices, including art. He posited that these ancient artworks might have been a way for early humans to impose order on the chaos of their world. Rather than simply documenting their environment, the cave artists could have been engaging in a ritualistic act of defiance, an attempt to ward off the threats posed by wild animals and the capriciousness of nature. This was not art for art's sake; it was a profound psychological maneuver, an early attempt to deceive the mind into believing it could control its fate.

The Lascaux Paintings: More Than Meets the Eye

The Lascaux cave paintings are often described in art history textbooks as the first masterpieces of humanity, celebrated for their beauty and realism. But what if we dig deeper? What if these paintings were the earliest examples of humans grappling with their existential anxieties through art? French philosopher Gaston Bachelard once remarked, "The human being in the grip of fear takes refuge in the imagination. He will imagine being dominated by forces against which there is no appeal." The Lascaux paintings could be seen as an early manifestation of this psychological need to confront and symbolically conquer the fears that plagued early humans.

In "The Cave Painters: Probing the Mysteries of the World's First Artists," Gregory Curtis delves into the theory that these images were not just records of daily life but served a deeper spiritual or ritualistic purpose. Curtis references the work of archaeologist Jean Clottes, who argued that the paintings might have been part of shamanic rituals. Shamans, believed to have the power to communicate with the spirit world, may have used these images as a means to connect with the supernatural, to negotiate with the forces that governed life and death in the harsh prehistoric world.

The shamanic interpretation suggests that these paintings were more than mere reflections of reality—they were attempts to alter reality. By depicting animals in the act of being hunted, the cave dwellers were not just recording what they had done but were perhaps trying to ensure future success in hunting, invoking the power of the depicted animals' spirits. It was a form of early sympathetic magic, a belief that by creating images of what they desired, they could influence the outcome. This is a far cry from the simplistic view of these paintings as mere decoration or documentation.

Art as Subversion: From Cave Walls to Modern Walls

This subversive use of art to challenge the status quo did not end with the cave dwellers of Lascaux. Fast forward several millennia, and we find similar acts of defiance in the works of artists who sought to challenge the prevailing narratives of their times. Consider Pablo Picasso's "Guernica," a powerful indictment of the horrors of war. Created in response to the bombing of the Basque town of Guernica during the Spanish Civil War, Picasso's monumental painting is a haunting depiction of the brutality and senselessness of conflict. Picasso himself once said, "Art is a lie that makes us realize the truth," and in "Guernica," he used art to force the world to confront the truth about the atrocities of war.

Picasso's statement echoes the sentiments of the German philosopher Friedrich Nietzsche, who believed that art was one of the most profound ways to engage with the truth. In his work *The Birth of Tragedy,* Nietzsche argued that art allows us to confront the darker aspects of existence, those truths that are often too difficult to face directly. Art, in Nietzsche's view, is not just a reflection of reality but a means of transforming it, of revealing truths that lie beneath the surface.

The power of art to challenge and subvert extends beyond the canvas and the cave wall. Street art, for instance, has become a modern medium for rebellion, a way for artists to speak truth to power in the most public of spaces. Banksy, the anonymous street artist, has made a career out of using art to challenge the status quo. His works, often laced with biting humor and irony, confront issues like consumerism, war, and political corruption. In one of his most famous pieces, "Balloon Girl," Banksy plays with the image of a child reaching for a red balloon, a seemingly innocent scene that, upon closer inspection, reveals a deep commentary on the loss of innocence and the fleeting nature of hope.

The Psychological Roots of Artistic Rebellion

But why do humans feel compelled to use art as a means of rebellion? The answer lies in the complex interplay between psychology and societal structures. Human beings have an inherent need for autonomy and self-expression, yet societies often impose constraints on these impulses, leading to tension and a desire to break free. According to the American psychologist Carl Rogers, creativity is a fundamental aspect of human nature, a drive toward self-actualization. When this drive is stifled by external pressures—whether from oppressive governments, restrictive cultural norms, or the harsh realities of life—art becomes a means of resistance.

Rogers' theory resonates with the ideas of the German psychoanalyst Erich Fromm, who argued that creativity is an essential aspect of human freedom. In his book *The Fear of Freedom,* Fromm discusses how individuals often feel trapped by societal expectations and norms, leading to a sense of alienation. Art, in this context, becomes a way to reclaim one's sense of self, to assert individuality in the face of conformity. By creating art, individuals can challenge the narratives that society imposes on them, offering alternative perspectives and, in the process, liberating themselves from the constraints of their environment.

This psychological need to resist and rebel through art is not limited to individuals. Entire movements have emerged from this impulse, challenging the dominant cultural and political narratives of their time. The Dada movement, for example, was born out of the horrors of

World War I, a reaction against the senselessness of the war and the societal structures that had led to it. Dadaists used absurdity and irrationality as tools of rebellion, creating works that defied conventional artistic norms and, in doing so, challenged the very foundations of Western culture.

Instances of Artistic Resistance

During World War II, the Nazis labeled modern art as "degenerate" and sought to suppress it? They organized an exhibition called "Entartete Kunst" ("Degenerate Art") in 1937, showcasing works by artists like Picasso, Kandinsky, and Chagall, which they deemed "un-German" and "corrupt." Ironically, this exhibition, intended to denigrate the artists, became one of the most popular art exhibitions in Nazi Germany, attracting over two million visitors. The public's interest in these so-called "degenerate" works was a clear indication that art has the power to transcend even the most oppressive regimes, challenging the narratives imposed by those in power.

Artistic resistance is not confined to Europe or the Western world. In Latin America, the Mexican muralists—artists like Diego Rivera, José Clemente Orozco, and David Alfaro Siqueiros—used their art to challenge social injustice and colonial oppression. Rivera, for example, painted murals that depicted the struggles of the working class, the history of Mexico, and the impact of capitalism and imperialism. His work was not just art for art's sake but a powerful tool for political change.

Rivera once said, "Art is not just art, it is a weapon for the people to fight against their oppressors."

In Africa, too, art has been a powerful tool for resistance. During the apartheid era in South Africa, artists like Gerard Sekoto and Dumile Feni used their work to expose the brutal realities of the regime and to inspire resistance. Sekoto's paintings, often depicting the daily lives of black South Africans, were a stark contrast to the idealized images promoted by the apartheid government. His work was banned in South Africa, but it continued to inspire those who saw it as a powerful indictment of the regime.

Breaking Away from the Past: Stories of Change

The story of how art has been used to challenge the status quo would be incomplete without mentioning those individuals who have harnessed the power of creativity to break away from the past and forge new paths. One such figure is Ai Weiwei, the Chinese contemporary artist and activist. Ai Weiwei's work is a direct challenge to the Chinese government's censorship and human rights abuses. His installation "Sunflower Seeds," which consists of 100 million porcelain sunflower seeds spread across the floor of London's Tate Modern, is a commentary on the mass production and conformity that characterized Mao's China. Each seed, hand-painted by Chinese artisans, represents the individuality that is often suppressed in totalitarian regimes.

Ai Weiwei's activism extends beyond his art. He has been a vocal critic of the Chinese government, using social media and his art to speak out against censorship and corruption. His outspoken nature has led to his arrest and imprisonment, but Ai Weiwei continues to create and inspire others to use art as a form of resistance. His story is a testament to the enduring power of art to challenge authority and inspire change.

Another artist who broke away from the past and used art as a tool for social change is Keith Haring. Emerging from the New York City graffiti scene in the 1980s, Haring's vibrant, cartoon-like figures quickly became iconic. But his art was not just about bright colors and playful images; it was a means of addressing serious social issues, including AIDS, apartheid, and the crack epidemic. Haring's work was deeply political, and he used his fame to raise awareness and funds for causes he believed in. His "Crack is Wack" mural, painted on a handball court in Harlem, was a bold public statement against the drug epidemic that was ravaging the city at the time.

Haring's art was a form of activism, and he believed in the power of art to change the world. He once said, "Art should be something that liberates your soul, provokes the imagination and encourages people to go further." Haring's legacy lives on, not just in his art but in the impact he had on public consciousness and the social issues he championed.

Art as a Mirror of Human Weakness

As we explore the subversive power of art, it is essential to acknowledge that the need for art to challenge the status quo arises from a fundamental aspect of human nature: our psychological weaknesses. Humans have a deep-seated desire for order and control, yet we live in a world that is often chaotic and unpredictable. Art, in many ways, serves as a coping mechanism, a way for individuals to exert some semblance of control over their environment, even if only symbolically.

Sigmund Freud, the father of psychoanalysis, believed that art is a way for individuals to reconcile the conflicting demands of the id, ego, and superego. In his essay "Creative Writers and Day-Dreaming," Freud argued that artists, like daydreamers, use their work to fulfill unfulfilled desires and to create a sense of order in a disordered world. This idea aligns with the notion that art, particularly subversive art, is a way for individuals to challenge the narratives imposed by society, to assert their own identity in the face of external pressures.

But there is also a darker side to this psychological need for control. The same desire that drives individuals to create art can also lead to self-deception. In our attempts to impose order on the chaos of the world, we may create narratives that, while comforting, are ultimately deceptive. This is particularly true in the realm of political art, where artists may present idealized visions of the world that gloss over its complexities. The danger lies in mistaking these visions for reality, in believing that art can provide a complete solution to the problems it depicts.

Art, then, is both a tool for resistance and a potential source of deception. It can challenge the status quo, but it can also reinforce it, depending on how it is used and interpreted. The same psychological weaknesses that drive us to create art also make us susceptible to the deceptions that art can perpetuate. This dual nature of art is what makes it such a powerful and complex force in human history.

The Power of Satire

It all started in Ancient Greece, a civilization often celebrated as the cradle of democracy and philosophy, yet one that was rife with political intrigue and corruption. It was in this complex societal backdrop that the playwright Aristophanes emerged as a fierce critic of the ruling elites, wielding his pen as both a scalpel and a sledgehammer. His work, particularly the play *Lysistrata,* written in 411 BCE, is a masterclass in the art of political satire, using humor not merely to entertain but to eviscerate the moral failings of those in power.

Aristophanes was no mere jester; he was a commentator on the human condition, a precursor to the modern satirist who uses wit to reveal uncomfortable truths. In "Lysistrata," he tackles the Peloponnesian War, a devastating conflict that had engulfed Greece for decades. The play's premise is both audacious and subversive: the women of Greece, led by the titular character Lysistrata, withhold sexual privileges from their husbands as a means to force them into negotiating peace. This comedic setup belies the seriousness of the message—war is not just a matter of national interest but also a personal tragedy, disrupting families and communities for the sake of political ambition.

Aristophanes' satire was not without risk. In ancient Athens, where the Assembly wielded immense power and the specter of ostracism loomed large, criticizing the government was a dangerous endeavor. Yet, Aristophanes persisted, understanding that comedy was a powerful vehicle for truth. As the philosopher and literary critic Mikhail Bakhtin later noted, "Laughter demolishes fear and piety before an object, before a world, making of it an object of familiar contact and thus clearing the ground for an absolutely free investigation of it." Aristophanes used laughter to break the chains of reverence that bound the citizens to their leaders, encouraging them to view their rulers not as infallible gods but as flawed men, susceptible to the same vices and errors as anyone else.

The play's impact was profound, not just as a piece of theater but as a social commentary that resonated with the Athenian public. Aristophanes' ability to blend humor with serious critique was a hallmark of his work and an early example of how art can serve as a mirror to society's ills. According to Plato, in his *Republic,* the role of the artist is to imitate life, but Aristophanes went further—he distorted it, exaggerated it, and in doing so, revealed its deeper truths. His satire was a form of resistance, a way of holding a mirror up to the powerful and forcing them to confront their own hypocrisy.

But why does satire, and particularly the satire of Aristophanes, resonate so deeply with us? The answer lies in a fundamental aspect of human psychology—our cognitive dissonance. As psychologist Leon Festinger described in his seminal work *A Theory of Cognitive Dissonance,* humans have an innate tendency to avoid mental discomfort by rejecting or rationalizing information that conflicts with their beliefs. Satire exploits this weakness, forcing us to confront the absurdities and contradictions in our own thinking. In

"Lysistrata," the absurdity of women seizing control of the political situation through a sex strike forces the audience to question the underlying assumptions about gender roles, power, and the justification for war.

The influence of Aristophanes' work can be seen throughout history, as satire has continued to be a powerful tool for social and political commentary. Jonathan Swift, in his famous essay "A Modest Proposal," used satire to highlight the callousness of British policy towards the Irish poor, proposing, with biting irony, that they sell their children as food to the rich. Like Aristophanes, Swift used humor to expose the moral failings of those in power, forcing his readers to confront the inhumanity of their own society.

Another example of the enduring power of satire is George Orwell's *Animal Farm,* a thinly veiled critique of the Russian Revolution and the rise of totalitarianism. Orwell, like Aristophanes, understood that satire could cut through the propaganda and lies of those in power, revealing the truth in a way that direct criticism often cannot. As Orwell himself wrote, "The point is that we are all capable of believing things which we know to be untrue, and then, when we are finally proved wrong, impudently twisting the facts so as to show that we were right. Intellectually, it is possible to carry on this process for an indefinite time: The only check on it is that sooner or later a false belief bumps up against solid reality, usually on a battlefield."

But satire is not just a tool for criticism; it is also a form of catharsis. In a world that often seems beyond our control, laughter is a way of reclaiming our agency, of asserting that, even in the face of absurdity and injustice, we retain the power to mock, to resist, to imagine something better. This is the power of "Lysistrata"—it allows the audience to laugh at the absurdity of war, to see the folly in the actions of their leaders, and, in doing so, to envision a world where peace is possible.

Aristophanes' work has also inspired countless others to use humor as a form of resistance. Consider the case of Charlie Chaplin, whose film "The Great Dictator" was a bold and dangerous satire of Adolf Hitler and the rise of fascism in Europe. At a time when the world was teetering on the brink of war, Chaplin used his platform to ridicule one of the most feared men in history, exposing the absurdity and danger of totalitarianism through humor. As Chaplin later wrote in his autobiography, "I was determined to go ahead, for Hitler must be laughed at." Like Aristophanes, Chaplin understood that laughter could be a weapon, a way of cutting through the fear and propaganda to reveal the truth.

The impact of Aristophanes' work can also be seen in the modern world, where satire continues to be a powerful tool for social and political commentary. Shows like "The Daily Show" and "Last Week Tonight" use humor to critique the news and hold those in power accountable, much like Aristophanes did in ancient Greece. These modern satirists follow in the footsteps of Aristophanes, using comedy to expose the absurdities of the world around them and to encourage their audiences to think critically about the information they are being presented with.

The Renaissance

The Renaissance, that dazzling period when art, science, and humanism began to reshape the Western world, was also a subtle battleground for ideas, particularly when it came to the hallowed halls of the Church. Artists like Leonardo da Vinci and Michelangelo, often revered for their celestial masterpieces, were more than just creators of beauty—they were, in many ways, covert critics of the ecclesiastical orthodoxy of their time.

Leonardo da Vinci's "The Last Supper," completed between 1495 and 1498, is often seen through a lens of religious reverence, but it may well be more than meets the eye. The painting depicts a pivotal moment: Jesus revealing that one of his disciples will betray him. However, da Vinci's inclusion of Judas Iscariot—depicted as reaching for the same bowl as Jesus, a sign of his betrayal—can be interpreted as a critique of the Church's hypocrisy. As the historian Kenneth Clark suggests, "Da Vinci's masterpiece subtly questions the nature of betrayal and loyalty, themes that were just as relevant to the Renaissance viewer as they were to the biblical narrative" (Kenneth Clark, Civilization). The painting's composition, its use of perspective, and the emotional tension captured all contribute to a complex interplay of symbolism that may have subtly undermined the Church's control over interpretation and authority.

Michelangelo's "The Last Judgment," painted on the altar wall of the Sistine Chapel between 1536 and 1541, offers another intriguing example. This monumental fresco is a cacophony of chaos and divine judgment, a stark portrayal of salvation and damnation. What is particularly striking is the figure of Christ, who, as art historian Helen Gardner notes, appears almost indifferent to the fate of the damned, "A reflection of the growing skepticism and the emergent individualism that questioned the Church's omnipotence" (Helen Gardner, Art Through the Ages). The fresco's depiction of the damned—an eclectic mix of mythological and biblical figures—can be read as a commentary on the nature of divine justice and human frailty, subtly challenging the Church's rigid interpretations of salvation.

The Renaissance was also a period of psychological upheaval, wherein the human psyche's vulnerability to manipulation and authority was laid bare. The era's art reflects this vulnerability. Just as da Vinci and Michelangelo embedded critiques within their masterpieces, they were also tapping into a broader questioning of authority that characterized the Renaissance. This questioning was, in part, a reaction to the Church's dogmatic control, which had long stifled intellectual and artistic freedom. As the philosopher Michel de Montaigne observed, "The greatest deception men suffer is from their own self-delusion and the manipulation of those in power" (Montaigne, Essays). The psychological interplay between artist, viewer, and authority is a reminder of how the quest for understanding can be both a personal and collective struggle against dominant ideologies.

Stories of individuals breaking away from such constraints are numerous and varied. One such figure is Martin Luther, whose 95 Theses sparked the Protestant

Reformation, challenging the Church's sale of indulgences and the very nature of ecclesiastical authority. Luther's defiance was not just a personal rebellion but a broader societal shift, illustrating the profound impact of questioning and reinterpreting established norms. In *The Reformation: A History*, Diarmaid MacCulloch writes, "Luther's challenge was as much a psychological battle against the fear of eternal damnation as it was a theological dispute" (Diarmaid MacCulloch, The Reformation: A History). His actions exemplify how individual courage and critical thinking can provoke profound change in the face of established dogma.

In examining Renaissance art and its implicit critiques of the Church, it becomes clear that these works were not mere reflections of contemporary religious sentiment but active dialogues with the Church's power. They tapped into psychological themes of doubt, rebellion, and the quest for personal truth, which were manifesting in various forms across the period. These works, therefore, were more than religious iconography; they were revolutionary statements wrapped in the guise of traditional art forms.

The Renaissance also saw the rise of humanism, a movement that emphasized the value of human experience and rationality. This shift is mirrored in the art of the period, which often celebrated human potential and questioned the rigid doctrines that had previously stifled intellectual exploration. The humanist philosopher Erasmus, for example, argued that "the very foundation of human knowledge is the ability to question and to doubt" (Erasmus, In Praise of Folly). His perspective aligns with the subtler critiques found in Renaissance art, where questioning the status quo was both a form of personal enlightenment and a challenge to the collective power structures of the time.

Art as a Mirror to Society: The Case of Francisco Goya

One of the most glaring examples of art as a mirror to society is the work of Francisco Goya, the Spanish painter and printmaker whose career spanned the late 18th and early 19th centuries. Goya lived through a tumultuous period in Spanish history, marked by the Napoleonic Wars, the Inquisition, and the decline of the Spanish Empire. His art reflects the horrors of these times and serves as a powerful critique of the social and political systems that caused them.

Goya's series of etchings titled "Los Caprichos," published in 1799, is a searing indictment of the corruption, superstition, and hypocrisy he saw around him. The famous etching "The Sleep of Reason Produces Monsters" depicts a man asleep at a desk, surrounded by nightmarish creatures. It is often interpreted as a warning of the dangers of abandoning reason and falling prey to irrational beliefs—a message that resonates as much today as it did in Goya's time.

Later, during the Peninsular War, Goya created another series of etchings titled "The Disasters of War" (1810–1820), which depicted the brutal realities of conflict. Unlike the glorified images of war often produced by official propaganda, Goya's work presented the suffering, death, and destruction in stark, unflinching detail. His art was a powerful form of resistance, challenging the romanticized narratives of war and exposing the human cost of imperial ambition.

Music as a Weapon: The Power of Protest Songs

Music has long been a powerful catalyst for social change, acting as a sonic protest against the injustices and delusions perpetuated by oppressive systems. In the 20th century, the role of protest songs as instruments of political and social upheaval cannot be overstated.

Billie Holiday's "Strange Fruit," recorded in 1939, remains one of the most poignant examples of how music can confront societal horrors. The song, written by Abel Meeropol, a Jewish schoolteacher from the Bronx, was a lyrical indictment of the lynchings that plagued the American South. Meeropol's composition and Holiday's soulful delivery combined to create a potent protest against the systemic racism that underpinned American society.

The psychological impact of "Strange Fruit" was profound, as it bypassed rational defenses and appealed directly to the emotional core of its listeners. The discomfort and outrage elicited by the song served to confront the willful blindness that allowed such violence to persist. The song's haunting melody and stark lyrics challenged listeners to confront their own complicity in perpetuating racial injustices, thereby revealing a collective psychological weakness: the tendency to deny uncomfortable truths.

In the 1960s, music became an integral part of the struggle for civil rights and anti-war protests. Bob Dylan's "Blowin' in the Wind" (1962) and "The Times They Are a-Changin'" (1964) emerged as anthems for a generation questioning authority and demanding change. Dylan's songs were not mere reflections of the times but active agents of social transformation. These songs became emblematic of the civil rights movement, inspiring and uniting activists across the globe in their quest for equality and justice.

In South Africa, the fight against apartheid was similarly fueled by music, which served as both a form of resistance and a means of raising international awareness. Hugh Masekela's "Bring Him Back Home" (1968) became a rallying cry for the movement to free Nelson Mandela, reflecting the deep yearning for liberation from an oppressive regime. Miriam Makeba's "Soweto Blues" (1977) memorialized the 1976 Soweto Uprising, a tragic event in which police violence against protesting students highlighted the brutality of apartheid. As the political analyst and writer South African Steven Biko famously said, "The most potent weapon in the hands of the oppressor is the mind of the oppressed" (Steven Biko, I Write What I Like). Music, in this context, was not just a form of artistic expression but a weapon of psychological resistance, combating the pervasive delusion of racial superiority and systemic oppression.

The psychological dimension of music as protest is crucial. Music's capacity to convey complex emotions and ideas in an accessible form can dismantle psychological defenses that maintain societal delusions. Stories of individuals who have used music to challenge and dismantle oppressive systems abound.

Consider the case of the band Rage Against the Machine, whose 1990s activism and politically charged lyrics provided a soundtrack to the anti-globalization and anti-corporate movements. Their music was not just a form of artistic rebellion but a direct challenge to the economic and political structures they critiqued.

Music's role in social movements demonstrates how the arts can engage with and address deep-seated psychological and societal issues. By challenging the status quo and confronting oppressive systems, music not only provides a voice for the marginalized but also serves as a mirror reflecting the uncomfortable truths that society might prefer to ignore. As the poet and musician Gil Scott-Heron observed, "The revolution will not be televised; it will be live" (Gil Scott-Heron, The Revolution Will Not Be Televised). In this sense, protest music becomes a living, breathing embodiment of resistance, an ever-present reminder of the power of art to inspire, unite, and effect change.

The Birth of Rap: A New Voice for the Marginalized

Rap music, with its rhythmic and poetic style, was born in the Bronx during the 1970s—a period marked by economic decline, rising crime rates, and a city grappling with neglect and decay. This new genre emerged from block parties, where DJs would loop breakbeats and MCs would rap over them, turning the microphone into a tool of storytelling and social commentary. For the black and Latino youth of the Bronx, rap was more than just a new musical style; it was a form of expression that articulated their frustrations and aspirations in a world that had largely marginalized them.

Rap quickly evolved into a powerful cultural movement, challenging the status quo and giving a voice to those who had been silenced by mainstream society. As Tricia Rose points out in her seminal work *Black Noise: Rap Music and Black Culture in Contemporary America,* "Rap music is a black cultural expression that prioritizes black voices from the margins of urban America. These voices, in turn, critique the dominant notions of identity, race, and power."

Rap as a Mirror to Social Reality: The Case of "The Message"

One of the earliest and most influential examples of rap's role as a social commentator is Grandmaster Flash and the Furious Five's 1982 hit "The Message." This track was a departure from the party anthems that characterized early rap music. Instead, it offered a stark portrayal of life in the inner city, with lyrics that spoke to the frustration and despair felt by many black Americans. The refrain, "It's like a jungle sometimes, it makes me wonder how I keep from going under," encapsulated the daily struggle for survival in neighborhoods ravaged by poverty, drugs, and violence.

"The Message" was groundbreaking in its directness, using vivid imagery to highlight the harsh realities faced by black communities. It addressed issues such as unemployment, crime, and the lack of opportunities, making it one of the first rap songs to focus explicitly on social issues. As Rose argues, "The Message' transformed rap music by providing a blueprint for how the genre could be used to articulate the lived experiences of black Americans in a manner that was both political and poetic."

Gangsta Rap: The Unfiltered Truth of Urban Life

As rap continued to evolve, the late 1980s and early 1990s saw the rise of gangsta rap, a subgenre that further pushed the boundaries of social commentary. Gangsta rap was characterized by its raw, unfiltered depiction of life in America's ghettos, where violence, drugs, and systemic oppression were everyday realities. Artists like N.W.A, Ice-T, and Tupac Shakur used their music to expose the conditions in black neighborhoods, often provoking controversy for their explicit lyrics and confrontational style.

N.W. A's 1988 album Straight Outta Compton is a seminal example of gangsta rap's power to challenge authority and highlight social injustices. The album's most infamous track, "F*** tha Police," was a searing indictment of police brutality and racial profiling, issues that were rampant in black communities. The song's lyrics— "They have the authority to kill a minority"— resonated deeply with listeners who had experienced such brutality firsthand. While the track was condemned by law enforcement and banned from many radio stations, it also sparked important conversations about police violence and systemic racism.

Tupac Shakur, one of the most iconic figures in rap, used his music to explore the complex realities of black life in

America. Songs like "Brenda's Got a Baby" and "Keep Ya Head Up" addressed issues such as teenage pregnancy, poverty, and misogyny, highlighting the struggles faced by black women in particular. Shakur's lyrics were often deeply personal, reflecting his own experiences with poverty and violence. As Jeff Chang notes in Can't Stop Won't Stop: A History of the Hip-Hop Generation, "Tupac's music was a reflection of his own life, but it was also a reflection of the broader black experience in America—a life marked by pain, struggle, and a relentless fight for dignity."

The Cultural and Political Impact of Rap

Rap music's ability to rebel against established norms and fight oppression is not limited to its lyrical content. The very existence of rap as a dominant musical genre represents a defiance of traditional music industry standards. Rap challenged the dominance of rock and pop, genres that had historically been dominated by white artists and audiences. It brought the voices of black youth to the forefront of popular culture, forcing mainstream society to confront issues that it had long ignored.

Furthermore, rap's influence extends beyond music; it has become a cultural and political force that has inspired movements for social justice around the world. The Black Lives Matter movement, for example, has drawn heavily on the themes and rhetoric of rap music to articulate its demands for racial justice and police reform. Songs like Kendrick Lamar's "Alright" have become anthems for the movement, with lyrics that speak to the resilience and hope of black communities in the face of systemic oppression.

Visual Arts and Political Change: From Guernica to Banksy

Visual art has long served as a dynamic medium for political expression, often pushing boundaries and challenging the status quo. From Pablo Picasso's harrowing "Guernica" to Banksy's subversive street art, artists have used their craft to voice dissent, critique political systems, and inspire change. This tradition of using art to engage with political and social issues extends globally, with each era and region reflecting its unique struggles and aspirations through its artistic expression.

Pablo Picasso's "Guernica," painted in 1937, is a quintessential example of art as political protest. This monumental mural was Picasso's response to the bombing of the Basque town of Guernica during the Spanish Civil War, and it vividly captures the horrors of warfare and the suffering inflicted on civilians. The mural's distorted figures, agonized expressions, and stark monochrome palette serve as a powerful condemnation of the brutality of conflict and a critique of the fascist forces responsible. Art historian Robert Hughes describes "Guernica" as "not merely a painting but an urgent plea for the end of violence, a visual manifesto of anguish and resistance" (Robert Hughes, The Shock of the New). The painting's global impact was immediate, transforming into a universal symbol of anti-war sentiment and a rallying cry for those opposed to fascism.

Similarly, street art has emerged as a potent and accessible form of protest in the modern era, with artists like Banksy leading the charge. Banksy, the enigmatic British street artist, has used his work to challenge societal norms and critique political systems through satirical humor and provocative imagery. His art often appears in public spaces, where it disrupts the everyday flow of life and engages directly with viewers. Banksy's "Balloon Girl," painted in London in 2002, depicts a young girl reaching out for a heart-shaped balloon, an image interpreted as a poignant commentary on lost innocence and hope amid societal conflicts. The artwork's popularity, evidenced by its recognition as the UK's favorite artwork in a 2014 poll, underscores the profound effect street art can have on public consciousness.

Globally, the tradition of using visual art as a tool for political change can be seen in various forms. In the United States, the Harlem Renaissance of the 1920s and 1930s saw African American artists like Jacob Lawrence and Aaron Douglas use their work to challenge racial injustice and celebrate Black identity. Lawrence's "Migration Series," which chronicles the migration of African Americans from the rural South to the urban North, vividly depicts the struggles and aspirations of a community seeking greater freedom and equality. The series was described by art historian Jeanetta Cochrane as "a powerful visual narrative that not only documents but also critiques the systemic racism that plagued American society" (Jeanetta Cochrane, The Harlem Renaissance and Its Legacy).

In Latin America, the Mexican Muralism movement, spearheaded by artists Diego Rivera, David Alfaro Siqueiros, and José Clemente Orozco, used large-scale murals to address social and political issues. Rivera's murals in the National Preparatory School in Mexico City, for instance, depict the struggles of the working class and the impact of imperialism. His work, as noted by art critic Octavio Paz, was "an unflinching portrayal of the historical struggles and social inequities that defined Mexican society" (Octavio Paz, The Labyrinth of Solitude). These murals were instrumental in shaping public discourse and rallying support for revolutionary causes.

In the Middle East, visual art has also played a significant role in political resistance. In Iran, the 1979 Islamic Revolution saw the rise of politically charged street art and graffiti as a means of challenging the Pahlavi regime. Artists like Shirin Neshat have used their work to address issues of gender, identity, and political repression. Neshat's "Women of Allah" series, which juxtaposes images of women in traditional Islamic attire with powerful, often contradictory symbols, critiques the complex interplay between religion, politics, and gender in contemporary Iran. As Neshat has remarked, "Art is a way to make visible the invisible, to give voice to those who have been silenced" (Shirin Neshat, Art and Identity).

In South Africa, the struggle against apartheid was vividly captured through the work of artists like William Kentridge. Kentridge's animations and drawings, such as those in "Drawings for Projection," address the pervasive impact of apartheid and the complexities of post-apartheid reconciliation. His work has been described by cultural critic Mark Gevisser as "a poignant and unsettling exploration of the ways in which personal and political histories intersect and shape one another" (Mark Gevisser, Lost and Found in Johannesburg). Kentridge's art serves as a powerful reflection of the nation's ongoing struggle with its past and its search for a more equitable future.

The stories of artists who have used their work to challenge oppressive systems are as varied as they are inspiring. Consider the case of Ai Weiwei, whose activism and art have consistently challenged the Chinese government's policies on censorship and human rights. Ai's installation "Sunflower Seeds," featuring millions of handcrafted porcelain seeds, critiques not only the homogenization of Chinese society but also broader global issues of consumerism and production.

Similarly, the Cuban artist Tania Bruguera has used her performance art to engage with themes of freedom and censorship, creating works that confront the political realities of her home country. Her piece "Tatlin's Whisper #6," which involved creating a space for free speech that was subsequently shut down by authorities, demonstrates the ways in which art can serve as a form of political intervention.

Visual art, from Picasso's "Guernica" to Banksy's "Balloon Girl," serves as a powerful medium for political commentary and protest. By tapping into psychological vulnerabilities and challenging dominant ideologies, art continues to play a crucial role in advocating for change and confronting the deceptions of oppressive systems.

Literature as Liberation: The Impact of Books and Writers

Literature has often served as a mirror reflecting society's flaws, a tool for social critique, and a catalyst for political change. This transformative power of written words has shaped and inspired movements across the globe. From George Orwell's stark dystopian visions to Aleksandr Solzhenitsyn's harrowing accounts of political repression, literature has consistently challenged entrenched systems and inspired calls for justice. Its influence is profound, spanning various cultures and epochs, demonstrating the unique ability of books to illuminate truths and provoke societal introspection.

George Orwell's *1984* (1949) remains a seminal work in the annals of political literature, offering a chilling portrayal of a totalitarian regime where individual freedom is obliterated by pervasive surveillance and thought control. Orwell, writing under the shadow of post-World War II anxieties and the rise of Soviet communism, crafted a narrative that resonates far beyond its historical context. The novel's impact is enduring, often invoked in discussions about modern surveillance, censorship, and authoritarianism, and its themes have permeated cultural and political debates worldwide.

In parallel, Aleksandr Solzhenitsyn's *The Gulag Archipelago* (1973) provided a damning expose of Soviet labor camps, meticulously detailing the grim reality of life under Stalin's regime. The book's unflinching account of political persecution and the dehumanizing effects of the gulag system contributed significantly to international condemnation of Soviet practices and played a role in the broader discourse on human rights. *The Gulag Archipelago* became a vital piece of evidence in the global discourse on totalitarianism and inspired a wave of solidarity with those fighting against oppressive regimes.

Literature has served as a potent force for social change. In Latin America, Gabriel García Márquez's *One Hundred Years of Solitude* (1967) challenged political and social injustices through its magical realist narrative. Márquez's depiction of the fictional town of Macondo serves as an allegory for the tumultuous history of Colombia and Latin America at large. As literary scholar and García Márquez biographer Gerald Martin points out, "Márquez's novel not only captured the political and social upheavals of his time but also offered a profound critique of the cyclical nature of history and power in Latin America" (Gerald Martin, Gabriel García Márquez: A Life). The novel's impact extended beyond literary circles, influencing political thought and cultural identity throughout the region.

In South Africa, the anti-apartheid movement found a significant voice in the works of Nadine Gordimer. Her novel *Burger's Daughter* (1979) provided a nuanced portrayal of the complexities of resistance against apartheid. Gordimer's writing offered a critical perspective on the struggle for liberation, highlighting the personal sacrifices and moral dilemmas faced by activists. Her contributions were instrumental in raising international awareness about the injustices of apartheid and garnering support for the anti-apartheid cause.

In Japan, Yoko Ogawa's *The Housekeeper and the Professor* (2003) provides a subtle yet profound critique of societal norms and personal relationships. While the novel's primary focus is on the unique bond between a housekeeper and a mathematics professor, it subtly addresses issues of societal expectations and personal identity. Ogawa's work reflects the complexities of modern Japanese society and the challenges faced by individuals in navigating traditional expectations.

The impact of literature on societal change is not confined to any single genre or style. For instance, the speculative fiction of Margaret Atwood in *The Handmaid's Tale* (1985) provides a dystopian vision of a future where women's rights are systematically stripped away. Atwood's narrative serves as a stark warning about the dangers of religious extremism and the erosion of gender equality.

The stories of writers who have used their work to break away from the past are as varied as they are impactful. Consider the story of Salman Rushdie, whose novel *The Satanic Verses* (1988) led to significant political and cultural upheaval, including fatwas and threats to his life. Rushdie's defiant stance in the face of censorship and violence underscores the risks that writers face in challenging dominant ideologies and the broader implications of their work for freedom of expression.

Literature, therefore, continues to be a powerful tool for challenging authority and questioning societal delusions.

From Orwell's stark dystopian visions to Roy's poignant critiques of social norms, writers have consistently used their craft to illuminate truths and inspire change. Through their exploration of human psychology and societal structures, these authors demonstrate the enduring impact of literature in shaping and challenging the world.

The Evolution of Cultural Expression: New Mediums, New Voices

The 21st century has witnessed a revolutionary transformation in the way cultural expression challenges societal illusions, driven by the rapid evolution of digital mediums. As we navigate this digital landscape, it's clear that new technologies are not just expanding the reach of art and activism but also reshaping how these forms engage with truth and perception. From social media's democratizing force to the immersive realms of virtual and augmented reality, the evolution of cultural expression reflects both the possibilities and the complexities of our modern world.

Social media platforms such as Twitter, Instagram, and Tik Tok have become arenas where cultural expression is not merely broadcast but actively engaged with. This democratization has amplified voices that were historically marginalized or suppressed. For instance, the #MeToo movement, which gained momentum through social media, revealed the widespread nature of sexual harassment and assault, giving a platform to countless individuals who had previously been voiceless.

A particularly poignant example of this is the role of social media in the Arab Spring, which utilized platforms like Facebook and Twitter to mobilize protests and challenge authoritarian regimes. The spontaneous and decentralized nature of these movements was greatly facilitated by the immediate and far-reaching capabilities of social media, illustrating how technology can expedite and amplify social and political change.

Digital art, too, has pushed the boundaries of traditional media, creating new ways to engage with and challenge perceptions of reality. Virtual Reality (VR) and Augmented Reality (AR) are at the forefront of this transformation, offering immersive experiences that invite users to confront complex and often uncomfortable truths. For instance, "The Enemy," a VR project by photojournalist Karim Ben Khelifa, allows users to engage with combatants from conflict zones, providing an intimate look at their experiences and perspectives. This project exemplifies how VR can bridge the gap between distant conflicts and personal understanding, challenging viewers to grapple with the human cost of war in a deeply engaging manner.

The global reach of these new mediums is further exemplified by artists like Hito Steyerl, whose work often addresses the intersection of technology, politics, and society. In her video installation "How Not to Be Seen: A Fucking Didactic Educational .MOV File" (2013), Steyerl explores themes of surveillance and digital visibility through a satirical and self-reflexive lens. Steyerl's work underscores the ways in which digital technologies shape our perceptions of reality and challenge traditional notions of visibility and invisibility.

Similarly, in the realm of augmented reality, the artist and technologist Jeff Koons has employed AR to create interactive art experiences that challenge conventional boundaries of perception. His installation "Bouquet of Tulips" (2019), which utilizes AR to transform public spaces, prompts viewers to question their relationship with both the physical and digital worlds. Koons's work highlights how AR can expand the possibilities of artistic engagement and challenge viewers to reconsider their interaction with art and reality.

The rise of these new mediums also brings to light the psychological vulnerabilities that can influence and complicate our engagement with art and activism. The immersive nature of VR and AR, while powerful, can also lead to a form of "virtual empathy," where the intensity of the experience might obscure the complexities of the issues being represented. This phenomenon can create a deceptive sense of understanding or engagement without addressing the underlying realities.

Moreover, the rapid dissemination of information on social media can sometimes lead to a phenomenon known as "information overload," where the sheer volume of content makes it difficult to discern credible sources from misleading ones. This can contribute to the spread of misinformation and create a distorted perception of social and political issues.

As we continue to explore these evolving forms of expression, it is crucial to remain vigilant about the potential pitfalls and to harness these tools in ways that truly advance understanding and foster meaningful change.

Future Generations and the Power of Art: A New Era of Liberation

The future promises an exhilarating evolution in how art and culture challenge societal illusions and pursue liberation. As we stride further into the 21st century, it's evident that future generations are poised to utilize art not merely as a form of expression but as a potent tool for instigating change. The fusion of technology with artistic and cultural endeavors is setting the stage for a new era of activism and innovation.

Digital art is breaking new ground in how we think about and respond to issues. In Hong Kong, the pro-democracy protests were not just marked by physical demonstrations but also by a vibrant display of digital art and symbols. Protesters used augmented reality (AR) to create interactive, virtual murals and sculptures that critiqued authoritarianism and inspired solidarity. This merging of art and technology offered a way to circumvent censorship while amplifying their messages. For example, AR installations displayed animated scenes of protest and resistance that could be viewed through smartphones, creating a layer of engagement that traditional media struggled to match.

Blockchain technology is also making waves in the art world, promising to revolutionize how intellectual property is protected and how art is distributed. Cryptocurrencies and NFTs (non-fungible tokens) are being explored to ensure that artists receive fair compensation and that their work remains authentic and untampered with. One notable instance is the collaboration between artist Beeple and the NFT platform Foundation. Beeple's digital collage, "Every day's: The First 5000 Days," sold for a staggering $69 million, underscoring how blockchain can create new revenue streams and ownership models in the art world.

Further afield, the intersection of art and social justice continues to evolve in fascinating ways. In India, street art has become a powerful form of protest and social commentary. The Delhi-based artist Baadal Nanjundaswamy has gained acclaim for his politically charged murals that address issues from climate change to corruption. His work often uses humor and satire to critique societal problems, such as his mural depicting a giant cockroach (a symbol of corruption) scuttling across a luxury apartment building. Nanjundaswamy's approach highlights how street art can challenge norms and spark conversation in a visually arresting way.

These developments are not without their psychological implications. The increasing immersion in digital and virtual worlds can sometimes create a false sense of participation and engagement, leading to what might be called "activist fatigue." While technology provides new tools for expression, it can also lead to an oversaturation of information, where the sheer volume of content dilutes its impact.

Moreover, the rapid pace of digital change can foster a phenomenon known as "technological determinism," where technology is seen as the sole driver of societal progress. This view can obscure the complexities of human psychology and social dynamics that influence how art is perceived and acted upon. This blurring can lead to a deceptive sense of engagement and progress, where the spectacle of digital activism overshadows tangible, real-world impact.

Future generations will undoubtedly continue to push the boundaries of art and activism, leveraging these tools in ways that can both inspire and complicate our understanding of truth and change. The evolving landscape of cultural expression thus represents both an exhilarating frontier and a field requiring careful navigation.

In the hands of future generations, these powerful catalysts for change will undoubtedly lead to new and exciting forms of expression, helping to create a world where truth and liberation are not just ideals, but realities.

Chapter 10

Navigating the New Age of Threats and Transformation

Civilizations rise, flourish, and sometimes crumble like ancient statues worn by time. Our 21st-century global civilization, intricate and interconnected, teeters on the precipice of unprecedented change. In this era of unparalleled technological advancements, we are simultaneously besieged by existential threats that challenge the very essence of human survival. Climate change ravages our planet, nationalism stokes division, the specter of nuclear war looms large, and bioengineered pandemics threaten to unleash devastation. These perils, compounded by the erosion of our attention spans and the depletion of vital resources, demand a profound shift in our collective consciousness. Humanity stands at a crossroads, facing the dire consequences of our past actions and the urgent need to manage these agents of change for a better future. To overcome these existential perils, we must break free from the chains of ignorance and fear that have bound us for too long, forging a new path defined by resilience, compassion, and audacity. The alternative is clear: adapt or perish.

As the twenty-first century progresses, humanity finds itself besieged by a multitude of challenges that threaten our very existence. These forces, while diverse in their nature and impact, share a common thread: they demand a radical shift in human thinking. The unyielding fury of climate change, the seductive allure of right-wing nationalism, the looming specter of geopolitical wars, and more—all these agents of change force us to reconsider our path. Will we rise to the occasion, or will we succumb to the forces that seek to unravel our world?

Climate Change

The story of climate change is not just a narrative of environmental decline; it is a tale of human resilience, innovation, and, at times, sheer audacity. While the scientific consensus has warned of the dire consequences of unchecked emissions, the world is still grappling with how to effectively address this global crisis. In every corner of the globe, however, there are stories of individuals and communities who are pushing back against the tide of environmental degradation, challenging the status quo, and redefining what is possible in the fight against climate change.

Take, for instance, the island nation of Fiji, which, despite being one of the countries that are most vulnerable to climate change, has emerged as a leader in global climate advocacy. In 2017, Fiji became the first small island state to preside over the United Nations Climate Change Conference (COP23), where it championed the cause of vulnerable nations and pushed for more ambitious global climate action. Fiji's Prime Minister, Frank Bainimarama, coined the term "Talanoa Dialogue," a Pacific tradition of inclusive, participatory, and transparent dialogue, to describe the approach needed to tackle climate change. This approach emphasizes empathy and collective action, underscoring the idea that climate change is not just a scientific or political issue but a deeply human one.

Moving from the Pacific Islands to the African continent, we find another powerful story of climate action in the Great Green Wall initiative. This ambitious project aims to combat desertification and land degradation across the Sahel region by planting a mosaic of trees, vegetation, and green spaces spanning 8,000 kilometers from Senegal in the west to Djibouti in the east. The Great Green Wall is not just about reforestation; it is a bold attempt to restore ecosystems, create jobs, and enhance food security for millions of people living in one of the most climate-affected regions on Earth. The initiative has already had a significant impact, with millions of hectares of degraded land restored, and it serves as a testament to what can be achieved when communities come together to address the challenges posed by climate change.

While these stories inspire hope, they also highlight the psychological barriers that continue to hinder meaningful action. One of the most pernicious of these barriers is the "normalcy bias," a cognitive bias that leads people to underestimate the possibility and impact of a disaster. This bias is particularly relevant in the context of climate change, where the gradual nature of environmental degradation can lull societies into a false sense of security. The normalcy bias is compounded by the "optimism bias," where individuals believe that they are less likely than others to experience the negative impacts of climate change. These psychological tendencies are often exploited by those with vested interests in maintaining the status quo, leading to widespread denialism and apathy.

However, history has shown that when confronted with undeniable truths, people can overcome these biases and take bold action. A compelling example of this can be found in the story of the Ozone Hole crisis of the 1980s. When scientists discovered that chlorofluorocarbons (CFCs) were depleting the ozone layer, there was initially widespread skepticism and resistance, particularly from the chemical industry. Yet, the evidence became too overwhelming to ignore, and in 1987, the world came together to sign the Montreal Protocol, an international treaty to phase out the production and use of CFCs. The success of the Montreal Protocol, which has led to the gradual recovery of the ozone layer, is a powerful reminder that collective action, driven by scientific evidence and public awareness, can avert environmental catastrophe.

In the realm of individual action, few have made as significant an impact as Wangari Maathai, the Kenyan environmental activist and Nobel Peace Prize laureate. In 1977, Maathai founded the Green Belt Movement, a grassroots organization that focused on tree planting, environmental conservation, and women's rights. Through her tireless efforts, Maathai mobilized thousands of women to plant over 51 million trees across Kenya, helping to combat deforestation, restore ecosystems, and empower rural communities. Her work not only transformed the landscape of Kenya but also inspired environmental movements around the world, demonstrating the power of individual initiative in the fight against climate change.

Maathai's story, like those of many other climate activists, underscores the importance of addressing the psychological roots of inaction. Cognitive dissonance, the mental discomfort experienced when holding two or more contradictory beliefs, is a common response to the realities of climate change. People often find themselves caught between the desire to protect the environment and the convenience of unsustainable practices. Maathai's approach was to bridge this gap by making environmental conservation a matter of personal and communal identity, thereby aligning people's actions with their values.

As we look to the future, it is clear that the battle against climate change will require not just technological innovation and political will but also a profound shift in human consciousness. The rise of the youth climate movement, spearheaded by figures like Greta Thunberg, is a testament to the growing awareness and urgency among younger generations. These young activists are not only demanding action from world leaders but are also challenging the deep-seated psychological and cultural norms that have contributed to the climate crisis.

One striking example of this is the Sunrise Movement in the United States, a youth-led organization that advocates for a Green New Deal to address climate change and economic inequality. The Sunrise Movement has successfully mobilized thousands of young people to participate in direct actions, lobbying, and public demonstrations, pushing climate change to the forefront of the national political agenda. Their efforts have highlighted the intersectionality of climate justice, emphasizing that the fight against climate change is also a fight for racial, economic, and social justice.

In Europe, the Extinction Rebellion (XR) movement has taken a more radical approach, using nonviolent civil disobedience to force governments to take decisive action on climate change. XR's tactics, which include mass protests, roadblocks, and even the occupation of government buildings, have garnered significant media attention and sparked debates about the effectiveness of direct action in the face of a global crisis. The movement's emphasis on "telling the truth" about the severity of the climate emergency has resonated with many, leading to the declaration of climate emergencies by numerous local and national governments.

These movements, and the broader shift in public consciousness they represent, are critical in overcoming the psychological barriers to climate action. The "tragedy of the commons," a concept popularized by ecologist Garrett Hardin, describes the phenomenon where individuals, acting in their self-interest, deplete shared resources to the detriment of the whole community. Climate change is the ultimate tragedy of the commons, where the atmosphere, oceans, and forests are being exploited with little regard for the collective consequences. Overcoming this requires a radical rethinking of how we relate to the planet and to each other, moving from a mindset of exploitation to one of stewardship.

In exploring the psychology of climate inaction, it is impossible to ignore the role of misinformation and deliberate deception. The fossil fuel industry, in particular, has played a significant role in sowing doubt about the science of climate change, using tactics reminiscent of the tobacco industry's denial of the health risks of smoking.

The challenge of climate change is not just a scientific or technological one; it is a deeply human one that requires us to confront our psychological weaknesses, challenge entrenched interests, and reimagine our relationship with the natural world. The stories of those who have made a difference, from grassroots activists to global movements, offer a blueprint for how we can rise to this challenge.

Right-Wing Nationalism: The Siren's Call

The resurgence of right-wing nationalism in recent years is not just a fleeting political trend but a haunting echo from the past—a siren's call that has seduced societies into the dangerous waters of authoritarianism, xenophobia, and exclusionary politics. This ideology, which promises to restore a glorified past, often does so by scapegoating the "other" and glorifying a homogenous national identity. While it may seem like a modern phenomenon, the seeds of this ideology have been sown throughout history, flourishing in times of uncertainty, fear, and economic distress. The existential threat posed by right-wing nationalism is not new; it has plagued both the past and present, and its shadow looms large over the future.

The allure of right-wing nationalism lies in its simplicity. It offers clear, albeit simplistic, answers to complex problems. In a rapidly globalizing world where borders are increasingly porous and identities more fluid, the idea of returning to a "pure" and "unadulterated" past appeals to many. Yet, as George Orwell astutely noted, "Nationalism is power-hunger tempered by self-deception." This self-deception is perhaps the most dangerous aspect of right-wing nationalism, as it blinds societies to the true cost of exclusionary policies and the erosion of democratic values.

One of the most chilling examples of right-wing nationalism's resurgence can be found in the heart of Europe. Hungary, under Viktor Orbán's leadership, has become a laboratory for illiberal democracy. Orbán, who once championed democratic reforms in the post-Soviet era, has since transformed Hungary into a quasi-autocratic state. His government has curtailed press freedoms, weakened the judiciary, and enacted laws that explicitly target immigrants, LGBTQ+ individuals, and political opponents. In his quest to create an "illiberal state," Orbán has invoked the rhetoric of nationalism, presenting himself as the protector of Hungarian identity against the so-called dangers of multiculturalism and immigration. His strategy has not only solidified his grip on power but has also inspired a wave of right-wing movements across Europe, each echoing the call for a return to a mythical past.

Beyond Europe, right-wing nationalism has taken root in the Americas. Brazil, under Jair Bolsonaro, witnessed a dramatic shift towards authoritarianism, with Bolsonaro often referred to as the "Trump of the Tropics." His administration was marked by a blatant disregard for democratic norms, environmental protections, and human rights. Bolsonaro's rhetoric, deeply nationalistic and often tinged with racism and homophobia, resonated with a significant portion of the Brazilian population disillusioned by corruption scandals and economic stagnation. He portrayed himself as the savior of Brazil, a strongman who would restore order and national pride. The consequences were severe: under Bolsonaro, the Amazon rainforest faced unprecedented destruction, indigenous rights were trampled, and the COVID-19 pandemic was catastrophically mismanaged. His brand of right-wing nationalism, like Orbán's, thrived on fear and division, promising security at the cost of freedom.

The United States, once a beacon of democracy, was not immune to the allure of right-wing nationalism. The election of Donald Trump in 2016 marked a significant shift in American politics, with Trump espousing a brand of nationalism that was overtly exclusionary and xenophobic. His campaign's slogan, "Make America Great Again," was a masterstroke of nationalist rhetoric, invoking a nostalgic vision of an America that never truly existed. Trump's presidency was characterized by policies that targeted immigrants, sowed division, and undermined democratic institutions. His refusal to accept the results of the 2020 election and the subsequent insurrection on January 6th, 2021, underscored the dangers of a leader who prioritizes personal power over democratic principles.

The psychological underpinnings of right-wing nationalism are deeply rooted in human nature. Social identity theory suggests that people derive part of their self-esteem from their group memberships, leading them to favor their in-groups and view out-groups with suspicion or hostility. Nationalist leaders exploit this psychological tendency by portraying their nations as besieged fortresses, under threat from foreign influences, immigrants, or ideological enemies. This binary worldview, where the "us" is pitted against the "them," discourages critical thinking and fosters intolerance. It is a classic example of how psychological weaknesses can lead to societal deception, trapping people in prisons of delusion.

Yet, history also offers hope that these prisons can be broken. Nelson Mandela's fight against apartheid in South Africa stands as a powerful testament to the possibility of overcoming nationalist and racist ideologies. Mandela, who spent 27 years in prison for his opposition to apartheid, emerged not as a man consumed by hatred, but as a leader committed to reconciliation. His vision of a "Rainbow Nation," where people of all races could live together in harmony, was a direct challenge to the divisive nationalist rhetoric of his time. Mandela's autobiography, Long Walk to Freedom, captures the essence of his struggle and his unwavering belief in the power of inclusive, democratic ideals. His legacy continues to inspire those who resist the siren call of nationalism, reminding us that the future need not be a repetition of the past.

As we look to the future, the question remains: will the next generation succumb to the same nationalist delusions, or will they find a way to break free? The rise of digital technology and social media has created new battlegrounds for nationalist ideologies. On the one hand, these platforms have enabled the rapid spread of disinformation and nationalist propaganda, fueling division and hatred. On the other hand, they have also provided tools for activists to organize, educate, and resist. The future of nationalism may well be determined by who masters these tools and how they are used.

In some ways, the existential threat posed by right-wing nationalism may become more acute in the future. Climate change, economic inequality, and the pressures of globalization are likely to create conditions that nationalist leaders can exploit. However, there is also reason for cautious optimism. The younger generation, often referred to as digital natives, is more connected and more aware of global issues than any generation before them. They have grown up in a world where diversity is the norm, and they are less likely to buy into exclusionary nationalist narratives.

Moreover, the global nature of many of the challenges we face—from climate change to pandemics—requires international cooperation and collective action. The very problems that nationalist leaders decry as threats to sovereignty may ultimately be what forces nations to work together. If the past and present have taught us anything, it is that the future will be shaped by those who are willing to challenge the status quo, who refuse to be imprisoned by the delusions of nationalism.

Right wing nationalism remains a powerful and dangerous force, one that has deep roots in human psychology and history. However, history also shows that it can be resisted, and the future offers both challenges and opportunities in this regard. Whether the next generation will continue to be seduced by the siren's call or will chart a new course remains to be seen. What is certain is that the struggle between nationalism and inclusive, democratic ideals will be one of the defining battles of our time—and the stakes could not be higher.

Geopolitical Wars and Nuclear Shadows

The geopolitical stage has always been a theater of power struggles, with nations jockeying for supremacy through both overt conflict and subtle diplomacy. Yet, in the shadow of nuclear weapons, these contests have taken on a new, terrifying dimension. The existential threat posed by nuclear warfare has loomed large since the mid-20th century, a specter that has haunted the past, stalked the present, and threatened to shape a bleak future. This ever-present danger raises the question: Are we on a path to inevitable destruction, or can humanity break free from this prison of delusion?

The Cold War may have officially ended with the dissolution of the Soviet Union in 1991, but the nuclear arsenals it spawned remain, a chilling reminder that the capacity for global annihilation is just a button-push away. The doctrine of Mutual Assured Destruction (MAD) has kept this apocalyptic potential in check, operating on the assumption that no rational actor would dare initiate a conflict that would result in their own destruction. Yet, the history of human conflict is littered with irrational decisions made under pressure, decisions that could easily spell disaster in the nuclear age.

Take, for instance, the incident of 1983, when the world came perilously close to nuclear war due to a simple computer error. On September 26th of that year, Soviet lieutenant colonel Stanislav Petrov was on duty at a nuclear early-warning station when the system reported an incoming missile strike from the United States. The logical, protocol-driven response would have been to launch a retaliatory strike, effectively starting World War III. But Petrov hesitated. Despite the overwhelming pressure, he decided the alarm was a false one—an error in the system. His decision, later confirmed as correct, likely saved millions of lives. Petrov's story, documented in David Hoffman's The Dead Hand, is a testament to how a single, cool-headed individual can prevent catastrophe, even in the midst of geopolitical chaos.

The Cuban Missile Crisis of 1962 remains one of the most studied examples of how close the world has come to nuclear war. For thirteen tense days in October, the United States and the Soviet Union teetered on the brink of disaster. The crisis began when American reconnaissance flights revealed Soviet nuclear missiles stationed in Cuba, just 90 miles from the U.S. mainland. The discovery triggered a standoff that saw both superpowers prepared to unleash their full nuclear arsenals. However, the crisis was averted not by military might but by careful diplomacy. President John F. Kennedy and Premier Nikita Khrushchev, despite the immense pressure from their respective governments and military establishments, chose to pursue a diplomatic resolution. Their negotiations, as recounted in Graham Allison's Essence of Decision, pulled the world back from the brink of annihilation and highlighted the critical importance of dialogue in defusing nuclear tensions.

The lessons of the Cuban Missile Crisis seem clear: diplomacy, dialogue, and a willingness to compromise are essential in preventing nuclear catastrophe. Yet, these lessons are often ignored in the current geopolitical climate, where the pursuit of military superiority and national pride frequently overrides common sense. The ongoing rivalry between the United States and China, the nuclear ambitions of North Korea, and the fragile state of arms control agreements all suggest that the world remains dangerously close to another nuclear standoff.

The current era of geopolitical conflict is not just about traditional warfare but also involves economic struggles, cyber-attacks, and disinformation campaigns. The rise of cyber warfare has added a new layer of complexity to international relations. Cyber-attacks can disable critical infrastructure, steal sensitive information, and even disrupt democratic processes, all without a single shot being fired. In this environment, the line between war and peace becomes increasingly blurred. The Stuxnet virus, a sophisticated piece of malware developed by the United States and Israel to sabotage Iran's nuclear program, is a prime example of how cyber weapons can be used to achieve geopolitical objectives without direct military engagement. While Stuxnet may have delayed Iran's nuclear ambitions, it also set a dangerous precedent for the use of cyber warfare in international conflicts.

But perhaps the most concerning development is the breakdown of arms control agreements that have, for decades, kept the nuclear threat in check. The 1987 Intermediate-Range Nuclear Forces (INF) Treaty, which eliminated an entire class of nuclear missiles, was one of the most significant achievements of the late Cold War era. However, in 2019, the United States formally withdrew from the treaty, citing Russian violations. The collapse of the INF Treaty has led to fears of a new arms race, with both the U.S. and Russia now free to develop and deploy intermediate-range missiles. The demise of the treaty, detailed in Jeffrey Lewis's The 2020 Commission Report on the North Korean Nuclear Attacks Against the United States, signals a return to the dangerous brinkmanship of the Cold War, where the threat of nuclear war was never far from the public consciousness.

The psychological underpinnings of this relentless pursuit of power are deeply ingrained in the human psyche. The desire for dominance, the fear of vulnerability, and the belief in one's own righteousness all contribute to the geopolitical posturing that has brought the world to the brink of disaster time and again. The theory of deterrence, which underpins much of modern nuclear strategy, is based on the assumption that all actors involved will behave rationally in the face of mutually assured destruction. Yet, history has shown that leaders do not always act rationally, especially when under extreme pressure. The Cuban Missile Crisis, for instance, was fraught with miscalculations and misunderstandings on both sides, any one of which could have led to a catastrophic outcome.

Moreover, the very existence of nuclear weapons creates a sense of inevitability about their use. As long as these weapons exist, the possibility of their use remains, whether by design, accident, or miscalculation. The story of Vasili Arkhipov, another unsung hero of the Cold War, illustrates just how close we have come to nuclear war due to miscommunication and panic. During the Cuban Missile Crisis, Arkhipov was the lone officer aboard a Soviet submarine who refused to authorize the launch of a nuclear torpedo, despite orders from his superiors. His refusal, documented in Red November by W. Craig Reed, prevented a direct confrontation with the U.S. Navy and likely averted a full-scale nuclear war.

As we look to the future, the question of whether these geopolitical tensions and the nuclear shadow they cast will grow darker or brighter remains uncertain. The proliferation of nuclear weapons, once the purview of a few superpowers, is now a global issue, with countries like North Korea and potentially Iran seeking to join the nuclear club. The more actors that possess these weapons, the greater the risk of their use, either intentionally or accidentally. The lack of progress in nuclear disarmament, coupled with the erosion of international norms and agreements, suggests that the threat of nuclear war may indeed become more acute in the coming decades.

In this uncertain future, the key to breaking free from the delusion of inevitable conflict may lie in reimagining what it means to be a powerful nation. Power need not be measured solely in terms of military strength or economic dominance. Instead, true power could be defined by a nation's ability to champion peace, promote justice, and build a sustainable future for all. This redefinition of power is not just a lofty ideal but a necessary evolution if humanity is to survive the nuclear age.

The prisons of delusion that have held humanity captive for so long—delusions of invincibility, superiority, and righteous power—must be dismantled if we are to navigate the challenges of the 21st century. The future will be shaped not by those who cling to the past but by those who dare to imagine a different path, one that leads away from the shadow of nuclear annihilation and towards a brighter, more peaceful world.

Bioengineered Pandemics: Pandora's Vials

In the labyrinth of modern science, where possibilities are endless, one might find a sense of wonder. Yet, it's equally a Pandora's box, holding within it threats as terrifying as they are unpredictable. The dawn of bioengineering has bestowed humanity with the tools to manipulate life at its most fundamental level. On one hand, it promises cures for diseases, enhanced crops, and even the extension of human life. But lurking in the shadows of these advancements is a specter far more sinister: the potential for bioengineered pandemics.

The COVID-19 pandemic has already illustrated how a microscopic organism can bring even the most powerful nations to their knees. Yet, COVID-19, devastating as it was, emerged naturally—at least as far as current evidence suggests. But imagine a pathogen that doesn't evolve through natural processes but is instead crafted in a laboratory. The power to create such a pathogen is no longer the stuff of science fiction; it's the reality of 21st-century biotechnology.

The Global Tapestry of Biothreats

Historically, the threat of pandemics has always been with us. The Black Death in the 14th century wiped out a third of Europe's population, and the Spanish Flu of 1918 claimed millions of lives across the globe. But unlike these natural outbreaks, bioengineered pandemics are a deliberate creation. Take, for example, the Soviet Union's Biopreparat program, a clandestine initiative that sought to develop biological weapons during the Cold War. Even after the Biological Weapons Convention of 1972, which was supposed to curtail such efforts, reports have surfaced about continuing research into bioweapons by various nations, often under the guise of defense.

The danger lies not only in state-sponsored programs but also in the democratization of technology. CRISPR-Cas9, a gene-editing tool once restricted to high-end labs, is now accessible to many. While this democratization has led to remarkable medical breakthroughs, it also opens the door for non-state actors, including terrorist groups, to engineer deadly pathogens. The implications are chilling. In "The Dead Hand," David E. Hoffman explores the legacy of the Cold War arms race, including biological weapons, and how close humanity has come to self-annihilation. In our present day, the barriers to creating a weapon of mass destruction have been lowered significantly, increasing the risk manifold.

The Dual-Edged Sword of Biotechnology

Biotechnology, with its promise of curing diseases, improving crops, and even extending human lifespan, is a double-edged sword. While these advances are undoubtedly beneficial, they also introduce new risks. For example, the ability to synthesize viruses from scratch, something that was once the domain of a select few, is now more widespread. Researchers at the University of Alberta, for instance, synthesized horsepox virus, a close relative of smallpox, using mail-order DNA in 2017. While their goal was to develop new vaccines, the potential for misuse is clear.

Consider also the case of the H5N1 avian flu virus. In 2011, researchers in the Netherlands and the United States created a version of the virus that could spread more easily between mammals. While their research aimed to understand how the virus might evolve in nature, it also sparked a debate about the wisdom of such experiments. As Laurie Garrett, a Pulitzer Prize-winning science writer, has pointed out in her book *The Coming Plague,* our technological prowess has outpaced our understanding of its potential consequences. The line between beneficial research and dangerous experimentation is razor-thin.

Psychology of Fear and the Spread of Misinformation

Pandemics, whether natural or engineered, tap into deep-seated human fears. The invisible nature of a virus, combined with its often-lethal consequences, creates a perfect storm of anxiety and paranoia. This fear, in turn, can lead to societal breakdown. During the COVID-19 pandemic, we saw how quickly misinformation could spread, exacerbating fear and mistrust. Social media platforms became breeding grounds for conspiracy theories, ranging from the virus being a hoax to it being a deliberate creation of a government or corporation.

This is not new. During the bubonic plague in the 14th century, rumors spread that Jews were poisoning wells, leading to massacres across Europe. In 1918, the Spanish Flu was often blamed on foreigners or other marginalized groups. The psychological weakness that drives humans to seek scapegoats in times of crisis is a constant throughout history. It is this same psychology that makes the threat of bioengineered pandemics particularly dangerous. In a world where trust in institutions is already eroding, the introduction of a man-made pathogen could push societies to the brink.

The Silver Lining: Stories of Resilience and Innovation

Yet, amid the darkness, there are also rays of hope. The rapid development of COVID-19 vaccines was nothing short of miraculous. Researchers like Katalin Karikó and Drew Weissman, whose work on mRNA technology laid the groundwork for these vaccines, exemplify the potential of scientific collaboration. As Walter Isaacson chronicles in "The Code Breaker," the race to develop these vaccines was a testament to human ingenuity and perseverance.

Similarly, the global eradication of smallpox, achieved through a coordinated vaccination campaign, serves as a reminder that humanity is capable of overcoming even the most daunting challenges when united by a common goal. This effort, detailed in William H. Foege's "House on Fire," was a triumph of global cooperation and a model for how future pandemics might be tackled.

The Future: A World on Edge

Looking forward, the question is whether the threat of bioengineered pandemics will worsen or improve. On one hand, technological advancements will likely continue, making it easier to create and manipulate pathogens. The accessibility of these technologies means that the threat will not be confined to state actors but will also include rogue scientists and terrorist groups.

In the end, whether bioengineered pandemics become a more significant threat or a manageable risk will depend largely on our ability to learn from history, trust in science, and cooperate across borders. The challenge is immense, but so too is the potential for resilience and innovation. As we peer into Pandora's vials, the contents may terrify, but they also hold the promise of progress—if we are wise enough to use them judiciously.

Resource Depletion, and Food Scarcity

Resource depletion is not merely an environmental issue; it is an existential crisis that threatens the very fabric of human civilization. For centuries, humanity has operated under the dangerous delusion that Earth's resources are infinite, believing that technological advancements and economic growth would perpetually sustain us. This mindset has led to rampant overconsumption and environmental destruction, with severe consequences for both our present and future. As we continue to deplete the planet's resources at an alarming rate, the future generations will inherit a world marked by scarcity, conflict, and instability.

The Illusion of Endless Growth

Throughout history, civilizations have risen and fallen based on their ability to exploit natural resources. From the deforestation of ancient forests to the over farming of fertile lands, the pattern is clear: societies repeatedly fall into the trap of believing that their resources will last forever. This belief, fueled by the notion that human ingenuity can always overcome natural limitations, has driven us to push the boundaries of what the Earth can sustain.

The Industrial Revolution marked a significant turning point, sparking an unprecedented surge in the consumption of coal, oil, and natural gas—resources that took millions of years to form but are being consumed within a few centuries. Today, our reliance on fossil fuels continues to deplete these reserves rapidly. According to the International Energy Agency, global oil production is expected to peak in the near future, leading to higher prices, economic uncertainty, and geopolitical tensions as nations compete for control over the remaining supplies. This depletion is not just an energy crisis; it signals a broader societal collapse if we do not shift to more sustainable practices.

The Ravaging of Forests

Deforestation represents another critical aspect of resource depletion, with far-reaching consequences for both the environment and human populations. The Amazon Rainforest, often referred to as the "lungs of the Earth," is being cleared at an alarming rate—approximately 10,000 square kilometers per year—for agriculture, logging, and urbanization. This deforestation contributes significantly to climate change, as forests play a vital role in absorbing carbon dioxide and regulating the global climate.

Beyond environmental degradation, the loss of forests threatens global biodiversity, with countless species facing extinction due to habitat loss. The World Wildlife Fund (WWF) reports that nearly 60% of all vertebrate species have been lost in the last 50 years, largely due to deforestation and habitat destruction. Additionally, indigenous communities who have lived in harmony with these forests for centuries are being displaced as their lands are destroyed. Future generations will inherit a world where the consequences of deforestation are fully realized—where climate change is more severe, biodiversity is diminished, and the planet's capacity to support human life is gravely compromised.

The Oceans' Empty Nets

The depletion of ocean resources is another manifestation of our unsustainable relationship with the Earth's natural wealth. Overfishing has led to the collapse of some of the world's most important fisheries, with devastating consequences for both the environment and coastal communities. The North Atlantic cod fisheries, for instance, have been severely depleted, leading to economic hardship and the loss of livelihoods for thousands of people. The once-abundant cod population has been reduced by over 95% from historical levels, demonstrating the catastrophic impact of overfishing.

As global demand for seafood continues to rise, the pressure on marine ecosystems increases. Industrial-scale fishing operations are decimating fish populations, pushing many species to the brink of extinction. According to the United Nations Food and Agriculture Organization (FAO), over 34% of the world's fish stocks are overexploited, while 60% are fully exploited, leaving little room for recovery. If current trends continue, the future of the world's oceans looks bleak. Marine ecosystems could collapse, leading to the loss of biodiversity and the disruption of the food chain. This, in turn, could exacerbate global food scarcity, as fish and other marine resources become increasingly scarce.

Water Scarcity: The Ticking Time Bomb

Water is perhaps the most critical resource of all, yet it is also one of the most threatened. Water scarcity is already affecting billions of people worldwide, with regions like the Middle East, North Africa, and parts of Asia facing severe challenges. According to the World Resources Institute, nearly one-quarter of the world's population lives in regions of extremely high water stress, where the demand for water far exceeds the available supply. The depletion of freshwater resources, driven by overuse, pollution, and climate change, is leading to a crisis that threatens both human survival and geopolitical stability.

The situation is expected to worsen as climate change exacerbates drought conditions and reduces the availability of freshwater. For instance, the Intergovernmental Panel on Climate Change (IPCC) projects that by 2050, more than 5 billion people could suffer water shortages due to climate change, increasing the likelihood of conflicts as nations and communities vie for access to this vital resource.

In 2018, Cape Town, South Africa, faced the terrifying prospect of "Day Zero," when the city's water supply was expected to run dry. Although the crisis was averted through drastic water-saving measures, it served as a stark warning of the potential consequences of water scarcity. In the coming decades, similar crises are likely to become more common as the impacts of climate change intensify. Future generations will face the full brunt of this crisis, with the potential for conflict over water resources leading to social unrest and instability.

Ecological Overshoot: The Limits of Growth

The concept of "ecological overshoot" is central to understanding the broader implications of resource depletion. Humanity currently uses the equivalent of 1.7 Earths to sustain its consumption, meaning that we are depleting resources faster than the planet can regenerate them. This phenomenon is a stark reminder that our current trajectory is unsustainable and that we are living beyond the planet's means.

The consequences of ecological overshoot are far-reaching. Environmental degradation, loss of biodiversity, and increased carbon emissions are just some of the symptoms of this unsustainable path. As the planet's resources continue to dwindle, the strain on natural systems will only increase, leading to more frequent and severe environmental crises.

Future generations will inherit a world where the consequences of ecological overshoot are fully realized. They will face greater challenges in securing the resources needed for survival, leading to increased competition and conflict. To prevent this outcome, we must fundamentally change our relationship with the Earth's resources, adopting more sustainable practices and reducing our overall consumption.

Future Unrest and the Path Forward

The continued depletion of the Earth's resources will inevitably lead to future unrest if current trends persist. As resources become scarcer, competition for what remains will intensify, leading to conflicts between nations and within communities. The social and economic consequences of resource depletion will exacerbate existing inequalities, leading to greater instability and the potential for widespread violence.

However, there is still hope for future generations if we take action now. The key to addressing resource depletion lies in recognizing the limits of growth and adopting more sustainable practices. This requires a fundamental shift in how we think about progress and development, moving away from the pursuit of endless growth toward a more balanced and sustainable approach.

Future generations can tackle the challenge of resource depletion by investing in renewable energy sources, promoting sustainable agriculture and fishing practices, and improving water management. Additionally, efforts to reduce consumption and waste, protect natural ecosystems, and restore degraded environments will be essential in ensuring that the planet can continue to support human life.

Education and awareness will also play a crucial role in shaping the future. By understanding the consequences of resource depletion and the need for sustainable practices, future generations can avoid the mistakes of the past and build a more resilient and equitable world.

The path forward will not be easy, but it is necessary. The survival of future generations depends on our ability to confront the delusions that have led us to this point and to embrace a more sustainable and responsible way of living on this planet. The choices we make today will determine whether we leave behind a world capable of sustaining life and prosperity or one marked by conflict, scarcity, and collapse.

Psychological Drivers

The psychological issues that plague humanity are far more complex than they appear on the surface. As we delve into the existential threats they pose to our past, present, and future, we uncover a myriad of cognitive barriers that have consistently hindered progress. These barriers, deeply rooted in human psychology, not only drive individual behaviors but also shape the collective actions of societies. The central question that arises is whether future generations will be able to overcome these barriers, or if they will succumb to the same delusions that have trapped us for centuries.

The Tragedy of the Commons

The "tragedy of the commons" remains a powerful illustration of how human behavior often disregards long-term sustainability in favor of short-term gains. Garrett Hardin's concept, introduced in 1968, has found application in a wide range of scenarios, from environmental degradation to overfishing. The essence of this tragedy lies in individuals acting in their own self-interest, ultimately depleting shared resources that are critical for the survival of the collective.

This tragedy is not just a historical phenomenon; it continues to manifest in modern times. For instance, the overuse of antibiotics has led to the rise of antibiotic-resistant bacteria, a global health crisis that threatens to undermine decades of medical advancements. The agricultural sector also falls prey to this pattern, where excessive use of chemical fertilizers and pesticides has resulted in soil degradation and loss of biodiversity, endangering food security for future generations.

One of the most poignant examples of this tragedy is the ongoing destruction of the Amazon rainforest. Despite widespread awareness of its importance as the "lungs of the Earth," deforestation continues at an alarming rate, driven by logging, agriculture, and infrastructure development. According to the World Wildlife Fund (WWF), the Amazon lost over 17% of its forest cover in the last 50 years, with approximately 13,235 square kilometers (5,108 square miles) lost in 2021 alone. This depletion not only contributes to climate change but also threatens countless species and indigenous communities that rely on the forest for survival.

Hyperbolic Discounting

Cognitive biases, such as hyperbolic discounting, exacerbate the tragedy of the commons by influencing how individuals perceive time and rewards. Hyperbolic discounting describes the human tendency to prefer smaller, immediate rewards over larger, delayed ones, even when the latter are objectively more beneficial. This bias plays a significant role in decision-making processes, leading to behaviors that are detrimental in the long run.

For example, consider the global response to climate change. Despite overwhelming scientific evidence that reducing carbon emissions is essential to prevent catastrophic outcomes, many governments and corporations continue to prioritize short-term economic gains over long-term environmental sustainability. This is evident in the persistent reliance on fossil fuels, which, according to the International Energy Agency (IEA), accounted for 80% of the world's energy consumption in 2020. The immediate benefits of economic growth and energy security often overshadow the future costs of environmental degradation and climate-related disasters.

Hyperbolic discounting is not confined to environmental issues. It also influences personal health decisions, such as the choice to indulge in unhealthy foods or engage in sedentary behavior, despite knowing the long-term risks of obesity, diabetes, and cardiovascular diseases. A study published in the journal Psychological Science found that individuals with a stronger tendency towards hyperbolic discounting were more likely to make poor health choices, leading to higher rates of chronic illnesses and reduced life expectancy.

The Attention Span Crisis: A Modern Plague

The digital age has introduced a new cognitive barrier: the dwindling attention span. The constant barrage of information from smartphones, social media, and 24/7 news cycles has significantly altered our cognitive abilities, leading to a decline in deep thinking and sustained focus. According to a 2015 study by Microsoft, the average human attention span has dropped to just 8 seconds—shorter than that of a goldfish. This alarming statistic highlights the extent to which digital distractions have permeated our lives.

Nicholas Carr, in his book *The Shallows: What the Internet Is Doing to Our Brains,* argues that this shift is not merely superficial but has profound implications for how we process information. The design of digital platforms, which exploit psychological vulnerabilities such as the reward circuitry of our brains, has created addictive feedback loops. Notifications, likes, and social media interactions trigger dopamine releases, reinforcing the habit of "continuous partial attention." This state of perpetual alertness prevents deep engagement and critical thinking, leading to a society that is more reactive than reflective.

The consequences of this attention span crisis are far-reaching. In the educational sector, teachers report that students struggle to maintain focus during lectures, with many resorting to multitasking on their devices. This trend has been linked to declining academic performance and reduced ability to engage in complex problem-solving tasks. A 2018 study published in Educational Psychology found that students who frequently used digital devices during lectures scored 5% lower on exams compared to those who did not.

In the workplace, the attention span crisis has manifested in the rise of "busy work," where employees are constantly switching between tasks without making meaningful progress on any of them. This phenomenon, known as "task switching," is estimated to reduce productivity by up to 40%, according to research by the American Psychological Association (APA). The cumulative effect of these distractions can lead to burnout, job dissatisfaction, and a decline in overall well-being.

Digital Minimalism

In the realm of technology, the concept of "digital minimalism" has gained traction as a response to the attention span crisis. Cal Newport's book *Digital Minimalism* presents numerous examples of individuals who have drastically reduced their digital consumption, finding greater fulfillment and productivity as a result. These digital minimalists prioritize intentional use of technology, setting boundaries around their online activities and rediscovering the value of offline experiences. By reclaiming their attention, they have not only improved their mental health but also enhanced their ability to engage in meaningful work and relationships.

Will We Break Free?

There is reason for both optimism and concern. On the one hand, advancements in psychology, neuroscience, and behavioral economics have provided us with a deeper understanding of cognitive biases and their impact on decision-making. This knowledge has the potential to inform policies and interventions that promote long-term thinking and sustainability. For example, "nudging" strategies, popularized by behavioral economists Richard Thaler and Cass Sunstein, have been used to encourage healthier choices, such as saving for retirement or reducing energy consumption, by subtly altering the choice architecture.

On the other hand, the rise of artificial intelligence (AI) and big data presents new challenges. These technologies, while powerful, also have the potential to exacerbate existing cognitive biases and create new ones. For instance, AI algorithms that prioritize engagement over accuracy can spread misinformation and reinforce echo chambers, further polarizing societies and eroding trust in institutions. The challenge for future generations will be to harness these technologies in a way that enhances human well-being without falling prey to the same delusions that have trapped us in the past.

Volatile Economics: The Dance of Chaos

In an era marked by rapid transformations and unpredictability, the global economy is increasingly volatile, impacting nations and individuals alike. This volatility stems from a myriad of factors, including financial crises, trade wars, technological disruptions, and pandemics. A poignant example of this is the 2008 financial crisis, a seismic event that exposed the fragility of the global financial system. The crisis was fueled by speculative bubbles and systemic risks, compounded by complex financial instruments and a glaring lack of regulatory oversight. Michael Lewis's "The Big Short" vividly details the unraveling of this catastrophe, painting a picture of a world where greed and short-sightedness led to widespread devastation.

In the realm of economics, decisions are often driven by psychological factors rather than purely rational considerations. Behavioral economics, championed by thinkers like Daniel Kahneman and Richard Thaler, delves into these cognitive biases. Concepts such as "loss aversion" and "herd behavior" explain why markets can be inefficient and unstable. For instance, during the 2008 crisis, the fear of loss prompted massive sell-offs, exacerbating the downturn. Similarly, herd behavior often leads investors to follow trends blindly, creating bubbles that eventually burst.

Yet, amidst the chaos, there are tales of resilience and adaptation. Iceland's recovery from the 2008 crisis stands out as a testament to the power of transparent governance, social solidarity, and innovative policy measures.

Chronicled in Michael Lewis's "Boomerang," Iceland's story is one of a small nation implementing radical reforms to stabilize its economy. In the wake of the crisis, Iceland took the unconventional route of letting its banks fail, thereby avoiding the trap of moral hazard and forcing a rapid restructuring of its financial system. This bold approach, combined with measures like capital controls and fiscal austerity, helped Iceland recover more swiftly than many other affected nations.

The dance of economic chaos is not just a modern phenomenon. Throughout history, economies have ebbed and flowed, influenced by wars, technological advancements, and societal shifts. The Tulip Mania of the 17th century, often cited as the first recorded speculative bubble, saw the price of tulip bulbs skyrocket in the Netherlands before crashing spectacularly. This event serves as an early illustration of the irrational exuberance and subsequent panic that can drive economic cycles.

In more recent times, the COVID-19 pandemic has once again underscored the interconnectedness and vulnerability of the global economy. Supply chain disruptions, lockdowns, and shifts in consumer behavior have created new challenges and uncertainties. However, the crisis has also accelerated technological adoption and innovation, with remote work and digital transformation becoming more prevalent.

Understanding the underlying psychological factors that drive economic behavior, coupled with transparent and innovative policy-making, can help mitigate the impact of future shocks. The dance of chaos, with all its unpredictability, is an integral part of the economic narrative, impacting the fortunes of nations and individuals alike.

Navigating the Shadows: The Darknet, and Cyber Threats

In an age where our lives are increasingly intertwined with the digital realm, the rise of the darknet, cyber-attacks, and cyber fraud represents a formidable existential threat. These phenomena highlight the vulnerabilities that have plagued our past and continue to menace our present, raising critical questions about how future generations will confront and possibly mitigate these dangers. Will they fall deeper into the prison of digital delusion, or will they rise to the challenge and build a safer, more secure digital future?

The Darknet: A Hidden Abyss

The darknet, often referred to as the underbelly of the internet, is a network of hidden websites accessible only through specialized software like Tor (The Onion Router). While the surface web—what most people use daily—constitutes just a small fraction of the entire internet, the darknet and its broader cousin, the deep web, represent the vast majority of online content. The darknet, however, is where the shadows truly reside.

This hidden corner of the internet has become a breeding ground for illicit activities. It's where drug traffickers, arms dealers, human traffickers, and other criminals operate with relative impunity. Silk Road, one of the most notorious darknet marketplaces, facilitated the sale of illegal drugs, weapons, and even assassination services before its eventual shutdown by the FBI in 2013. Its founder, Ross Ulbricht, was sentenced to life in prison, but the closure of Silk Road only led to the emergence of countless other similar platforms, underscoring the resilience and adaptability of darknet operations.

The scale of illegal activity on the darknet is staggering. A 2019 study by the RAND Corporation found that 57% of darknet sites were used for illegal trade, including drugs, counterfeit currency, and stolen data. Another report by Europol highlighted that the darknet is increasingly being used for child exploitation, with a significant rise in the number of forums and marketplaces dedicated to child pornography.

Despite these grim realities, the darknet is not entirely a cesspool of criminality. It has also been a refuge for activists, journalists, and whistleblowers in repressive regimes, where anonymity is a matter of life and death. For example, Edward Snowden used the darknet to communicate with journalists while leaking classified information about the NSA's surveillance programs. Similarly, in countries like China and Iran, where internet censorship is rampant, the darknet offers a lifeline for those seeking to bypass government restrictions and access uncensored information.

Yet, the existential threat posed by the darknet is not merely in its existence but in the psychological allure it holds. The anonymity and freedom it offers are double-edged swords, providing a space for both liberation and corruption. The question that looms large is whether future generations will harness the darknet for good or whether it will continue to be a haven for the darkest aspects of human nature.

Cyber Attacks: A Growing Menace

As the world becomes increasingly digitized, cyber-attacks have evolved from mere nuisances to full-blown crises capable of crippling entire nations. These attacks range from ransomware, which locks up crucial files until a ransom is paid, to sophisticated breaches that target sensitive personal, corporate, and even governmental information.

One of the most significant cyber-attacks in recent history was the 2017 WannaCry ransomware attack, which affected more than 200,000 computers across 150 countries. The attack exploited a vulnerability in Microsoft Windows, encrypting files and demanding ransom payments in Bitcoin. Hospitals, businesses, and government agencies were among the hardest hit, with the UK's National Health Service (NHS) particularly affected—disrupting patient care and costing millions of pounds in damages. The source of the attack was later traced to North Korean hackers, highlighting the growing role of state actors in cyber warfare.

Another alarming example is the 2020 SolarWinds cyber-attack, a breach that infiltrated numerous U.S. government agencies, including the Departments of Defense, Homeland Security, and the Treasury. The attackers, believed to be linked to the Russian government, used a software update from SolarWinds, a U.S. IT firm, as a Trojan horse to gain access to these agencies' networks. The breach went undetected for months, exposing the fragility of even the most secure systems and underscoring the far-reaching consequences of cyber espionage.

The financial cost of cyber-attacks is astronomical. According to a 2021 report by Cybersecurity Ventures, global cybercrime costs are expected to reach $10.5 trillion annually by 2025, up from $3 trillion in 2015. This staggering figure includes the costs of damage and destruction of data, stolen money, lost productivity, theft of intellectual property, and reputational harm. Yet, the true cost of cyber-attacks is not just financial; it is also psychological. The fear and uncertainty that these attacks generate can erode trust in digital systems and institutions, leading to a more paranoid and fragmented society.

Cyber-attacks also have a profound psychological impact on individuals. Victims of identity theft, for example, often report feelings of violation and helplessness, as their personal information is used to commit fraud or other crimes. A 2018 study by Javelin Strategy & Research found that 16.7 million Americans were victims of identity theft in the previous year, with total losses amounting to $16.8 billion. The emotional toll of these crimes is often long-lasting, as victims struggle to reclaim their identities and restore their financial standing.

Cyber Fraud: The Invisible Predator

While cyber-attacks capture headlines, cyber fraud is the more insidious threat that preys on unsuspecting individuals. Phishing schemes, identity theft, and online scams are just a few of the tactics used by cybercriminals to exploit the vulnerabilities of the digital age.

Phishing, in particular, has become a pervasive problem. These schemes typically involve fraudulent emails or websites that appear legitimate, tricking users into providing sensitive information such as passwords or credit card numbers. Despite widespread awareness, phishing remains highly effective; in 2020 alone, the Anti-Phishing Working Group (APWG) recorded over 200,000 unique phishing sites each month, a significant increase from previous years.

One of the most infamous phishing attacks targeted John Podesta, the chairman of Hillary Clinton's 2016 presidential campaign. In March 2016, Podesta received an email that appeared to be from Google, warning him that his account had been compromised and urging him to change his password. The email was, in fact, a phishing attempt, and when Podesta clicked on the link, he inadvertently gave hackers access to his email account. The stolen emails were later published by WikiLeaks, causing significant political damage and influencing the outcome of the U.S. presidential election.

Identity theft is another widespread form of cyber fraud. In the digital age, personal information has become a valuable commodity, and criminals are constantly finding new ways to steal and exploit this data. In 2017, the credit reporting agency Equifax suffered a massive data breach, exposing the personal information of 147 million Americans, including Social Security numbers, birth dates, and addresses. The breach, which was caused by a vulnerability in Equifax's website software, resulted in a $700 million settlement, one of the largest in U.S. history. However, the damage to victims was immeasurable, as many spent years dealing with the fallout of having their identities stolen.

Online scams, too, have evolved in sophistication. From romance scams that prey on the lonely to investment fraud schemes that promise high returns with little risk, cybercriminals have become adept at exploiting human psychology. One notorious example is the case of Anna Sorokin, a Russian-born con artist who posed as a wealthy socialite in New York City. Sorokin used social media to cultivate an image of wealth and success, convincing her victims to lend her money or cover her expenses. Her scams, which totaled hundreds of thousands of dollars, were eventually exposed, and Sorokin was sentenced to prison in 2019. Her story, chronicled in the Netflix series Inventing Anna, is a stark reminder of how easily people can be deceived in the digital age.

Human Weakness and the Deception of Cyber Threats

The existential threat posed by cyber threats is not merely a function of technology but also of human psychology. Cybercriminals often exploit cognitive biases and psychological vulnerabilities to carry out their schemes, turning human weaknesses into their greatest weapons.

One such psychological weakness is the tendency to trust familiar or authoritative sources, a bias that phishing schemes exploit to great effect. Cybercriminals often impersonate trusted entities, such as banks, government agencies, or even colleagues, to trick individuals into revealing sensitive information. This exploitation of trust is particularly dangerous in a digital world where face-to-face interactions are increasingly rare, making it difficult to verify the legitimacy of online communications.

Another cognitive bias that cybercriminals exploit is the "optimism bias," the belief that bad things are more likely to happen to others than to oneself. This bias leads individuals to underestimate the risk of cyber threats and to neglect basic security measures, such as using strong passwords or enabling two-factor authentication. A 2020 survey by IBM found that 40% of respondents believed they were unlikely to be targeted by cybercriminals, despite the growing prevalence of cyber-attacks and fraud.

The illusion of control is another psychological trap that cybercriminals leverage. People tend to believe that they have more control over their online activities than they actually do, leading to complacency in digital security. This illusion is shattered when individuals become victims of cybercrime, as they realize how easily their personal information can be stolen or their accounts compromised. The sense of powerlessness that follows can be devastating, leading to a loss of confidence in digital systems and a reluctance to engage in online transactions.

Stories of Digital Resistance

Amidst the growing menace of cyber threats, there are stories of individuals and organizations that have successfully navigated the digital shadows, turning the tide against cybercrime and setting an example for future generations.

One such story is that of J. Trevor Hughes, the CEO of the International Association of Privacy Professionals (IAPP). Under his leadership, the IAPP has grown into the world's largest privacy organization, dedicated to helping professionals manage and protect personal information in an increasingly digital world. Hughes has been a vocal advocate for stronger privacy laws and better cybersecurity practices, emphasizing the need for individuals to take control of their digital lives. His work, chronicled in his book *Privacy is Power*, has inspired a global movement towards greater digital responsibility and awareness.

Another inspiring figure is Marcus Hutchins, the British cybersecurity researcher who famously stopped the WannaCry ransomware attack in 2017. Despite his troubled past—he was later arrested for creating malware as a teenager—Hutchins used his skills to identify and activate a "kill switch" that disabled the ransomware, preventing further damage. His story, documented in his memoir Saved by the Code, highlights the potential for redemption and the importance of using one's talents for the greater good.

In the corporate world, companies like IBM and Microsoft have taken proactive measures to combat cyber threats and promote digital security. IBM's X-Force Command Center, for example, is a state-of-the-art facility where cybersecurity experts simulate cyber-attacks and develop strategies to defend against them.

Microsoft, on the other hand, has been at the forefront of developing advanced security technologies, such as biometric authentication and AI-powered threat detection, to protect users from cybercrime.

The Future of Cybersecurity

As we look to the future, the question remains whether future generations will be able to overcome the cyber threats that have plagued their predecessors or whether they will become even more entangled in the web of digital deception.

On one hand, advancements in technology offer hope. Artificial intelligence (AI) and machine learning (ML) are being increasingly used to detect and prevent cyber-attacks, with AI-powered systems capable of identifying threats in real-time and responding to them faster than any human could. Blockchain technology also holds promise as a means of securing digital transactions and preventing fraud, with its decentralized and tamper-proof nature making it difficult for cybercriminals to manipulate.

On the other hand, the same technologies that offer hope also pose new challenges. As AI and ML become more sophisticated, so too do the cyber-attacks that use them. AI-driven phishing attacks, for example, are becoming increasingly difficult to detect, as they can mimic human behavior and personalize attacks based on individual data. Similarly, the rise of quantum computing threatens to render current encryption methods obsolete, potentially exposing even the most secure systems to cyber threats.

Future generations must be equipped with the knowledge and skills to navigate the digital world safely, from understanding the basics of cybersecurity to recognizing the psychological tactics used by cybercriminals. This will require a cultural shift towards digital responsibility, where individuals take ownership of their online presence and prioritize security in their daily lives.

Moreover, governments and institutions will need to play a more active role in protecting citizens from cyber threats. This includes implementing stronger cybersecurity laws, investing in digital infrastructure, and fostering collaboration between the public and private sectors to develop innovative solutions to the ever-evolving threat landscape.

The battle against cybercrime is far from over, but with vigilance, education, and innovation, future generations have the potential to turn the tide and break free from the prisons of delusion that have kept us trapped in the shadows for so long.

Human Psyche: The Veil of Illusion

The human psyche is a complex landscape, often clouded by illusions and biases that shape our perceptions and actions.

Cognitive biases such as confirmation bias, where individuals favor information that confirms their preconceptions, and the Dunning-Kruger effect, where people overestimate their abilities, illustrate how our minds can deceive us. As Daniel Kahneman explains in "Thinking, Fast and Slow," these biases affect everything from personal decisions to political judgments.

These cognitive distortions can have profound implications. For instance, the illusion of invulnerability can lead to risky behaviors, while groupthink can stifle innovation and perpetuate flawed policies. Understanding these psychological tendencies is crucial for developing critical thinking and informed decision-making.

Yet, there are stories of individuals who have transcended these limitations. Viktor Frankl's experiences, as described in "Man's Search for Meaning," highlight the power of resilience and self-awareness in overcoming psychological challenges. Frankl's insights into the human capacity for finding meaning and purpose, even in the face of extreme adversity, offer valuable lessons for navigating the complexities of the modern world.

As we confront these multifaceted challenges, it becomes clear that new questions and new thinking are essential. The old world, with its entrenched beliefs and practices, cannot provide the solutions we need.

As existential threats mount, intolerance is likely to rise. Fear and uncertainty often drive societies to scapegoat minorities and resist change. This reactionary stance, however, is counterproductive and undermines efforts to address global issues.

To move forward, humanity must embrace change and cultivate a culture of open-mindedness and innovation. This requires rethinking education, governance, and societal norms. As Yuval Noah Harari argues in "21 Lessons for the 21st Century," we must develop new narratives and frameworks to navigate the future.

History is replete with examples of transformative thinking. The Renaissance, for instance, marked a period of profound intellectual and cultural change, driven by figures like Leonardo da Vinci and Galileo Galilei. Their willingness to question established knowledge and explore new ideas paved the way for significant advancements in science, art, and philosophy.

As dawn breaks on our fragile world, we stand at the crossroads. The chains of ignorance, fear, and apathy bind us. But perhaps, just perhaps, the convergence of these existential forces will awaken a new generation. Let us write our own story—one of resilience, compassion, and audacity. Let us break free.

If future generations do not awaken from the numbing stupor of endless screen time and other addictions, if they remain indifferent to the existential crises that threaten humanity, if they fail to shatter the fallacies and falsehoods that obscure our vision, if they cannot break free from the vicious cycles of slavery to fear, greed, and lies, then they will be doomed to remain in the Prisons of Delusion. Furthermore, it is imperative that they break the chains which have bound previous generations, for they possess the tools, energy, and resources to do so. The time to act is now, to reclaim our minds, to confront the harsh truths, and to forge a path toward a more enlightened and liberated future. The chains of delusion can be broken, but only if we muster the courage and clarity to do so. The destiny of generations yet unborn hangs in the balance.

Epilogue

As we conclude this exploration, it is essential to reflect on the journey we've embarked upon. From the outset, we drew a parallel between the tragic fate of the Titanic and the perilous course humanity navigates today. This comparison serves as a stark reminder of the dangers inherent in overconfidence and the willful ignorance of critical warnings.

Throughout this book, we've unraveled the complex web of deceptions that have shaped human history and continue to influence our present. We've examined the grand narratives that obscure our understanding of the past, the dogmas and doctrines that dictate moral and social norms, and the subtle and overt ways state power exerts control. We have also shed light on the societal constructs that perpetuate illusions and maintain oppressive systems.

The delusions we've uncovered are not merely historical artifacts but active forces shaping our contemporary world. They blind us to existential threats and limit our potential for meaningful change. By dissecting these false beliefs, we've sought to empower you, the reader, to question, understand, and ultimately transform the world around you.

In the first part of our journey, we confronted the foundational myths and systemic manipulations that have distorted our understanding of history, religion, government, media and society. These chapters revealed the profound impact of these deceptions on our collective consciousness and highlighted the urgent need for a critical re-examination of our beliefs.

The second part of the book shifted focus to the catalysts for change. We explored the transformative power of education, the potential for economic reforms to expose and rectify systemic injustices, and the promise of technological advancements to support greater transparency and understanding. We also critiqued how art and culture brought about revolutionary thinking. Finally, we looked ahead to future challenges and opportunities, emphasizing the need for a more truthful and liberated society.

As we stand at the threshold of a new era, the lessons of this book are more relevant than ever. The existential crises we face—climate change, superintelligence, depleting resources, geopolitical conflicts, and new pandemics—demand urgent and concerted action. To overcome these challenges successfully, we must break free from the delusions that have held us back and embrace a mindset grounded in truth, integrity, and evidence-based understanding.

The path to liberation from these delusions is neither easy nor swift. It requires courage, resilience, and a relentless commitment to questioning the status quo. But the rewards are profound. By shedding the chains of ignorance and embracing a more enlightened perspective, we can create a world that is not only more just and equitable but also more resilient and adaptive to the challenges of the future.

Let us remain vigilant against the allure of comforting illusions and steadfast in our pursuit of truth. The journey ahead is fraught with challenges, but it is also rich with possibilities. Together, we can forge a future where humanity is no longer a prisoner of delusion but a beacon of enlightenment and progress.

Bibliography

Acemoglu, Daron, and Robinson, James A.

Why Nations Fail: The Origins of Power, Prosperity, and Poverty. Crown Business, 2012.

Apple, Michael W.

Ideology and Curriculum. Routledge, 2004.

Banks, James A.

Teaching Strategies for Ethnic Studies. Allyn and Bacon, 1997.

Bostrom, Nick.

Superintelligence: Paths, Dangers, Strategies. Oxford University Press, 2014.

Bregman, Rutger.

Utopia for Realists: How We Can Build the Ideal World. Little, Brown and Company, 2017.

Brynjolfsson, Erik, and McAfee, Andrew.

The Second Machine Age: Work, Progress, and Prosperity in a Time of Brilliant Technologies. W.W. Norton & Company, 2014.

Chang, Ha-Joon.

23 Things They Don't Tell You About Capitalism. Bloomsbury Press, 2010.

Church, George, and Regis, Ed.

Regenesis: How Synthetic Biology Will Reinvent Nature and Ourselves. Basic Books, 2012.

Daly, Herman E., and Cobb, John B.

For the Common Good: Redirecting the Economy toward Community, the Environment, and a Sustainable Future. Beacon Press, 1989.

Diamond, Jared.

Collapse: How Societies Choose to Fail or Succeed. Viking Penguin, 2005.

Dawkins, Richard.

The God Delusion. Bantam Books, 2006.

Ellul, Jacques.

Propaganda: The Formation of Men's Attitudes. Vintage Books, 1973.

Ferguson, Niall.

Empire: How Britain Made the Modern World. Allen Lane, 2003.

Freire, Paulo.

Pedagogy of the Oppressed. Bloomsbury Academic, 1970.

Giroux, Henry A.

Schooling and the Struggle for Public Life: Critical Pedagogy in the Modern Age. University of Minnesota Press, 1988.

Giddens, Anthony.

The Consequences of Modernity. Stanford University Press, 1990.

Graeber, David.

Debt: The First 5,000 Years. Melville House, 2011.

Harari, Yuval Noah.

Homo Deus: A Brief History of Tomorrow. Harvill Secker, 2016.

Harvey, David.

A Brief History of Neoliberalism. Oxford University Press, 2005.

Harris, Sam.

The End of Faith: Religion, Terror, and the Future of Reason. W.W. Norton & Company, 2004.

Hobsbawm, Eric.

On History. Weidenfeld & Nicolson, 1997.

The Age of Extremes: A History of the World, 1914–1991. Vintage Books, 1994.

Hitchens, Christopher.

God Is Not Great: How Religion Poisons Everything. Twelve, 2007.

Howard, Zinn.

A People's History of the United States. Harper & Row, 1980.

A People's History of the American Empire: The Stories of Resistance. Metropolitan Books, 2008.

Jung, Carl G.

Psychology and Religion: West and East. Princeton University Press, 1969.

Keay, John.

India: A History. HarperCollins, 2000.

Kincheloe, Joe L.

Critical Pedagogy Primer. Peter Lang Publishing, 2004.

Kurzweil, Ray.

The Singularity is Near: When Humans Transcend Biology. Viking, 2005.

Ladson-Billings, Gloria.

The Dreamkeepers: Successful Teachers of African American Children. Jossey-Bass, 1994.

Lanier, Jaron.

Who Owns the Future? Simon & Schuster, 2013.

Loewen, James W.

Lies My Teacher Told Me: Everything Your American History Textbook Got Wrong. Touchstone, 1995.

Lovelock, James.

The Revenge of Gaia: Why the Earth Is Fighting Back - and How We Can Still Save Humanity. Basic Books, 2006.

Malthus, Thomas Robert.

An Essay on the Principle of Population. J. Johnson, 1798.

McKibben, Bill.

The End of Nature. Random House, 1989.

Mazower, Mark.

Dark Continent: Europe's Twentieth Century. Vintage, 1998.

Mann, Charles C.

1491: New Revelations of the Americas Before Columbus. Alfred A. Knopf, 2005.

Monbiot, George.

Heat: How to Stop the Planet from Burning. South End Press, 2006.

Nieto, Sonia.

Affirming Diversity: The Sociopolitical Context of Multicultural Education. Pearson, 2012.

Nietzsche, Friedrich.

The Antichrist. Penguin Classics, 2005.

Nye, Joseph S.

The Future of Power. PublicAffairs, 2011.

Orwell, George.

1984. Harvill Secker, 1949.

Animal Farm. Secker & Warburg, 1945.

Piketty, Thomas.

Capital in the Twenty-First Century. Belknap Press, 2014.

Polanyi, Karl.

The Great Transformation: The Political and Economic Origins of Our Time. Beacon Press, 1944.

Postman, Neil.

Amusing Ourselves to Death: Public Discourse in the Age of Show Business. Penguin Books, 1985.

Raworth, Kate.

Doughnut Economics: Seven Ways to Think Like a 21st-Century Economist. Chelsea Green Publishing, 2017.

Reich, Wilhelm.

The Function of the Orgasm: Sexuality, Repression, and Liberation. Viking Press, 1945.

Rockström, Johan, et al.

A Safe Operating Space for Humanity. Nature, 2009.

Rushkoff, Douglas.

Media Virus! Hidden Agendas in Popular Culture. Ballantine Books, 1994.

Said, Edward W.

Orientalism. Pantheon Books, 1978.

Schell, Jonathan.

The Fate of the Earth. Alfred A. Knopf, 1982.

Schmitt, Carl.

The Concept of the Political. University of Chicago Press, 1996.

Stenger, Victor J.

God: The Failed Hypothesis – How Science Shows That God Does Not Exist. Prometheus Books, 2007.

Stiglitz, Joseph E.

The Price of Inequality: How Today's Divided Society Endangers Our Future. W.W. Norton & Company, 2012.

Stoler, Ann Laura.

Along the Archival Grain: Epistemic Anxieties and Colonial Common Sense. Princeton University Press, 2009.

Tegmark, Max.

Life 3.0: Being Human in the Age of Artificial Intelligence. Knopf, 2017.

Tilly, Charles.

Coercion, Capital, and European States, AD 990–1992. Blackwell Publishing, 1992.

Tocqueville, Alexis de.

Democracy in America. University of Chicago Press, 2000.

Venter, J. Craig.

Life at the Speed of Light: From the Double Helix to the Dawn of Digital Life. Viking, 2013.

Wachowski, James.

The Evolution of God: A Study of Religion in Modern Society. University of Chicago Press, 2008.

Wiener, Norbert.

Cybernetics: Or Control and Communication in the Animal and the Machine. MIT Press, 1948.

Wolin, Sheldon S.

Democracy Incorporated: Managed Democracy and the Specter of Inverted Totalitarianism. Princeton University Press, 2008.

Žižek, Slavoj.

The Sublime Object of Ideology. Verso, 1989.

Zuboff, Shoshana.

The Age of Surveillance Capitalism: The Fight for a Human Future at the New Frontier of Power. PublicAffairs, 2019.

Zinn, Howard.

A People's History of the United States. Harper & Row, 1980.

Berners-Lee, Tim.

Weaving the Web: The Original Design and Ultimate Destiny of the World Wide Web by Its Inventor. HarperSanFrancisco, 1999.

Mary Beard and Classical History

Beard, Mary. SPQR: A History of Ancient Rome. Liveright, 2015.

Hasan Kwame Jeffries and Public History

Jeffries, Hasan Kwame. Teaching Hard History: American Slavery. Southern Poverty Law Center, 2018.

Shashi Tharoor and Colonial History

Tharoor, Shashi. Inglorious Empire: What the British Did to India. Scribe Publications, 2017.

Roxanne Dunbar-Ortiz and Indigenous Histories

Dunbar-Ortiz, Roxanne. An Indigenous Peoples' History of the United States. Beacon Press, 2014.

Priyamvada Gopal and Decolonizing the Curriculum

Gopal, Priyamvada.

Insurgent Empire: Anticolonial Resistance and British Dissent. Verso Books, 2019.

www.ingramcontent.com/pod-product-compliance
Lightning Source LLC
LaVergne TN
LVHW091658070526
838199LV00050B/2196